The Rise of the Mutant Ego

John Faupel

I met a traveller from an antique land,
Who said, "Two vast and trunkless legs of stone
Stand in the desert ... Near them, on the sand,
Half sunk a shattered visage lies, whose frown,
And wrinkled lip, and sneer of cold command,
Tell that its sculptor well those passions read
Which yet survive, stamped on these lifeless things,
The hand that mocked them, and the heart that fed;
And on the pedestal, these words appear:
My name is Ozymandias, King of Kings;
Look on my Works, ye Mighty, and despair!
Nothing beside me remains.Å Round the decay
Of that colossal Wreck, boundless and bare
The lone and level sand stretches far away."

'Ozymandias' by Percy Bysshe Shelley, 1818

.

ACKNOWLEDGMENTS

Although these essays are the culmination of a long and solitary search, they began in 2000, when Robert Kane, Professor of Philosophy at the University of Texas, Austin, very kindly promoted my enquiries concerning the subject of 'free will', so I would first like to express my appreciation to him. I would also like to show my gratitude to the parapsychologist, Susan Blackmore, whose encouragement concerning that same subject and its relation to 'consciousness ' was of great help. My writing these essays however, began in 2007, when I set up a philosophy group at our local U3A organisation. About 12 of us met at regular fortnightly intervals, and from these meetings many enjoyable and stimulating discussions followed for the next seven years. I am therefore deeply indebted to each and every one of those members for all the ideas, suggestions and critical appraisals they offered and which have, no doubt contributed to my writing of this book. I am also indebted to the authors of the numerous publications referred to in my text, but especially to Leonard Katz, who edited the *Evolutionary Origins of Morality*, to V.S. Ramachandran, author of *The*

Tell-tale Brain, to Steve Taylor, who wrote: *The Fall, The Insanity of the Ego in Human History*, and to Ian McGilchrist, for his *The Master and his Emissary*. I should especially also like to thank my faithful friend, Mark Thackeray, for his continued help and encouragement in the editing of these essays, for Brian Barban for his IT advice and unfailing support over many years. My profoundest thanks however must surely go to my long-suffering wife, for her non-judgmental counseling and guidance, and with whom I persistently tested out many of these ideas, surely to the limits of her patience, kindness and understanding.

CONTENTS

INTRODUCTION

Each of these essays can be read autonomously but there is a common theme running through them. They are all premised on the belief that we are evolving neurologically in much the same way as we are physiologically, and that the whole course of human history has been an indeterminate process of trial and error.

Many believe they are in charge of their destinies but perhaps that's only because they have been conditioned to think they are. In other words, it is our thoughts that determine our beliefs, but maybe it's our feelings determine our thoughts. We may think we're free but we're not free to think we are. We seem to believe in the 'the ascent of man' and that we're superior to other species because we have the ability to think, but is it any more valid claiming we're superior to, say, a butterfly because it can't think, than it is claiming a butterfly is superior to us because we can't fly? Since comparisons are often chosen to validate our beliefs they can be misleading.

It has been suggested our unashamed vanity has been dealt three serious blows. The first was cosmological, dealt by Copernicus in 1543, who showed that we were not at the center of the Universe; the second was biological, dealt by Darwin in 1859, who showed that we were just one small branch of the evolutionary tree of life, and the third was psychological, dealt by Freud in 1900, who showed that the unconscious mind had a far greater influence on us than we had ever believed possible. To these might be added yet a fourth blow to our vanity. It is a blow that is gradually being exposed by our continued enquiry into what makes us feel and think and act the way we do and how much our heredity and environmental experiences have shape our behavior.

So, perhaps we're not quite so much in charge of our destinies as we thought we were. Most of us think we learn from our experiences but this process is usually retrospective, and less about learning than conditioning. This would undermine the very foundations upon which civilized society has been built, namely that we are responsible for our behavior and should be held accountable for it. So it's assumed those that conform to the standards that society approves of should be rewarded and those that don't should be punished.

If, however, it could be shown that this ten-thousand-year old experiment in social conditioning is based upon one of the most wide-spread and long-lasting delusions in the history of civilization, we might eventually begin to come to terms with the fact that we're evolving by chance alone and without any overall direction or purpose. The realization of this would cast a very different light upon, not only our understanding of consciousness but upon how we relate to one another and the nature of ourselves within in the World. If any prescription for corrective action were possible, it would be a consequence of your appreciating the exploration of these problems in the following essays.

1. WHO'S IN CHARGE?

On May 1st 2011, Osama Bin Laden, 'the glowering mastermind' behind the 9/11 terrorist attacks on the World Trade Centre in New York, was hunted down and killed. When the news broke, a jubilant crowd gathered outside the White House and the U.S. President announced: 'justice has been done'. This type of reaction is not unusual. Societies everywhere believe that those who have committed anti-social acts need to be punished; yet don't seem to think it necessary to delve too deeply into the reasons why such acts have been committed. In courts of law, case histories and mitigating circumstances are sometimes taken into account, even questions of insanity are occasionally raised, but retributive justice is premised upon the belief that adults are free to choose whether they are going to act in a socially acceptable way or not and should be held accountable for their actions. As it is assumed we are all free agents, we ought to behave responsibly and if we don't we must be prepared to accept the consequences. Law and order can only be maintained through fear of punishment.

In fact, ever since spiritual and secular codes of

conduct were first laid down in writing thousands of years ago, no other method of social control has ever been seriously tried and tested. Everyone believes they are free to choose between what society believes is 'good' and should be commended, or what society believes is 'bad' and should be condemned. Consequently, in an attempt to establish conformity and order, authority-figures everywhere, and at all levels within societies have been applying this method of social control for the last ten thousand years or so. Reward for 'good' behaviour usually results in credit, praise, even adulation, along with all sorts of rewards, prizes, honours and promotions, whereas punishment for 'bad' behaviour usually involves various forms of retribution, ranging from fines, imprisonment, to unbearable torture and death; even of mass slaughter and the extermination of whole towns, cities and nation states. Although such attempts to control the way people think and act, both within, and between societies and countries, may sometimes help to create order and conformity, it is questionable as to whether they actually make people any more responsible for their actions. Indeed, such rewards might only encourage pride, arrogance and hypocrisy, whereas punishment may only create low self-esteem, resentment and revenge. It's possible punishment might inhibit vice but it certainly won't promote virtue.

Nevertheless, we still feel sure we have the freedom to choose how we behave, even though we never seem quite so sure what made us choose. Why some people do bad things while others radiate goodness, is far from obvious. From time to time, we've all said or done hurtful things to one another, then afterwards felt regret and wondered why we ever said or did them in the first place. We often don't know why we're bad tempered at certain times and companionable at others. In fact, we don't seem to have much control over our mood swings at all, even when they seriously affect our behaviour. Most of our work and pleasure pursuits, along with our preferences for food, fashion and entertainment are often hard to explain; their origins might go back a long way, even to infancy or earlier. And why some people just go with the flow, or turn out to be loyal patriots, while others become committed terrorists or freedom fighters or just social misfits, is far from obvious.

Although we like to think we are rational human beings who exercise common sense in our decision-making, all sorts of unidentifiable feelings, superstitions and prejudices shape and influence the way we live our lives. We automatically perform many mannerisms, gestures and rituals, while being quite unaware that we are doing so, and many of the things we believe in that affect the way we feel and think, and subsequently act upon, turn out to be quite misguided or fundamentally erroneous.

Without realising it, much of our behaviour is culturally conditioned, while the origins of many of our social practices have been traced back even further.[1] The reason why we eat together around dinner tables, for example, may be because our distant ancestors ate communally together around fires thousands of years ago. Many of the things we do instinctively, nudge us one way or another through life and can mould whole patterns of social behaviour and change the values, practices and beliefs of communities, societies, cultures and even nation states.

Various experiments[2] have shown how group conformity can convince people that their own sound judgements are misguided if they realise they differ from those of other group members and sometimes people can even be persuaded to inflict pain on others, simply because they have been told to do so by authority figures,[3] and, of course, the hidden powers of persuasion are demonstrated

---

[1] Morris, D: *The Naked Ape*, 1967, also *The Human Zoo*, 1967 & *Manwatching*, 1977 by the same author, contain many examples.

[2] Asch, S: *Opinions and Social Pressures*, Scientific American, Vol. 193 No.5, 31-5, 1955 and its derivatives.

[3] Milgrim, S: *Obedience to Authority: an Experimental View*, 1974.

by advertising, upon which corporations spend vast amounts of money in order that they might be profitably reimbursed from increased sales revenue. The average American is exposed to over thirty thousand adverts on TV every year, each of which has to be paid for by the consumer, so it's evidently an effective method of mind-bending.

Curiously enough, we don't seem to mind being told what to buy and are even prepared to pay to be told, because the cost of marketing is included in the purchase price. In one extreme case, a seventeen-year-old, who had shot dead another youth, admitted he had done so out of jealousy, simply because he had seen the fashionable shoes his victim was wearing advertised on TV. Our heads are full of all sorts of mythological beliefs that can unwittingly affect our actions and how we interpret them. Things like dowsing, telepathy, astrology or Ouija Boards that many people believe in but can't explain, might turn out to be far less mysterious than they thought.[4] Even our love of mystery and the paranormal might reveal a deep-seated bias against rational explanation.

Propaganda, based on the flimsiest of evidence and often of a more emotional than rational kind, can influence whomsoever we vote for, the spiritual and secular leaders we follow, or the celebrities we most admire and try to emulate. History is plagued with political and religious despots whose ideologies have indoctrinated the minds of populations of people throughout whole nations and empires, who might otherwise have lived more peaceful and happier lives.

In times of threat from invasion, when self-aggrandisement and posturing are believed to enhance the chance of winning, 'the first casualty of war is truth'. In fact, entire populations can be persuaded to kill or be killed by people of other nations or ethnic groups, about

---

[4] Heap M: *The Ideomotor Effect*, 2002

whom they have no personal knowledge, simply because they have been told to do so by charismatic leaders, or from loyalty to ideological beliefs they might have only arbitrarily acquired because of their location at birth. Although we might be inclined to think 'murderers should be punished' rather than helped, it has been found that some have inherited a 'warrior gene' which, when evoked, can make them uncontrollably violent,[5] while others who 'kill in large numbers to the sound of trumpets and flag-waving, are usually honoured, rather than punished.' [Voltaire]

It is perhaps easy to accept how these things affect other people but are we so very different? Let's start at the beginning. Because we don't choose our parents, we have no say in the genes we inherit from them. All our pre- and post-natal experiences are beyond our control too, even though there is increasing evidence that they can play a significant part in shaping the rest of our lives.[6] There is, for example, a risk of mental illness in later life when children experience serious adversities such as bullying or other forms of abuse.[7] "Decades of research has given us robust evidence that the risk of developing schizophrenia goes up with experience of childhood adversity."[8]

Many sexually deviant crimes are committed by adults who themselves have suffered sexual abuse in childhood, and crimes of violence are often committed by those who have been exposed to violence or bullying during their early upbringing. Even acquisitiveness or vanity in later life may have their genesis in basic feelings of insecurity or low self-esteem because of a poor or emotionally deprived

---

[5] Brunner, H et al: *Abnormal Behaviour associated with point mutation* ..., Science, 262, 1993, 578-80

[6] Shonkoff, J & Phillips, D (Eds.): *From Neurons to Neighbourhoods: the Science of early Childhood Development*, Committee on Integrating the Science of early *Childhood* Development Board on Children, Youth and Families, 2002

[7] Myers, D: *Psychology*, 10th edn., 2011

[8] Gold, J & I: *Suspicious Minds: How Culture Shapes Madness*, 2014

childhood. As that great observer of human nature, Henrik Ibsen said: 'What we inherit from our mothers and fathers haunts us with all kinds of defunct theories and beliefs... it's not that they actually live on in us; they are simply lodged there and we cannot get rid of them'.

Then, as we grow up and mature, all those friends, colleagues and acquaintances that influenced us, for better or for worse over the years, were probably the result of an initial chance encounter or some common interest or mutual attraction, rather than because of any premeditated, rational or objective choice. How otherwise could we have known the effect they were going to have on us? Any advantages or disadvantages that resulted from those we knew personally were acquired only retrospectively from our experiences of them; first from the influences of our parents and siblings, then later on from our education or as a result of chance conversations, the books we'd read, the films or plays we'd watched, the events we witnessed, and so on and so forth. This is how our inherited biology and neurology allow us to interact with each other and with our environment and in the way we process the data we accumulate from these experiences. It shapes the way we feel, think and act and is changing unpredictably all the time.

But what about our conscience, to which theologians or lawyers are inclined to attribute credit or blame? Doesn't that provide us with a free and independent will that knows the difference between 'right' and 'wrong' and helps us to monitor our behaviour accordingly? If it were as simple as that it would be easy for the sinner to become the saint. Darwin evidently struggled with the problem of 'conscience' when he wrote that:

> At the moment of action, man will no doubt be apt to follow the stronger impulse; and although this may occasionally prompt him to the noblest deeds, it will far more commonly lead him to

gratify his own desires at the expense of other men. But after ... will then feel dissatisfied with himself, and will resolve with more or less force to act differently for the future; this is conscience, for conscience looks backwards and judges past actions, indicating that kind of dissatisfaction, which if weak we call regret, and if severe remorse.[9]

In other words, the feeling that we could have done otherwise comes after we have already acted, because 'at the moment of action' we are not consciously aware of what we are doing. And, although Darwin doesn't specifically say so, deliberation and conscious choice are not the cause of our actions. All our feelings about our behaviour are acquired unconsciously at first by example from the way we were treated in infancy and youth, then more consciously as we matured, according to how we were educated, persuaded, conditioned, cajoled or even hoodwinked or brainwashed over the years. And the process of alteration to the way we feel and think about our actions, for better or for worse, always occurs retrospectively.

Those who still insist they have the 'will' to make choices that are not just their chemistry or chance conditioning, must identify what else it is that allows them to escape these influences, even if only partially. If they believe they didn't have some chance biological or experiential origin, and that they possessed the independent willpower to freely override such prejudicial influences, they need to identify where else this 'willpower' came from. They might argue, for example, that they had gradually acquired enough wisdom or reasoning-power from their life-experiences to make wiser choices, in which case they would still need to explain what independent

---

[9] Darwin, C: The Descent of Man, 1871, 91

control they had had over those life-experiences that allowed them to do so; or otherwise, what had given them the basic ability to develop that wisdom in the first place. And surely all those respectable and law-abiding citizens, who are inclined to act in accordance with the spiritual or secular rules of the society within which they find themselves, must have been conditioned thus to abide by those self-same rules.[10]

Moreover, the codes of conduct of every society have themselves only been culturally or politically conditioned over the generations too, and as history has shown, such conditioning has sometimes led to horrible crimes being committed by these law-abiding citizens in the name of obedience to authority.[11] The fact that people in different countries everywhere are inclined to act according to the practices and beliefs of that country's culture or tradition, because they believe them to be the right ones, is surely proof enough of these geographical or cultural biases. Those who identify with their own race, religion or nationality are unwittingly inclined to feel the rest of mankind is misguided and a threat to their beliefs. In attempting to view the world less subjectively, it soon becomes clear that no race, religion or nationality has a monopoly of truth or virtue over its rivals, each of which should be recognised as merely one among many.

So it turns out that we are not quite as free and independent in our decision-making as we thought we were. From the moment of conception onwards, we become inescapably bound up and influenced by the world around us and there's absolutely nothing we can do to escape from its influences. Our minds and bodies are interacting with our environment all the time, even though we are only consciously aware of very few of these influences, so most, perhaps all our decisions are made for

---

[10] Double, R: *The Non-Reality of Free Will*, 1991

[11] Kelman H & Hamilton V: *Crimes of Obedience*, 1989

us.

In fact, it has been suggested that four conditions are necessary before anyone can even begin to consider whether they are in charge of an action. These are: "That they could fully envisage alternate courses of action; were fully aware of the potential short and long-term consequences of the action; could have chosen to withhold the action; and wanted the results that ensued."[12]

Let's consider each of these in turn. Although we might have some rough idea what the 'alternative courses of action' are, we're almost certainly not aware of all of them. In any event, we can never be sure that they are all equally available to compare and choose impartially from, nor can we ever know what their 'short or long term consequences' are going to be. If we had 'chosen to withhold the action', were we fully aware of the reasons why we did so? Finally, if we 'wanted the result that ensued', were we aware and in control of what had made us want that result? Evidently there is a great deal more going on in our minds than we are aware of[13], let alone in charge of.

With brain-scanning techniques, neurologists might be able to see roughly what is happening when our minds are engaged in decision-making, but almost certainly not why it's happening. That also requires the services of psychologists, sociologists, ethnologists, anthropologists and other specialists; a multi-disciplinary approach is required before we can even begin to see the holistic picture more clearly.

The common perception we have of ourselves as free agents, trying to steer our way wisely and morally through life to the advantage of ourselves and of those whom we love and care for, is evidently a delusion. Focusing our attention on what we think are wise choices, rather than on what has made us think they were, should lead us into

---

[12] Ramachandran, V: *The Tell-Tale Brain*, 2011, 286
[13] Bargh, J et al: *Direct Effects of Trait Constructs*, Journal of Personality & Social Psychology 71, No. 2 230-44, 1996

areas that have hitherto been inhibited by the widely held belief that we have freedom of choice over our behaviour. So, in an attempt to become more responsible, and law-abiding citizens, we are often persuaded by means of praise or blame, administered by authorities about what they believe we should or should not do, because we assume they are wiser and more responsible than we are in knowing how to live our lives.

However, before venturing into this largely uncharted, and for many, forbidden or unacceptable territory, we need to go back in our evolutionary history to a time before ideas about responsibility, authority and freedom of choice ever entered human consciousness. Only then might we begin to see how unwittingly we acquired these concepts in the first place and what devastating consequences have followed from believing in, and trying to abide by them.

2. CAN PEOPLE LIVE
PEACEFULLY TOGETHER?

We would probably all like to live in a society in which everyone treats everyone else fairly, but what does fairness really mean? The cynic might say it means 'being free to gain an unfair advantage over others', which highlights the incompatibility, hidden deep within all our natures, between egoism and altruism. When we think about the needs of others we become concerned for them and try to be more cooperative but sometimes we think more about our own needs and are inclined to be selfish and act competitively.

In small rural societies, people's communal needs form an important part of their lives, so they're more inclined to think of the common good and cooperate rather than compete with one another to achieve it, whereas in much larger urban societies there is often less community spirit, so people tend to focus more on their own needs and those of their immediate family and friends, so are more inclined to compete than cooperate with everyone else. As Oscar Wilde said: "anyone can be good in the country", to which he might have added: 'and anyone can be bad in the city', and because the city can have an affect on your mental health, it has been shows that:

> Schizophrenia interacts with the outside world, in particular with the social world ... the risk of illnesses increases in a near-linear fashion with the population of your city and varies with the social features of your neighbourhoods. Stable, socially coherent neighbourhoods have a lower incidence than neighbourhoods that are more transient and less cohesive.[1]

To make urban, or city life more tolerable, people sometimes form groups with a common interest in, say, football, tennis or dancing; but street gangs are often formed for the same reason. Although both nature and nurture influence our sense of fairness, the structure of the society we find ourselves in also has an influence on the way we treat each other.

In any event, there appear to be two quite distinct ways by which we learn how to behave towards one another. One way is simply 'tit for tat'; in other words, we instinctively tend to respond towards others according to how they respond to us. When they're nice to us we're usually nice back; if they're nasty we tend to respond in kind. The other way is to look for and find guidance in some prescribed spiritual or temporal 'rulebook'. The first of these ways probably formed a fundamental part of our gregarious natures millions of years ago and still contributes in part to the way we feel towards one another today, while the other way came much later in our social evolution, when our ancestors first began to identify, and prescribe in writing, codes of conduct for everyone to

---

[1] Gold, J & I: Gold, J & I: *Suspicious Minds: How Culture Shapes Madness*, 2014

follow.

The difference between these two ways in which we tend to conduct ourselves socially might best be illustrated by the way we drive our cars. In order to avoid accidents and arrive at our destination safely, we continually make adjustments to our driving by altering our speed and steering in accordance with how others around us drive. If everyone drives carefully, we tend to do so too and if they are aggressive, we tend to find ourselves responding in kind. At the same time, we need to be mindful of the road-signs, the speed limits and all the other rules and regulations specified in the Highway Code. So we're inclined to drive like others around us but, to reach our destination safely, we also try to abide by society's 'rulebook'.

Our ancient ancestors, of course, had no written rules to refer to; they simply relied on their personal encounters and how they instinctively felt about one another; it was the only way they could have learnt how to survive cooperatively together as a social species for so long. The codes of conduct that formed their customs and practices were handed down through the generations by example alone, and regulated almost entirely by what have been called 'positive or negative sanctions.'[2] Pro-social behaviour was reinforced by acceptance, friendship, kindness and praise, while anti-social behaviour was discouraged because it caused confusion, gossip, avoidance, even anger and aggression.[3] In other words, behaviour was responded to according to its degree of conformity to, or deviance from custom and tradition, rather than by reference to any consciously constructed spiritual or secular law-like rules of conduct. Those customs and practices that seemed to work best and remain stable were usually the ones that had the greatest

---

[2] Radcliffe-Brown, A: *Structure and Function in Primitive Society*, 1952, 205.
[3] Boehm, C: *Conflict and the Evolution*, Journal of Consciousness Studies 7, 1-2, 2000, 79-101.

survival value and the survival of the community was always greater than the survival of any individual within it. Traditions changed only gradually over time by trial-and-error in much the same way physical evolution does.

Evidently, some of our genetically closest non-human primates have evolved very similar methods of surviving cooperatively together. The way chimpanzees and apes behave, for example, involves:

> Resolving, managing and preventing conflicts of interest within their group [they exhibit] the very building blocks of moral systems, in that they are based on, and facilitate cohesion among individuals and reflect a concentrated effort by community members to find shared solutions to social conflict.[4]

For example, they appear capable of remembering received services, then selectively repaying whomsoever performs those favours, so just like humans, they evidently feel 'one good turn deserve another'. They also seem capable of expressing sympathy, in that they often console one another when distressed, so are able to empathise with others, just as we can. Darwin gives an example: when a troop of baboons were attacked they climbed up the mountain to escape but when a young one was left behind "one of the largest males, a true hero, came down again from the mountain and slowly went to the young one, coaxed him, and triumphantly led him away."[5]

Many of our own religious beliefs reflect such tendencies; for example: "blessed are they that mourn for they shall be comforted" [Matthew Ch.5: 4]. And various forms of reconciliation, along with impartial protective and pacifying intervention techniques observed in non-human

---

[4] Flack, J & de Waal, F: *Any Animal whatever* ..., Journal of Consciousness ..., 7, 1-2, 2000.

[5] Darwin, C: *The Descent of Man*, 1871, 75-6.

primates, such as: 'blessed are the peacemakers for they shall be called the children of God' [Matthew, Ch.5: 9] are also reflected in early religious folklore. Humans however, probably evolved to behave fairly towards one another by trial-and-error long before any of our spiritual and secular leaders thought about transcribing this behaviour into written codes of conduct and preaching about them.

Moreover, chimpanzees and apes seem capable of expressing 'disapproval' of negative behaviour, sometimes resulting in what we might interpret as 'retribution' or 'revenge'. Such words, however, are probably too anthropomorphic as, unlike humans their expressions of disapproval with conflict are usually only momentary impulses and are quickly resolved and forgotten about. Of course, even in small close-knit human groups, feelings of retribution or revenge probably existed too but, because everyone was so dependent upon everyone else in their communities, such feelings were usually only transient. If they had been more persistent, they would quickly destroy social bonding and threaten the survival of the whole group. Under our own more autocratic leadership however, whole societies can become thus affected, so control sometimes needs to be administered by the stringent enforcement of the law. Too much control can backfire though. In 1938, for example, there were sixteen dictatorships throughout Europe in which despotic methods of control were employed to "severely restrict personal liberties"[6], yet few of these lasted more than a generation and by 1975 they had all been replaced by more democratic governments.

From the Neolithic era onwards however, people seem to have increasingly believed the awesome mysteries of nature were the work of all-powerful deities. Favourable weather conditions and an abundance of food might have been interpreted as signs of approval by the gods, whereas

---

[6] Lee, S: *The European Dictatorships 1918-45*, 1987, xi- xv.

thunderstorms or drought were signs of disapproval. This, of course, may simply have been the transference of how young children looked to their parents for approval or disapproval[7] as these tendencies have strong instinctive survival value. In fact, people still seem to think "anything which manifests mysterious power is endowed with some form of life and with mental faculties analogous to our own."[8]

Relics of this anthropomorphism are still evident in the language we use today as we often refer to 'mother' nature or to God the 'father' and any feelings of sublimation to the powers of nature may have their genesis in the concept of a divine creator. Some still pray for rain in the hope their crops will grow, or when it's cold or overcast for the sun to shine. On the other hand, some might regard any "god whose creation is so imperfect that he must be continually adjusting it to make it work properly [to be] of relatively low order and hardly worth a worship"[9]

The marked decline in hunter-gatherers or band communities, in which order had been unilaterally maintained by tradition, occurred as they gradually became absorbed into larger, more urban communities in which order had to be maintained by hierarchically imposition. The gradual conversion of traditional customs into imposed regulations, rules and laws is what most distinguished so-called civilized societies from pre-civilized societies. There were practical reasons for this, of course. In all small egalitarian communities, "there was a limit to the size in which order could be maintained by direct personal contact" and studies have suggest that the

---

[7] Beaman, R & Wheldall, K: Vol 20, 4, 2000; Bugental, D & Love, L: *Nonassertive Expression of Parental Approval and Disapproval*, Child Development, Vol. 46, 3, 1975, et al.

[8] Darwin, C: *The Descent of Man ...*, 1871, Ch. 3.

[9] Gardner, M: *The Ambidextrous Universe* 1970

maximum number was about 150 members.[10] The change in size of these new groups, and hence in their structure, from unilateral tradition to hierarchical imposition, may have taken place over thousands of years but the larger these communities became, the more difficult it would have been for them to maintain unilateral standards of behaviour by direct person-to-person contact and influence.

Just for illustrative purposes, such standards of behaviour could be transmitted among a community of say, 50 members, by means of up to 1,225 person-to-person contacts, but, beyond that, this number grows exponentially to nearly half a million for a community of 1,000 members. Obviously, not all personal interactions would have been between pairs of individuals. Much group interaction would have occurred while eating together around fires or huddled together in caves, for example, but at least these figures indicate the enormous practical difficulties involved in trying to maintain stability and cohesion by face-to-face contact with everyone when people found themselves living in communities that had become too large.

So, as those small, self-regulated rural groups of people gradually became absorbed into larger urban societies, radical alterations to the way they were structured became increasingly necessary. If say, a society of 1,000 members, was reorganised hierarchically on four levels, with a ratio of one person in a dominant role to ten in subordinate roles, then, theoretically at least, less than just a 100 group-relationships would be required to establish common codes of conduct throughout that society. Jericho was one of the earliest of these urban settlements. It developed near the Jordan River from about 9,000 BCE onwards, from the migration of an increasing

---

[10] Dunbar, R: *Coevolution of Neocortical Size, Group Size and Language in Humans*, Behavioural and Brain Sciences, 1993 [16] 691.

accumulation of small band communities, and until the Bronze Age continued to grow into a municipality with a population of perhaps several thousand.

It's not surprising therefore that, as these societies increased in size, common standards of acceptable and unacceptable conduct, originally derived from the legends of folkloric mysticism, began to be transcribed into more ethical rules concerning 'right' and 'wrong' behaviour. Some of the earliest examples of these rules have been found in Samaria [3000 BCE] and among the hieroglyphs of ancient Egypt [c.2950 BCE] also in the Sanskrit texts of Vedic India [2500-1500 BCE], in Mesopotamia [2000 BCE] and, during the Shan Dynasty in ancient China [1600-1100 BCE]. All these codes of conduct seem to imply that they were authorised by anthropocentric deities and that 'justice', 'law' and 'order' were female: Maat or Mayet, the ancient Egyptian goddess of 'world order' for example, or Themis and Dike of ancient Greece, who 'passed judgement and executed retribution', or as Rta of early Indian mythology, who 'represented the eternal order of justice and law'.

At those times in our history, it began to be accepted that the cosmological laws of order in nature should be reflected in laws of conduct by men for maintaining order in human societies. Enuma Elish [1800-1600 BCE] from Babylonian myths, for example, was "he who could consult god for guidance about immediate problems." And "the father of the gods [was he] who ordered my rule,"[11] or "the great gods have called me ... I am the salvation-bearing shepherd". Meanwhile, the Pharaohs of ancient Egypt perceived themselves as 'living gods', or "he, who was protector of his people, was awesome in perfection" [Gilgamesh: 2750-2500 BCE]. And towards the close of the fourth millennium BCE, city-state rulers

---

[11] Hamarabi's Code of Laws: King of Babylonia c1700 BC, Epilogue, trans. L W King.

throughout Mesopotamia began claiming they had the right to administer justice by inflicting the most terrible punishments upon anyone who violated their divinely revealed codes of conduct. It may be worth noting however, that before these times, there was ample evidence "from men who have long resided with savages, that numerous races existed and still exist, who have no idea of one or more gods, and have no words in their language to express such an idea."[12]

With the gradual need to understand the mysterious forces of nature however:

> The belief in spiritual agencies easily passed into the belief in the existence of one or more gods. For savages would naturally attribute to spirits the same passions, the same love of vengeance or simplest form of justice, and the same affection, which they themselves experienced. ... The feeling of religious devotion is a highly complex one, consisting of love, complete submission to an exalted and mysterious superior, a strong sense of dependence, fear, gratitude, hope for the future, and perhaps other elements.[13]

So it is but a small step to see how such ideas became adopted by more structured societies in which the principal aim was to enforce order by 'the authoritative administration and maintenance of the law', and this was usually expressed in the form of commandments such as: 'thou shalt ...' or 'thou shalt not ...' by those who claimed they represented order in society, so 'it was the king's duty to destroy the wicked and inflict punishment on controverters of society'. Then, with the transference from spiritual to secular law, 'good' or 'virtuous' behaviour

---

[12] Darwin, C: *The Descent of Man*, 1871, 65.

[13] Pike, O: *The Psychical Elements of Religion*, Anthropology Review, 1879, lxiii

simply became reinterpreted as obedience, and 'bad' or 'evil' behaviour as disobedience to state authority, rather than to the authority of the god or gods it claimed to represent.

It was assumed that these laws had to be obeyed, not for any commonly accepted reasons of fairness or merit, but simply because they had the backing of supernatural power, as represented by the divine right of kings or emperors; consequently the punishments for not obeying them were often frighteningly severe. These included 'being beaten, flogged or struck a hundred times', 'broken into pieces'; or having one's 'hands cut off' or 'eyes gouged out', 'thrown into the fire', 'drowned' or 'decapitated', often with the added threat of 'eternal damnation' after death.

Understandably therefore, fear-induced feelings of submissiveness to authority, along with respect and admiration for the supreme powers claimed by these authorities, was simply the way order became enforced and maintained. And because fear is a universal emotion, despotic methods of social control sprang up and seem to have survived in many parts of the world to the present day, at least in principle, if not in degree, simply because this retributive method of justice is generally an effective way of keeping people under control.

In reality though, punishment often demonstrates little more than a difference of power and control between the opinion of the 'giver' and 'receiver'. Even in many more democratically organised societies, in which considerable effort may be made to ensure the laws are based on fairness and reason, citizens are still fearful of questioning authority because the power of "dominance and submission"[14] can always be called upon if it's ever seriously challenged. In fact, fear of punishment still remains the foundation stone upon which all forms of retributive justice ultimately depend.

---

[14] Fried, M: *The Evolution of Political Society*, 1967

Because these written records represented humanity's first attempts to define how citizens should, or should not behave under the absolute rule of a god-king figurehead, they might ironically be regarded as the original blueprints for civilization itself. Although a recognition that there were alternative ways of doing things, the idea that one could freely choose between them seems to have been assumed a justification for rewarding conformity and punishing deviance. In reality however, all it did was make citizens increasingly aware of, and become influenced by the consequences of their actions, whatever they were going to be.

Because people were constantly being reminded, by spiritual and secular law-makers, that there were 'right' and 'wrong' ways of doing things, it seems to have been assumed that the recognition of these alternatives somehow gave citizens the freedom to choose between them.[15] The great irony about all this is though, that such methods of control actually inhibit people's freedom rather than make it available to them. After all, it should be obvious that even a donkey's freedom becomes 'severely restricted' if it is constantly being enticed by its master's carrot and threatened by his stick. An independent observer of any retributive system of social control should immediately recognise that: "those who manipulate human behaviour are ... evil men, necessarily bent on exploitation. Control is clearly the opposite of freedom and if freedom is good, then control must be bad"[16]

---

[15] The concept of choice must have developed from conceptualising future events, even though comparing alternative probably occurred intuitively long before that.

[16] Skinner, B: *Beyond Freedom and Dignity*, 1971, 41

3. WHAT IS THE GOOD LIFE?

Any attempt to achieve the good life by administering codes of spiritual and secular conduct upon society, is not just questionable, it has serious moral implications. Nevertheless, with the birth of the city-state, this system began to be introduced by authority-figures who thought they knew best how to do so and it has remained with us ever since. It has polarised philosophical enquiry in two broadly different directions. One approach focused more on the emotional and spiritual needs of individuals, independently of all civic codes of conduct; the other more on how these needs might be best achieved within the organised rules of society, and in this respect a difference between Western philosophy and Eastern philosophy has emerged. To some extent this polarisation also distinguished those who focused more on the world 'with-out' and how it related to us, and the world 'with-in' and how we related to it.

There were areas of overlap, of course, as certain features of the Gita were concerned with social duties, while aspects of Confucianism also advised on the rituals of civic convention. But this approach might best be personified by ascetics such as the Indian sage, Yajnavalkya [c.1800BCE] or the Chinese mystic, Laozi [600BCE] or by Siddhārtha Gautama of northern India [c500BCE] who became known as the Buddha. In pursuit of a life of 'disinterested-action', he was reported to have surrendered all his worldly interests and public pleasures so as to 'neither hate nor rejoice' and, by 'relinquishing concepts of good and evil', came to 'be without self-pride'. In this way, he claimed one could attain universal compassion and live 'more in accordance with the natural harmony and continuity of things', his aim being a state of perpetual peace, called *nirvana*. This approach later became typified by Taoism, as represented by Chuang Tzŭ [c400BCE] among others, whose aim it was to free one's self from worldly goals, including all social norms and etiquettes.

There were echoes of this approach in Western philosophical thought too. The writings of Epicurus, for example, suggested that the desire for wealth and honour was futile and that it would be 'wise to flee from every form of culture'. Empathy for Eastern asceticism is also reflected in Montaigne's Essays, in which he frequently recommended following nature. No doubt he was inspired by contemporary accounts of voyagers to the New World, wherein the 'noble savages' were 'never forced, but only restrained in whatever they did'. Similar sentiments were expressed by Rousseau, who claimed "man is born free and everywhere he is in chains"[1]; and that "by nature he was good, yet corrupted and depraved by society"[2], sentiments that later became expressed in Existentialism, which favoured a general sense that 'existence precedes essence' and a contempt of all bourgeois organisations and practices.

The more general Western approach however, believed

---

[1] Rousseau, J: *Social Contract*, 1762 1:1
[2] Rousseau, J. *Discourse on the Sciences and Arts*, 1778

some form of authorised control of society was necessary but should always be open to critical appraisal. However, even before deciding whether these controls were valid or not, the Pre-Socratics [c.600 BCE] thought it was first necessary to question the god-given right of authority to administer them. Those who had already claimed this right however, saw this as a threat to their favoured position in society and were inclined to overrule any such criticism outright. Socrates, who questioned it, was one of the first to be sentenced to death on charges of 'impiety and corruption', while his pupil, Plato, managed to pre-empt a similar fate by leaving Athens for a long time and, even when he did return, was careful to confine his critical teachings to theory beyond the confines of the Athenian state. Later, Aristotle was also accused of 'impiety' but managed to escape persecution by spending the remainder of his days in self-appointed exile. Authority evidently felt that its need to protect its own interest was more important than questioning whether is was ever valid in the first place.

The Pre-Socratics had also tried to distinguish empirically between 'good' and 'bad' laws according to their consequences but came to the conclusion that some were mere conventions, sanctioned only by legal obligation. In the Homeric poems [750-550BCE] for example, the word 'good'[3] seemed to refer only to kings or noblemen who considered themselves custodians of the state, with the 'courage' and 'skill' to protect their citizens, along with the 'wealth' and 'power' to authorise laws for the maintenance of order and conformity as they defined it.

At a time when the city-state was under constant threat, this interpretation might well have been necessary, but in less bellicose times 'good' might have had an altogether more humanitarian connotation, connoting perhaps:

---

[3] Adkins, A: *Merit and Responsibility in Greek Ethics*, 1962, 32-3

'compassion', 'kindness' and 'trust'. And when applied to our more recent 'celebrity culture', the attribute of 'good' seemed to have acquired an entirely amoral connotation, based only on fame and fortune. Some might now even think the word 'courage' would be better applied to pacifists who faced public humiliation for their convictions, rather than to patriots who faced the enemy that threatened them. And others yet, might be more inclined to associate 'power' and 'status,' with 'greed' and 'exploitation', rather than 'care' and 'custodianship'. All these examples illustrate a transience in the meaning of these words and hence in the transience of our feelings and thoughts that express them.

Consider too how the word 'ownership' first came about. After all, before the agrarian revolution there didn't appear to be any presumption that anyone owned anything. Within those much smaller egalitarian communities at that time, the idea of personal ownership had evidently not been conceived of. If a community member made a spear and used it, or prepared a deer-skin and wore it, 'ownership' might have been thought valid by today's standards, yet before written laws gave any credence to the idea, such practices seem to have been regarded as mere customs or traditions, and most things people used or wore were considered communal property anyway. Words such as 'possession' or 'belong', which came to imply 'ownership', along with 'thief', 'steal' or 'rob', which implied their violation, only began to appear in the first written legal texts, so they became authorised only after possession of land and chattels had already been claimed by those who first acquired, and claimed possession of such things. Yet, to this day, no meaningful justification or validity for claiming ownership of anything seems to have been attempted before underwriting its validation by law in the first place.

Settlement and farming must have brought about a free-for-all acquisitiveness for land and chattels, particularly for crops, livestock and any natural resources contained within the boundaries of occupied land, along with its protection thereof. So, in an attempt to minimise endless feuding, along with jealousy, violence and revenge, such practices had to be validated retrospectively somehow, simply by force of law.

These days, it might seem perfectly fair and reasonable that whosoever had acquired property and chattels, which nobody else had hitherto claimed, had the right to own and retain them for themselves but, the process of acquiring any right to them only begs the question: how did they obtain that right in the first place? Then, with the age of exploration, discovery and colonialism, followed by claims of ownership of vast swathes of land and natural resources around the world, often at the expense of the indigenous peoples already living there, such acquisitiveness might have been what prompted Shakespeare to proclaim: "I see in a map the ruin of us all".

Indeed, could it ever be incontrovertibly shown that the loss to those who claimed ownership of their possessions was always going to be greater than the gain for others who decided to take possession off them for themselves? Should a starving man, for example, still be condemned for taking a loaf of bread from a rich man? Making ownership legal therefore, could not have been based on any reason of fairness such as equality, balance or practical necessity, but simply because it was thought by those who had the effrontery to claim it in the first place, to be preferable to its complete absence. The commandment: 'thou shalt not steal' might now seem inviolate to most people, yet only became so after the 'divine right of kings' and those with the power to enforce their acquisitiveness on others, insisted it was valid after they had already acquired it. The validity of ownership in law therefore, appears to have become a consequence, rather than a cause of acquisition, derived only from some spurious belief that 'possession was nine tenths of the law'. Now we implicitly believe in ownership because it has been an accepted practice since 'time immemorial', which literally means 'beyond the reach of memory', so is consequently, assumed to be also beyond question.

The difficulty of validating ownership is magnified out of all proportion however, when one considers the other benefits that somehow seem to have mysteriously accrued from it. These usually included 'status' and a favoured position in society, along with the 'power' to command obedience from others who owned less or nothing at all, and, in some respects, seemed also to imply the ownership of other people's minds and bodies. In fact, these accrued benefits infiltrated all levels of society, and included the ownership of servants or slaves by their 'masters', or of wives and children by their husbands and fathers. In fact: "The great sin of slavery has been almost universal, and slaves have often been treated in an infamous manner, [and] as barbarians do not regard the opinion of their women, [their] wives are commonly treated as slaves".[4]

Nevertheless, around the 5th century BC, when Athenian democracy was first born, Greeks generally didn't seem to think their ownership of 80,000 slaves was wrong.[5] Aristotle certainly seemed to believe it was an acceptable part of Athenian society, although Plato was more ambivalent. He could see that power claimed by those with authority, had no intrinsic merit and meant nothing more than an advantage of the strong over the weak, so would be better replaced by the 'philosopher-king', rather than abandoned altogether.

The Stoics argued that if state law was derived from natural law, then everyone, even slaves, had a right to their own freedom. Not surprisingly, as a consequence of 'ownership', all these accrued imbalances between people at first evoked a festering sense of unfairness, because they

---

[4] Darwin C: *The Descent of Man,* 1871, 94

[5] Thorley, J: *Athenian Democracy,* 2005, 74.

conflicted with natural feelings of 'equality' and 'balance', as symbolised sometimes by the 'scales of justice'. As the administration of 'justice' is essentially master-biased though, balance would turn this idea on its head because masters and slaves could swap places without its execution being altered. Although master-slave relationships may be less conspicuous these days, the inequalities of 'ownership' are manifest, not only in the controls employers have over their employees but, at every level within employment, between managers and their subordinates, and indeed more generally, at all levels throughout society. And although in modern life we don't call it slavery any more, in effect: "the State is a state of slavery in which a man does what he likes to do in his spare time but, in his working time, that which is required of him".[6]

Expediency alone, therefore, appears to have become the tenuous foundation upon which concepts such as 'ownership', 'status', 'power', 'control' and 'obedience', are all assumed to have some intrinsic validity. It might have been thought that by rewarding the 'good' and punishing the 'bad', imbalances in people's behaviour, and hence in their position in society, would eventually be ironed out and that the scales of justice would even out and become equal. Unfortunately though, the evidence tells a very different story. As Nietzsche had observed:

> In all higher and mixed civilizations there was a master-morality and a slave-morality .... The master morality was pleasantly conscious of being different from those they ruled. The rulers determine the conception of 'good'; it is their exalted, proud, disposition which [is] regarded as the distinguishing feature and that which determines the order of rank. The ruler rejoices over every good opinion which he hears about

---

[6] Gill, E: *Slavery and Freedom*, 1918.

himself ... and the slave immediately afterwards falls [and] prostrates himself before these opinions.[7]

It reality therefore, the very nature of all hierarchically structured societies had actually reinforced and even amplified differences between the 'good' and 'bad', rather than helped to level them out. After all, a 'master morality' can only exist if there is a 'slave morality' over which it can rule. These two moralities depend entirely upon each other for their own existence: those who dominate and those who are dominated are symbiotically related. "The noble type of man regards himself as a determiner of values; he does not require to be approved of; he passes the judgement, such morality equals self-glorification."[8]

To be 'good', the 'master morality' seemed somehow to claim 'strength', 'courage' and 'imperviousness to pain', whereas the slave-morality believed 'good' was more to do with 'humility', 'piety' and 'suffering'. These differences may have been more conspicuous in the Greek and Roman societies Nietzsche studied, but they are still just as relevant today, albeit in a somewhat more euphemistic form perhaps. Several different studies have shown that upper-class individuals were, for example: "More likely to exhibit unethical decision-making, take valued goods from others, lie in negotiation, cheat to increase their chances of winning a prize, and endorse unethical behaviour at work more than lower-class individuals.[9]

Before the agrarian revolution, however, our ancient ancestors appear to have survived fairly cooperatively together, with differentials less of status, power and authority, than of age, wisdom and natural ability. And these same features still remain prevalent amongst the few remaining hunter-gatherers and band communities that

---

[7] Nietzsche, F: *Beyond Good and Evil*, 1886, para. 260

[8] Ibid. Ch IX

[9] Piff, P et al: *Higher Social Class predicts increased unethical Behaviour*, 2012

exist today. They usually have extended family origins and each of their various activities contribute to the common good. In other words, their social needs, rather than their solitary needs, represent the essential part of their lives. There were and still are divisions of labour of course, but they are based on natural abilities or skill or wisdom and are not ranked hierarchically according to status, power or control, nor indeed do they generally give or take orders from one another since their aim is essentially for the community.

Although respect was, and still is attributed to those with particular skills, or to those who have accumulated knowledge with age and experience in resolving disagreements, but they still remain essentially egalitarian in structure.[10] Community leaders or village chiefs might gain respect but they do not command; they only advise on changes; they never enforce them. Any attempt to exert dominance or control is rarely tolerated, as the needs of the community are always rated as more important than those of any individual within it.[11] "Any control over an individual's behaviour is exercised almost entirely by their acceptance or rejection by other group members".[12] Moreover, their justice-systems are essentially 'restorative', rather than 'punitive' in nature, in that they focus more on compensating victims than on punishing offenders. This usually involved making good any damage or loss to injured parties, especially by means of sympathy and support; their aim, as far as possible, being the restoration of the community's *status quo*, rather than the enforcement of authority's *status quo*.

---

[10] Service, E: *Primitive Social Organisation* .. , 1962; Fried, M: *The Evolution of Political Society* ..1967; Knauft, B: *Violence and Sociality in Human Evolution*, Current Anthropology, 32; 1991, human egalitarianism could have started two million years ago; Boehm, C: *Conflict and the Evolution of Social Control*, Journal of Consciousness Studies 7, 89, 2000

[11] Cashdan, E: *Egalitarianism among Hunters and Gatherers*, American Anthropologist, 82, 116-20

[12] Drew, K: *The Lombard Laws*, 1973 edn., pp 51 & 62

So did these changes in society's social structure and in the way its members acted towards one another, come about accidentally as a result of the agrarian revolution or because of free and conscious choice? Nietzsche must have been familiar with evolutionary biology to suggest that it was "quite impossible for a man not to have the qualities and predilections of his parents and ancestors in his constitution".[13] After all, it is now known that: "...genes exert a statistical influence on human behaviour, while at the same time believing that this influence can be modified, overridden or reversed by other influences.[14] Indeed, some of these other influences might have had to be necessarily adopted by the significant increase in size of the societies within which people first found themselves. But it could also have been adopted by the concept of authority, as represented by the Babel story that appeared in mythology at about the same time. Before that it was believed everyone spoke the same language, but the building of a tower to reach heaven, caused a 'confusion of tongues' between metaphysicians and theologians about God and the immortality of the soul. Kant alluded to this story under 'The Doctrine of Method' in his first 'Critique', in which he claimed a confusion of languages prevented people for cooperating with each other, so a tower had to be built upon people's ignorance, forcing them to submit to what he called "the ridiculous despotism of the schools". Indeed, the birth of the city-state may have forced people to shift their perception of themselves from 'we', as part of an egalitarian community, to 'I', as part of a hierarchical society, and from 'us', as surviving cooperatively, with other members of the community, to 'me', as surviving in competition with other members of the society they found themselves in.

At one time people evaluated their own and each

---

[13] Nietzsche, F: *Beyond Good and Evil*, 1886, para. 264

[14] Dawkins, R: *The Selfish Gene*, 2006 edn., 331

other's survival skills, more in terms of how much or how little they could use them to contribute to the community, so perhaps 'comfort' and 'protection' was their only idea of 'the good life'. Now though, people think more about their own position in relation to the positions of others around them, as measured in terms of their personality, education, occupation, specialist knowledge, skills and so on. So perhaps the 'good life' depends on how best people exercises these abilities in order to survive. Surely though, they haven't deliberately chosen the society they find themselves in, so perhaps they haven't deliberately chosen how they should exercise these skills to survive either.

It has been suggested that the reason why kinship communities had been able to survive cooperatively together and without much change in their social structure for so long, was because of their high 'coefficient of relatedness',[15] resulting in a kind of instinctive 'reciprocal altruism'[16] amongst their members. This might be why parents feel altruistic towards their children and other members of their extended families. However, even sharing "hostile environments may [also] provide conditions conducive to the evolution of cooperation"[17], such as the great feeling of comradeship amongst soldiers facing a common enemy, even though it has nothing to do with genetics.

These days however, 'reciprocal altruism' often has an altogether more contractual meaning and implies an expectation of return from others in the form of goods and services, rather kindness and compassion. Understandably, people don't like to admit to this more materialistic form of 'tit-for-tat' expectation but, ever since

---

[15] Hamilton, W: *The Genetic Evolution of Social Behaviour*, 1964 Journal Theoretical Biology 7, 1-16.
[16] Trivers, R L: *The Evolution of Reciprocal Altruism*, Quarterly Review of Biology 46, 1971.
[17] Harms, W: *The Evolution of Cooperation in Hostile Environments*; Evolutionary Origins of Morality, ed. Katz, L, 2000, 308

behaviour became defined as 'good' or 'evil' and enforced upon society by means of 'rewards' and 'punishments', egoism began to replace altruism. This was a consequence of the more rational egocentric mind's attempt to enforce how it thought the 'good life' could be achieved, upon the more altruistic mind, which knew how to achieve it anyway. At one time therefore, only feelings of cooperation were needed to attain the 'good life', whereas now, only thoughts about how best to compete are required.

4. IS THERE A GOLDEN RULE FOR HOW TO LIVE?

The difficulties involved in living cooperatively together have encouraged philosophers to search for principles by which behaviour could be evaluated. Various criteria have been suggested: 'hedonism' and 'harmony of the soul' by Plato, 'temperance' and 'the golden mean' by Aristotle, 'empiricism' by Locke, Berkeley and Hume, 'utilitarianism' by Bentham and Mill, and 'positivism' by Comte, among many others. There have also been attempts to reconcile the rights of individuals with those of the state, but what were these rights? Locke was one of the first to define them as 'the right to life, liberty and property', which, in the American Declaration of Independence, became 'the right to life, liberty and the pursuit of happiness'.

Hegel, however, believed that the study of our history would reveal how strongly it had influenced our thinking about these things, and, by so doing, would give us the freedom to determine our own future, rather than have it determined for us. He summarised this claim with the phrase: 'the history of the world is none other than the progress of consciousness of freedom'.[1] He thought our conscious recognition of this would, in effect, give people the freedom to find a balance between the fulfilment of their own needs and those of the society within which they found themselves. In other words, the subjective desires of the individual and the objective desires of society could be unified in the form of a kind of communal spirit, or '*geist*', as he called it. In his attempt to solve this dilemma rationally however, he appears to have assumed our objective thoughts did not have a subjective origin. And even to this day, the relationship between, what appear to be *a priori* thoughts and *a posteriori* feelings has not been adequately resolved.

Nevertheless, the scientific age certainly seemed to have offered alternative courses of action from which people believed they could objectively choose the futures they wanted. Indeed, Leibniz suggested some 'concepts' of knowledge were *a priori* and therefore independent of experience, thus allowing us to "reason in metaphysics and morals in much the same way as in geometry and analysis".[2] As a result, he thought the 'concept' of judgement, which allowed us to "act ... in a way that no-one could complain about", was irrefutable.

This idea must have persuaded Kant to argue likewise, that 'pure reason' was just as valid as mathematical propositions, whereas 'practical reason', which was concerned with the inferences that could be drawn from it, was what we should all aim for.[3] So he thought it was our duty to follow moral law based on pure reason, and this became known as his 'categorical imperative', namely: "act

---

[1] Hegel, G: *The History of Philosophy*, published posthumously, 1837

[2] These philosophical conjectures were widely known through Leibniz's correspondence. Not until 1931 did Gödel's 'Incompleteness Theorems' show, at least mathematically, this claim was logically indefensible.

[3] Ernst Cassirer considered Leibniz's conception of justice pre-empted Kant's 'categorical imperative', which suggests Kant was more of a deductive than inductive thinker.

as if one's action willed that it were a law for everyone". If one were in any doubt about a particular moral issue, one need only appeal to the high court of reason to determine what the relevant 'categorical imperative' was, because reason transcended the bounds of personal judgement and applied, as a kind of universal 'rule' or 'law' of nature to all mankind equally, or so he thought. The great variety of cultural practices around the world, however, seem to demonstrate how overwhelmingly impractical this idea really was.

Although Hegel still seemed to think that reason gave us the freedom to sort out our differences on moral issues, in practice we were more often guided by our feelings and emotions about such things, which is precisely why it's often so difficult to break old habits. Reason might tell us that smoking shortens our lives, for example, yet how we feel emotionally about it may prevent us from giving up the habit. The 'thinking' and 'feeling' parts of our brain may try to synchronise with one another, yet they process data in such different ways it's hard to reconcile them; they might even be conceptually incompatible.

If, for example, three people had been alone together in a boat at sea for a long time and facing starvation, should a majority-vote allow the fittest or youngest to kill and eat the weakest or oldest, so that at least two of them might remain alive longer? Some might reason that saving two lives is better than none, whereas others might be horrified and leave it up to fate to determine the outcome. The nature of any problem depends on which part of our brain we're using. Many tend to rate objective thought or reason more highly then subjective feeling or intuition but it's sometimes very dangerous to do so. When we think carefully about a problem our solution might be more rational but when we respond without deliberating at all, our solution might turn out to be wiser.[4] Responding intuitively to traffic while driving a car, for example, is less likely to cause an accident than deliberating rationally all the time.

In a more materialistic world, some of our decisions require careful judgment and planning, sometimes also calculation or an appeal to prescription in law, but the sorts of problems our ancient ancestors faced were dealt with in a more intuitive, non-judgmental way. So perhaps the pre-frontal cortex, which is concerned with careful planning and judgement, is responsible for having brought about an ordered and more rational environment within which to act objectively, based on algorithms that influence the way we organised our lives these days. This reveals a strange irony in our neurology, because the conscious thinking parts of the brain developed later in our evolutionary history than the limbic system, which is more to do with sensual experiences.

> Very early in our evolution the brain developed the ability to create first-order sensory representations of external objects ... but as the human brain developed further, there emerged a second brain, a set of nerve connections, to be exact, that was in a sense parasitic on the old one ... by processing information from the first brain into manageable chunks that can be used for a wider repertoire of more sophisticated responses, including language and symbolic thought.[5]

Perhaps this 'second brain' had infected 'the old one', like some sort of toxoplasmosis with long-term detrimental consequences. Maybe the development of this

---

[4] Mikels, J et al: *Should I go with Gut?* Emotion 11(4) 743-53, 2011: found that for quick decisions, relying on emotional instinct tended to lead to better outcomes.
[5] Ramachandran, V: *The Tell-tale Brain*, 2011, 246

'second brain' convinced us that we had now 'progressed' further than all other species, because it gave us a greater capacity to think consciously about our environment and acquire recognisably objective knowledge from it with which to plan our futures. But before trying to assess this self-congratulatory piece of reasoning, we also need to give credence to what the limbic system might feel about the sort of world it was leading us into. Might the cultural diversity of all our feelings concerning 'right' and 'wrong' behaviour, for example, eventually become subjugated to some Kantian voice of universal reason that overrules all these feelings for moral imperatives that makes us emotionally sterile?

This *reductio ad absurdum* had already been dismissed thousands of years earlier by one of the founding fathers of scepticism, Sextus Empiricus [c.200 AD] who studied cultural differences in the customs and practices of the inhabitants of Rome, Ethiopia and Rhodes. As a result, he concluded that moral truths were always grounded in opinion. Despite societies' continued attempts to enforce their own moral truths on other societies, universal judgements should 'always be suspended' because our ethnocentric natures prevented us from ever knowing which customs and beliefs were the wisest. The cultural practices we were born into and influenced by before they were overruled by reason, were usually the ones we accept happily enough without having to constrict them to the rigors of critical appraisal. "Custom, then, is the great guide of human life". [David Hume]

Although both the 'feeling' and 'thinking' parts of our brain are subject to the same evolutionary processes, the feeling part evolved much earlier from sensory inputs. So all our thoughts about them, no matter how abstracted they may have become, must surely have originated from those self-same sensory inputs. Even people's most sacrosanct thoughts about how to live their lives surely originated from covert feelings that became transcribed into overt thoughts.

Despite our search for irrefutable moral truths, the way we feel we ought to act still precedes, and sometimes overrules the way we think we should act. Nature had ordained that our survival depended on balance, not only with our own species but, as far as possible, with everything else around us too, so if there was a universal morality, it would surely have its origins in this innate desire to act in harmony with everything. When we act in accordance with the way others act, we feel comfortable and safe; when disparities arise we feel insecure and threatened, so instinctively try to restore the balance. In fact, the extent to which people are able to coordinate with each other and with their environment is surely the source from which all our thoughts about moral principles of 'good' and 'evil' were originally derived.

Unfortunately though, feelings about what is harmonious or discordant can be distorted by thoughts about them being morally 'good' or 'evil'. If we act empathically towards others, we might feel a kind of 'authentic' pride that we were in harmony with them, on the other hand, if we won first prize in a sports competition against others, we might feel a kind of 'hubristic' pride that we were 'good' to have beaten them.[6] This illustrates how circumstances can change the meaning of our emotions, according to whether we feel cooperative or competitive with one another. If we feel we can trust others, we feel safe in their company and tend to cooperate with them; if we don't feel we can trust them, we unsafe and rely more on ourselves, so tend to be competitive and early conditioning usually determines our attitude.

Those who are fortunate enough to have been nurtured by loving and caring parents probably developed brains

---

[6] Weidman, A et al: *The Benefits of Following Your Pride*, Journal of Personality, 2016

that became wired to create loving and caring relationships with others. And, without needing to think about it, would have become conditioned to care about others in much the same way as others cared about them. On the other hand, those who suffered from neglect, molestation or physical abuse would probably have become conditioned to repeat those earlier transgressions by neglecting, molesting or abusing others too. And in more extreme cases, those who had not experienced empathy from anyone might become horribly cruel to others because they would surely not have developed any sense of shame or guilt about doing so. Without the "shame emotion as a source of self-control in social settings, and a feeling of concern for the well-being of others ... we would all be incorrigible sociopaths."[7]

Of course subsequent peer pressure and other forms of social conditioning, might encourage us to conform to the norms of society but, once the basic pathways by which we first learned to respond to human stimuli become imprinted in our minds, they are surely less likely to be susceptible to alteration. As an example: those who criticize others sometimes reveal more about them than about those they criticize.

In its positive form, the Golden Rule, namely 'treat others as you would like to be treated', assumes we should judge others by our own standards. And, in its prohibitive form: 'don't treat others in ways that you would not like to be treated', also assumes we should judge others by our own standards. Both seem to think everyone else should have the same standards as we do, which is a somewhat myopic view of human nature, to say the least. It would make sense only if we all felt the same as one another but not for people like 'Jack Sprat, who would eat no fat', nor for 'his wife, who would eat no lean.' And because they were evidently both happy to accept each other's

---

[7] Gintis, H: *Group Selection and Human Prosociality*, Evolutionary Origins of Morality, 2000, 218.

differences, 'they licked the platter clean'. Those theologians who promoted the Golden Rule evidently believed that, not only their own egocentric standards of moral conduct should apply to everyone else, but also that by convincing those simple enough to follow them, it would helped to validate their own belief that the should do so?

As a social species, our pre-linguistic ancestors learnt instinctively what to do and what not do by continually adjust their own behaviour according to how others responded to it. Empathy had allowed them to regulate their own behaviour according to how others with empathy felt about it, so had been able to maintain feelings of egalitarianism accordingly. They didn't need language to help them transpose these feelings into rational thoughts; facial expressions, body language and behaviour were usually quite enough. And thereby, common standards of empathy and trust helped them maintain common standards of conformity and equilibrium.

As the Chinese philosophies of Mencius and Laozi [c. 600 BCE] had suggested, our nature had taught us how to be personally kind to each other before our nurture had taught us how to be impersonally civilized towards each other. Genetic evolution functions on a much longer timescale than does cultural conditioning. Long before the Golden Rule became a twinkle in the minds of the theologians, the evolution of empathy had been enough to show us how to live gregariously together. As soon as the rational mind began moralising about human behaviour, it changed the focus of our attention away from egalitarian control, and more towards centralised control, which is probably why the Golden Rule became so appealing to those at the dawn of civilization who promoted it.

So there appears to be a disparity between how we instinctively feel we ought to behave and how society thinks we should behave. For example, we would probably instinctively feel we ought not to kill anyone of whom we had no personal knowledge, yet, in times of war, we might be ordered, by those who had the authority, to insist we should do so. Or we might feel the way the government spends our money was wrong, yet they would still insist we pay our taxes, and there are probably many things we would feel were right to do, even though they contravened the laws laid down by society.

If we are responsible for our behaviour, we need to ask: responsible to whom? At a personal level, 'responsibility' is defined as "the ability to act independently and take decisions without authorization". At an impersonal level it is "a thing, which one is required to do as part of a job or legal obligation".[8] If we accept the first definition and reject the second, we might privately feel contented within ourselves for acting according to our intuition but might have to face public condemnation for doing so. Alternatively, if we accept the second definition and reject the first, we might be publicly commended by society, yet privately condemn ourselves for allowing our instinct to be overruled.

This shows how the attribution of 'responsibility', which appears to be innately personal, has become increasingly overruled us by force of law. Yet history is replete with responsible people who have been punished for disobeying the law, along with irresponsible ones who have been rewarded for conforming to it. If disobedience is sometimes thought 'irresponsible' and condemned as immoral, then obedience should also sometimes be thought 'irresponsible' and condemned as immoral. For hundreds of years, many irresponsible people throughout the British Empire were admired and honoured for the riches they accrued from slavery, for example, until it became commonly accepted as abhorrent and made illegal in 1833. In fact there have been, and still are, and no doubt

---

[8] Definitions 2 and 3 respectively: Compact Oxford English Dictionary, 3rd edn., 2005.

will continue to be, numerous people who act irresponsibility within the confines of the law in pursuit of greed, exploitation and extreme self-promotion, until such time as their behaviour is eventually exposed as so outrageous that it has to be restrained by modification, or change of law. In the end though, it is usually those who are subjected to the law, rather than those who try to maintain it, that bring about these changes.

The customs a community practices invariably imply an unconscious consensus of agreement to follow them. "Custom reconcile us to everything" [Edmund Burke] and, in our desire to live in balance with one another, they are usually motivated by feelings of mutual trust. Conscious thought and legal obligation about how we should, or should not behave is an inevitable by-product of hierarchy. In other words, acceptable social behaviour is moulded and shaped instinctively, until such times as authorities start thinking about and defining it by legal obligation. Complete uniformity of behaviour, however, cannot be imposed upon society without negative consequences, because individuals can never be forced to act homogeneously for long. In small egalitarian communities, where everyone socialises personally with one another, acceptable standards of behaviour are far more easily established and kept in balance by on-going interaction and re-adjustment, whereas in larger and more pluralistic societies they have to be controlled and maintained by force of law.

In 1973 the Supreme Court of the United States legalise abortion, for example, but because neither pro- nor anti-abortionists could resolve their beliefs rationally, disagreement has continued to this day. In the final analysis, both beliefs depend upon contrary feelings about whether, or when a foetus has a right to life or not. Before people tried to rationalise the problem and it became a recognisable moral issue for everyone to think about. Women accepted the responsibility for themselves. As soon as we attempt to construct black and white categories about emotional issues such as these, we lose sight of our humanity.

> Self-styled 'pro-lifers', and others that indulge in footling debates about exactly when in its development a foetus 'becomes human', exhibit the same discontinuous mentality. It is no use telling these people that, depending upon human characteristics that interest you, a foetus can be 'half human' or a 'hundredth human'. 'Human', to the discontinuous mind, is an absolutist concept. There can be no half measures. And from this flows much evil.[9]

In fact, all judgements of human behaviour depend ultimately in origin upon subjective feelings of approbation or disapproval.[10] Whatever a community generally thinks is acceptable behaviour becomes defined as 'right' and whatever it thinks is unacceptable becomes defined as 'wrong', but these labels are conceived of retrospectively and defined inflexibly, despite our ever-changing experiences about them. They can never be rigidly defined in writing for all time, even though, under centralised control, lawyers and theologians continually try to do so. "In your search for moral truths ... you never can find [the answer] till you turn your reflections into your own breast and find a sentiment of [approbation] or disapprobation".[11]

It is only when certain actions begin to be conceived of as 'good' or 'bad' and become defined and ossified in writing in order to be obey, that problems arise. The

---

[9] Dawkins, R: *The Devil's Chaplain*, 2004 edn. 25-6.

[10] Ayer, A J: *Language, Truth and Logic*, 1936, Ch. 6, 'emotivism', viz. that "all moral judgements are emotional; expressed as sentiments of approval or disapproval".

[11] Hume, D: *A Treatise of Human Nature*, 1739-40

maxim: "father forgive them, for they know not what they do" [Luke: 23.34] for example, is self-contradictory because, if they knew not what they were doing they didn't need to be forgiven. It is premised on an assumption that they had not complied with rulers such as 'The Ten Commandments', and should be judged accordingly, even though long before Christianity entered our vocabulary, we controlled our behaviour non-judgmentally according to our feelings for one another. At one time these feelings were derived instinctively from on-going, two-way personal interaction, then later, when societies became more structured, they became rationalised and defined impersonally one-way by written laws. The validity of moral truths can never be found in reason or ideology and remain unaltered. Ultimately, they rest upon the quick-sands of personal sentiment in our on-going responses to changing circumstances.

How we evaluate our own behaviour in relation to each other's remains a socially evolving process that requires personal readjustment and alteration all the time. This was how our ancestors learnt to relate to each other gregariously and, evidently, the process survived for millennia well enough, that is until the focus of responsibility shifted away from personal intuition and more towards impersonal imposition, authorised ultimately by God, then by 'the divine right of kings or emperors' and finally by democratically elected governments. Thus, the old flexible codes of behaviour that unconsciously moulded and shaped people's lives became consciously transcribed into inflexible and ossified doctrinal beliefs. Unfortunately though, this only encouraged neurological laziness and inbred thinking that had to be defended from any more open-minded and less judgmental reappraisal.

So a clear distinction has emerged between sensual morality, based on personal *a posteriori* experiences of each other's behaviour within communities, and conceptual morality, based on *a priori* rules and laws, defined in law and enforced by punitive methods of social control. It is commonly assumed these two types of morality are independent of each other, in that perceptual morality derives from *a posteriori* experiences, whereas conceptual morality derives from *a priori* reason and logic. But *a priori* reason and logic must have had their genesis in our experiences no matter how far back we have to go to find them. Even if they have become genetically encoded, they must have had an *a posteriori* origin. Morality must ultimately bow to sentiment in an ever-changing and indeterminate world.

Unfortunately, we have become so committed to the imposition of prescribed spiritual and secular laws, under the usually unquestioned assumption that they must be true, that they now seem to rule our lives. Yet, the bigoted idea that the truth is unalterable, so needs to be universally complied with, has resulted in some of our most uncompromising conflicts in history. Doctrinal beliefs, such as those expressed in the name of Christianity, Islam or Judaism, or in the name of Capitalism, Socialism or Communism, may offer their advocates a tenuous sense of security and guidance but little else.

> Should we not, therefore, wreak vengeance upon our ignorance, for how often has that deceitful knave fooled the minds of innocent men who look out upon the same landscape from different viewpoints? Then, thinking their eyes cannot be deceiving them begin quarrelling with one another about what they each believe to be the one true picture of the world.[12]

All so-called 'inalienable moral truths' have gained too much credence in the hands of the egoists who promote them. In fact, egoism looks inwards and is quite incapable

---

[12] Pashoe, S: *A Painter in the Wilderness*, 1999, 218

of recognising the feelings of others, so denies the existence of two-way personal interaction based on mutual feelings of trust in one another. At one time this was all that was required to maintain stability, before law-like rules of conduct had to be introduced by egoists who could not trust others who thought differently. The consequences have resulted in an increasing sense of alienation between not only each other but between each of these so-called 'inalienable moral truths', with the inevitable confusion, misunderstanding and conflict that have followed from them.

5. HOW DO WE PROCESS DATA?

Evolution usually refers to biological changes as they occur over time but it can apply to cultural changes too. Studies of the relationship between biological evolution and cultural evolution, sometimes referred to as the 'dual inheritance theory', highlight some of those body-mind questions that have troubled philosophers for centuries.

How do the body and mind relate to one another? How can matter become mind? Do they affect us in different ways? In fact, is there really any clear distinction between them? At one time it was thought that biological changes were transmitted quantitatively and determined our physiology, whereas cultural changes were transmitted qualitatively by social interaction and determined our neurology. However, the distinction between the two is not so clear-cut, as the development or suppression of genes has been found to relate to our neurology too.

In 1864, William James noticed "a remarkable parallel ... between the facts of social evolution ... on the one hand, and of zoological evolution, as expounded by Mr. Darwin, on the other".[1] And Herbert Spencer, who in that same year coined the phrase 'survival of the fittest', thought the way things changed was as much to do with social evolution as it was to biological evolution. Then, Alfred Wallace suggested using this phrase as an alternative to Darwin's 'natural selection', and a few years later, the physicist, Ludwig Boltzmann, who was deeply committed to Darwin's ideas, became convinced that our:

> Laws of thought evolved according to the same laws of evolution as the optical apparatus of the eye, the acoustic machinery of the ear and the pumping device of the heart. In the course of mankind's development everything inappropriate was shed, and thus arose the unity and perfection that can give the illusion of infallibility ... In this simple process that is readily understood mechanically, we have heredity, natural selection, sense-perception, reason, will, pleasure and pain all together in a nutshell.[2]

More recently, it has been suggested genes: "Don't just issue instructions: they respond to messages coming from other genes, from hormones and from nutritional cues, and learning the methods by which genes make these responses often involves very small chemical modifications."[3]

Early models of cultural evolution implied the course of human history had some overall direction or purpose. Thomas Hobbes, for example, suggested society evolved from 'brutish' to 'stable' by means of 'endeavour'; Adam Smith: from 'hunting and gathering', or 'nomadic' and then to 'agricultural' and finally, to 'commercial'; whereas Lewis

---

[1] James, W: *Great Men and their Environment*, Atlantic Monthly 1880, 216.

[2] Cercignani, C: *Ludwig Boltzmann: The Man Who Trusted Atoms*, 2007, 179, 181

[3] Carey, N: *The Epigenetics Revolution*, 2011.

Morgan suggested from 'savagery' and 'barbarianism' to 'civilization'. Even Darwin seemed to believe cultural evolution had a progressive component, based primarily on intellect: "Comparison of the Mental Powers of Man and the Lower Animals [reveals] the difference in mind between man and the higher animals, great as it is, is certainly one of degree and not of kind."[4] It may be noted however, that all these models of cultural evolution are attempts to rationalise the process, on the assumption that they can be measured in terms of progress, whereas the way we sometimes experience it, based on criteria such as social stability or harmony and balance within our natural environment, may have a more or less stabilising than progressive connotation.

Some might argue that conscious thought has been progressively purposeful, because, by creating a more comfortable and convenient world, we have become less dependent upon those biological influences of 'chance mutation', 'natural selection', and 'genetic drift or flow', over which we felt we had little control. Others, however, might argue that our increasingly man-made and stressful environment has become so far removed from the one we originally accepted without question, that it has actually created more problems than it has solved. It's difficult to compare the state of 'well-being' of, for example, the hunter-gatherer with that of the supermarket shopper, as they mean different things to different people. So anthropologists tend to reject the idea that cultural changes can be evaluated in terms of progress. In any event, ethnocentrism makes the comparison of people, living in different places within different cultures, and at different times in our history, quite impossible.

Perhaps cultural evolution changes indeterminately in much the same way biological evolution does. This would seem to imply that both human societies, including the

---

[4] Darwin, C: *The Descent of Man*, 1781, 34-106.

individuals within them, were not really in more control of their destinies than any other species of fauna or flora. Maybe all our thinking and planning, not only at a social or organisational level, but at a personal level too, have been intuitive responses to our environmental experiences, rather than as a consequence of free and independent conscious choice to plan our futures. As Susan Blackmore wrote, in her introduction to *Conversations on Consciousness*: "I had rather expected, before I began that nearly everyone would intellectually reject the idea of free will ... with long practice, it becomes perfectly obvious that all the actions of this body are the consequences of prior events acting on a complex system; then the feeling of making free conscious decisions simply melts away."[5]

Before dismissing these rather provocative ideas out of hand, however, let us consider how new ideas become accepted and replicated in each other's minds. One suggestion is that such information is "acquired from other individuals via social transmission mechanisms such as imitation, teaching, or language".[6] Yet how do others acquire this information in the first place? Presumably it can only be acquired from their experiences; not just of others too, but of environmental factors such as climate and geography, along with the availability of natural resources, all of which must have had an enormous influence on our cultural heritage

Between 100,000 and 60,000 years ago perhaps, people began meandering out of Africa, in different directions, all over the world in search of more favourable conditions[7] This meandering probably involved following animal migrations, foraging the land for food and shelter, and, particularly during the Mesolithic, scavenging the seashores, in any direction that seemed favourable to

---

[5] Blackmore, S: *Conversations on Consciousness*, 2005; 8-9, 2006 edn.

[6] Mesoudi, A: *Cultural Evolution*, 2011, 2-3.

[7] Cavalli-Sforza, L: *Genes, People and Language*, 2000, Fig. 4, 94.

survival. There is some evidence[8] that in hunting and foraging, humans tended to follow fractal patterns for food resources that corresponded to random-walk models, or as 'Lévy flights' comprising short jumps in localised areas, combined with long leaps to new unexplored areas. Similar patterns have been observed in insects, birds, fish and land animals. This might explain how, for example, after crossing the Bering Straits before the end of the Ice Age, humans took little more than a thousand years to spread out and inhabit most of the Americas from Alaska to Patagonia. And settled farming could have begun only after the Ice Age, when more fertile regions of the world were gradually discovered. It has been claimed that: "At around 8,000 BCE, beginning in the Middle East, humans started to abandon the hunter-gatherer lifestyle. Instead of foraging for plants they started to cultivate them, and instead of hunting animals they started to domesticate them."[9] Then, farming gradually spread, with migration over the next few thousand years[10], from the Middle East into southern, and then into northern Europe. Meanwhile, with land claim, barter and trade eventually led to increasing differences in ownership, resulting in dominance, exploitation, bullying, slavery, conflict and warfare, all of which have continued, largely unabated, to this day.

Perhaps overall, every form of meandering, foraging, scavenging, exploration, discovery and acquisitiveness can be interpreted as mere chance opportunism in our ancestors' on-going struggle for survival, rather than because of conscious planning, with clearly defined goals or objectives in mind. With the development of tool-making, however, and subsequently since the

---

[8] Brown, C & Liebovitch, L: *Lévy Flights* ... Human Ecology 35, 2007; Humphries, N & Sims, D: *Optimal foraging Strategies* ..., Journal of Theoretical Biology, 356, 2014, 179-93
[9] Taylor, S: *The Fall- The Insanity of the Ego in Human History*, 2005, 38
[10] Cavalli-Sforza, L: *Genes, People and Language*, 2000. Fig. 5, 109

Enlightenment with the development of science and industry, we have increasingly learnt to plan ahead and try to control our environment.

It could be argued that this had been driven principally for the purposes of improving our chances of self-preservation and survival, but at an unanticipated cost that Thomas Malthus referred to as 'unsustainable growth'.[11] His epitaph reads as follows: "the power of population is indefinitely greater than the power in the earth to produce subsistence for man". It's a prophecy that has been largely overlooked or delayed in doing anything much about, but can't be ignored indefinitely.[12] Before the agrarian revolution however, the world's population remained sparse for thousands of generations, probably not exceeding 15 million but then began to increase steadily and, since the Industrial Revolution, has grown exponentially nearly 500 times, to about seven billion.

In attempting to understand how cultural evolution has come about, we first need to see how ideas grow or die, or change direction at a personal level within the nursery of the human mind, wherein are surely born the seeds of all human culture. Driven by environmental circumstances, and particularly by use of language, we simply can't help imprinting, conditioning, persuading, coercing, or even brainwashing one another by means of social interaction.

If we take the imitation and replication of a 'meme'[13] as the basic unit of information by which our feelings, opinions, beliefs or ideas, spread from one person to another, then like 'Chinese Whispers', they are inevitably subject to interpretational variances during transmission. So, just like physical evolution, all our feelings and

---

[11] Malthus, T: *An Essay on the Principle of Population*, 1798

[12] In 1972, The Club of Rome published: *Limits to Growth*, by Medows, D et al, with a forecast 'tipping point' in 2030 and although it has been updated, its forecasts still don't seem to have been taken seriously enough.

[13] Dawkins, R: *The Selfish Gene*, 2006 edn. 197-8.

thoughts must also be subject to random variations in transmission over time too. Moreover, our memories of these feelings will also change over time, even though 'it's a poor sort of memory that only works backwards'. [Lewis Carroll]. And even though our feelings and thoughts inevitably change with our experiences, they do not do so willingly. "The observer fills the gaps of his or her perception by the aid of what has been experienced before in comparable situations, or ... what are taken to be 'fit' or suitable to such situations. We may do this without being in the least aware that we are, either supplementing or falsifying the data of perception."[14]

Thus, it is by means of our sensual experiences of reality, along with the way we interpret these experiences, that our cultural inputs are constantly being moulded and modified. But herein lies a paradox, because sensations are neither evaluative nor judgmental, whereas our thoughts about them are. Even though our sensations, and our thoughts, attempt to communicate back and forth with each other, in an on-going struggle to cope with each other, they remain fundamentally different. In attempting to describe this mysterious demarcation of co-dependency between how we feel and how we think, Thomas Metzinger puts it like this: "The ebb and flow of autonomy and meta-awareness might well be a kind of attentional seesawing between our inner and outer worlds, caused by a constant competition between the brain networks underlying spontaneous sub-personal thinking and goal-orientated cognition."[15]

Our earliest ancestors' beliefs did not depend on reliable evidence but principally on their imagination. They were first recognisably expressed in their fantasies and folklore, and were passed on through the generations

[14] Bartlett, F C: *Remembering: A Study in Experimental and Social Psychology*, 1932, Ch. 2.
[15] Metzinger, T: *Cognitive Agency*, 'This Idea must Die', Ed. Brockman, J, 2015, 150

by word of mouth. But with the gradual development of cognitive thought and the acquisition of so-called facts about experience, such fantasies were continually being modified in the light of further experiences. We might convince ourselves that this has gradually resulted in a more reliable representation of reality but perhaps it is only less unreliable, as our acquisition of so-called facts still remains dependent on experiences, which have a sensual origin, and are both indeterminate and on-going.

In order to maintain or reinforce these representations of reality and the opinions, values and beliefs associated with them, they were originally conveyed and replicated horizontally between people by word of mouth. Within hierarchically structured societies though, they became replicated more downwards under pressure from above, then only sometimes subsequently modified upwards by pressure from below. At other times though, they appeared to replicate themselves without any obvious direction or purpose at all.

Most of the time these so-called units of information, or 'memes', are insignificant and soon forgotten but at other times they can have far-reaching consequences. They also sometimes appear to occur spontaneously, when unpredictable events occur. If Saul of Tarsus had been killed by that 'blinding flash of light' on the road to Damascus, or Columbus's ship had sunk in mid Atlantic, or Hitler had had a happier childhood, our history might have turned out very differently. Indeed, many apparently insignificant events can have far-reaching consequences and seem to occur without any rhyme or reason, in the same way mutations or tipping points act like 'the throw of the dice that never eliminates chance'. [Mallarmé]

Although it has been suggested that some of these changes might have a more 'meaningful basis' for selection, most, possibly all, have simply been the result of imperceptibly small random variances in replication between every link in the 'transmission chain' from one person to another. Research into how they have actually occurred is a complex subject but several field-studies have shown that differences in weaponry,[16] pottery designs,[17] food taboos,[18] even in the meanings of words and sentences,[19] appear to change aimlessly over time and tend to take the form of 'random-walks', whereby changes evolve probabilistically, step-by-preceding-step, without any predetermined objective to aim for. Put bluntly: the acquisition of data is always going to be biased by differences in experiences between transmitters and receivers, so random variances, no matter how inconspicuous, must surely be an inevitable feature of this process.

In the history of science, for example, some highly significant ideas have remained neglected before eventually being accidentally recognised or rediscovered, and replicated in others. Even the way scientific knowledge sometimes becomes more fully recognised depends upon the social network within which it is embroiled, rather than upon any intrinsic merit. One study found that the replication of scientific ideas in universities was less about their quality than about how scientists subjectively collaborated with one another to promote them.[20] In fact, the merit of individual bits of research is often measured more by the number of references and citations to it in other publications, and indeed, sometimes how popularised they might become in the media. But, as Popper suggested: the 'natural selection of hypothesis in science functions in exactly the same way as natural

---

[16] Bettinger, R & Eerkens, J: *Point Typologies, Cultural Transmission, and the Spread of Bow-and-Arrow Technology,* 1999 American Antiquity 64, 231-42.

[17] Bentley, A & Shennan, S: *Random Copying and Cultural Evolution,* 2005, Science 309, 877-9.

[18] Aunger, R: *The Life History of Cultural Learning in a Face- to-Face Society,* Ethos 28, 1-38.

[19] Chater, N et al: *Restrictions on Biological Adaption in Language Evolution,* 2009, National Academy of Science 106, 1015-20.

[20] Hull, D: *Science as a Process,* 1988, 353-7.

selection does in biology'. "It is ... the discovery and elimination of our errors that constitutes the positive experience which we gain from reality."[21]

Long before the emergence of rational thought and scientific thinking, cultural evolution had its origins in our on-going responses to our experiences, according to how we felt about them. These were, and still are represented by the ever-changing cognition-webs[22] of neurons in our minds. They are not fixed and unalterable though; they are more like amorphous networks that represent our experiences about our relationships with one another and with the world. Sometimes they trigger 'excitatory' or 'inhibitory' chemical cocktails of molecules, called neurotransmitters that make these experiences either increasingly well defined by repeated memory recall or less significant by neglect, so soon become weakened and are forgotten about. Neurological evolution is rather like biological evolution speeded up over time. The survival or extinction of these cognition-webs must surely depend on our attempt to maintain a balance between our own needs and the needs of others; in effect: between egoism and altruism.

As a gregarious species, our early ancestors could never have survived communally together for so long without common feelings of altruism. Expressions of egoism had no place in relationships at that time; the community was everything. Everyone accepted each other's different contributions to it non-judgmentally, and had no conception of these differences being better or worse than each other, just different. This open-minded and non-evaluative attitude to everything around them implied very little sense of self. So all their actions were primarily concerned with trying to keep in balance with each other.

---

[21] Popper, K: *Objective Knowledge* 1979 edn. 360 & also: *Logic of Scientific Discovery* 1977, 108.

[22] A phrase coined by Taylor, K in: *Brainwashing*, 2002, 302, which aptly describes 'hopes', 'desires', 'beliefs', 'ideas', 'concepts',' 'plans', &c.

In this way they instinctively adjusted their own behaviour according to how others responded to it; they existed in a permanent state of flexibility and readjustment, and the cultural customs, practices and beliefs that emerged from this process became imperceptibly re-moulded and re-shaped unpredictably over time, without any reference to clearly conceived of, or pre-planned rules or regulations.

This could be described as an unconscious process of 'induction' because their individual modes of behaviour, based on their individual experiences of one another, became automatically aggregated to form commonly accepted customs, practices and beliefs. No conscious reference to previously established modes of behaviour was necessary; they simply emerged from the way they felt about each other and the world at the time.

It has been suggested that ever since the recognition and emergence of the 'self', however, egoism gradually gained a controlling influence over this unpredictable altruistic process, by the increasing recognition of itself as being different from other selves, resulting in its judgment and increasing evaluation of these differences. And it is precisely the emergence of this non-empathic ego that gave rise to a growing neurological conflict of interests and imbalance between egoism and altruism. The more we focused on the self, the less we focused on others and *vice versa,* and in the case of extreme personality disorders that do not have feelings for anyone but them selves, egoism rules supreme over altruism.

This could be described as involving a process of 'deduction' whereby subjective experiences became blindly translated into rational thoughts, which subsequently gave rise to identifiable rules about how people should, and should not behave. And with the development of language, these became defined in writing in the form of fixed laws, or in the case of Judo-Christian folklore, more specifically in the form of the Ten Commandments. In other words, inductive forms of group conformity within egalitarian societies, gradually gave way to deductive forms of authorised conformity within hierarchically structured societies. This meant that altruistically controlled behaviour, that regulated itself by reference to experiences of each other, became increasingly replaced by egoistically controlled behaviour that had to be regulated by reference to those that authorised these fixed laws.

It is undoubtedly true that "common participation in rituals, coupled with a basic uniformity of beliefs, helped to bind people together and reinforce their identification with their group"[23] but 'binding people together and reinforcing their identification with their group' inductively, changed dramatically in nature when a few more egocentrically minded individuals began trying to bind people together and reinforcing their identification with them deductively, according to written laws of conduct administered and enforcement punitively. Although it is still generally accepted that induction and deduction are fundamentally different ways of processing data, they have become entangled with one another in the following way. The inductive process of subjectively recognising generalised patterns from particular experiences has come to involve also the deductive process of objectively constructing particular conclusions from generalised patterns. And buried within this symbiosis is the demarcation problem, between subjective feelings and rational thoughts.

Our ancient ancestors had been intimately in touch with each other and with their natural environment, so their on-going, self-regulatory way of processing data inductively didn't involve any form of rational thought. It wasn't until the emergence of the ego that rational thoughts and deductive reasoning were first used to process data, which then became transcribed into law and enforced upon society under threat of violation. The fact

---

[23] Haviland, W: *Cultural Anthropology*, 9th edn. 1999, 406.

that all these laws must originally have been premised on experiences seems to have been overlooked or denied by those who authorised them, as this would have invalidated their enforcement, which was probably why the 'divine right of kings' had to try and crush any such thoughts of insurrection so ruthlessly.

However, by deliberately "binding people together and reinforcing their identification with their group" in this way only encouraged tunnel-vision, bigotry and 'confirmation bias'[24] as a refuge against threat from rival belief-systems, which had to be assumed erroneous, rather than just different.[25] Yet history has shown that these differences had to be dealt with overtly, in much the same way as they were dealt with covertly in the minds of individuals who became committed to them; namely by defence, avoidance, denial or even conflict; the preservation and propagation of their conditioned beliefs being the sole motivation for such reactions. No wonder, most of the blood shed on the battlegrounds of history has been the result of unquestioned obedience to authority's claim in its absolute truths.

Of course, both induction and deduction are caught up in the same loop feedback process, but some people tend to be more question-biased and process information inductively, while others are more answer-bias and favour deduction. Those who are more 'question biased' may have an unclear sense of self and place greater emphasis on their on-going experiences about a world they feel is only indeterminate, and forever changing. On the other hand, those who are more 'answer-biased' gain comfort from clearly defined beliefs and values, especially those that have the backing of authority.

At one time a passionate desire to cooperate was all

[24] Nickerson, R: *Confirmation Bias: a Ubiquitous Phenomenon in many Guises*, 1998 Review of General Psychology 2, 175-220, et al.
[25] Whitehead, N & Ferguson, B: *Deceptive Stereotypes about tribal warfare*, Chronicle of Higher Education, Nov. 1995, A48

that our ancestors needed to keep themselves in continual balance with each other and their environment. With the development of the self and language however, egoism and rational thought has provided us with reasons to try and change this environment to our own advantage. But, as Hume had realised: "Reason is, and ought to be the slave of the passions and can never pretend to any other office than to serve and obey them".[26] So, perhaps both egoism and altruism compete neurologically for their own survival in much the same way our genes compete biologically for their own survival, but are programmed independently to ensure the survival of hosts', namely us, who are harbouring them. In fact, the 'selfish meme' may function in much the same way as the 'selfish gene'. And, if both 'we' and 'they' comprise one and the same thing, namely the 'self', then does the 'self' really have any more control over the destiny of its cultural evolution than it does over the destiny of its biological evolution?

---

[26] Hume, D: *An Enquiry Concerning Human Understanding*, 1748

6. DOES CAUSE EQUAL EFFECT?

We live in a turbulent world. Some things, like the clouds above or the waves around our shores, change before our very eyes, but hills and mountains change too, but so slowly we hardly notice. So what exactly is the essence of change, from past 'cause' to future 'effect' perhaps? Although we rarely think consciously about why or how changes come about, we often speculate about the future. Is it going to rain? Who will turn up at the party? What will our holiday de like? And although we can't change the past, we sometimes try to plan, to change our futures. What career should we pursue? What should we plant in the garden this year? Which investment would give us the best return? These questions are based on the idea that what we choose to do now might 'cause' some planned-for 'effect' in the future.

Planning for the future is common practice these days, yet our ancient ancestors probably didn't think about how they could change things to their advantage at all; they simply accepted the turbulent state of the world and responded to its changes instinctively. They were probably very sensitive to changing weather patterns and responded to them without thinking consciously about them at all. They didn't consciously plan where they might find food or shelter, or how to avoid danger; they 'knew' intuitively by following their instincts. Just like our closest non-human primates, their emotions 'told' them what to do.

Only later in our evolutionary history did we begin to think consciously about the changing seasons and where to look for food and water, or where to find shelter. As our ancestors gradually became more consciously aware of their environment, they started to question how such changes came about. They would have begun to recognise patterns in nature that appeared orderly and used this knowledge to predict the futures. The right part of the brain, which is more focused on feelings is able to appreciate the waves of the sea or the wonder of the stars, whereas the left part recognises regularities in these things, such as the rise and ebb of the tides, or the rotation of stars, and gradually learnt how to translate them into recognisably ordered patterns, defined by laws that have help us plan our futures. To assume these laws actually exist in nature though, rather than in our minds, is a misconception because they are still only provisional or temporary regularities that occur from chance events and sometimes they don't conform to these laws at all.

The world around us presents two fundamentally different forms of patterns: those that appear random and those that appear ordered. As adults we appreciate these two types of patterns tend to arise from very different sorts of causal processes. Typically, we expect that, whereas agents can increase the orderliness of a system, inanimate objects can cause only increased disorder. Thus, one major division in the world of causal entities is between those that are capable of "reversing local entropy" and those that are not. In the present studies we find that sensitivity to the unique link between agents and order emerges quite early in development. Results from three experiments suggest that by 12 months of age, infants associate agents with the creation of order and inanimate objects with the creation of disorder. Such expectations appear to be robust in children's preschool years and are hypothesized to result from a more general understanding that agents causally intervene on the world in fundamentally different ways from inanimate objects.[1]

With the recognition of the 'self' in our evolution, we gradually became increasingly hard-wired to believe that there had to be a designer behind the ordered patterns we recognised in nature. Self-awareness and conscious thinking grew very slowly at first with tool making and the development of language, and only began to be taken more seriously from the dawn of civilization onwards, with the discovery of fertile land, followed by settled farming. New problems that required organisation and planning arose at this time with problems such as the feeding of livestock or the cultivation of crops, along with social problems relating to the development and construction of villages, towns and cities.

By attempting to live together in this more organised way, required thinking consciously about how best to transform their new environment for their future advantage. Agent-based thinking, premised on models of 'cause' and 'effect', gradually became the way they began processing data rationally in their on-going attempt to understand and interact with the world according to how they wanted it to be. And, in order to check the validity of this model, people needed to monitor the successes and failures of their conjectures, which probably gave rise to

---

[1] Newman, C et al: *Early understanding of the link between agent and order,* 2010 Abstract.

ideas such as classification, numerology, measurement and calculation. Foods needed to be classified or counted and bartered for, land had to be measured and divided up, and houses had to be designed and built, all of which necessitated the development of a more rational and logical form of thinking. By observing the effects their plans were having on their environment, people must have become increasingly aware of the cause-effect relationship they were having upon it. So, with their on-going desire to change their environment to their advantage, this relationship eventually became the bedrock of scientific enquiry, particularly during the Age of Enlightenment. Investigations into the properties of matter, concerning heat, light, sound, magnetism and electricity, led to the discovery of laws that expressed measurable correlations between temperature, pressure, volume, mass, energy, force, acceleration, distance, time and so on, all of which took the logical form: 'if cause then effect'.

The fact that many of these laws appeared to be good predictors of the future brought about the Industrial Revolution and accelerated the use of harnessing nature's resources and energy for the production of goods and services. Indeed, the world had seemed to resemble a giant machine or clock that operated according to mechanical laws of logic and reason. The growing acquisitiveness that followed began to transform the natural world into an increasingly man-made one, and hence appeared to further substantiate the belief that this 'cause and effect' relationship must be a fundamental law of nature.

By the turn of the nineteenth century however, serious doubts about its validity were beginning to be expressed. Perhaps the most serious of these concerned the origin of causation. If every effect was the result of a previous cause then that cause itself must have been the effect of an even earlier one, and so on, leading back in time to a single first cause for everything, which somehow needed to be exempt from any previous cause if this model of reality could be substantiated. But then, if that first cause did not need any antecedent cause, why should any of the subsequent effects need causes? Furthermore, a single first cause would seem to imply everything had been predetermined from the beginning of time, suggesting an inflexible universe, with all plant and animal life, even people's thoughts and actions, must have been planned out mechanistically in advance according to the laws of nature. Some seemed happy enough with God as an explanation for this, while others found it hard to accept everything had been predetermined in this way.

To doubt the validity of a precise relationship between cause and effect though, would be to doubt the validity of science itself, which repeatedly, had appeared to demonstrate the existence of this cause-and-effect relationship between the properties of matter. It also seemed to validate the assumption that there really were discrete identities that could be counted and classified, and that there really were laws in nature that could be measured, it was simply a question of identifying them. Yet, on closer inspection, this simplistic way of modelling the world turned out to be suspect, for the more precisely these laws were defined, the less precisely nature appeared to conform to them. In reality, of course, no perfect patterns could be found and no two objects were ever identical, so could never be classified as if they were; other than approximately. Even Darwin admitted the classification of species was 'a purely subjective invention of the taxonomist'.

Nevertheless, predictions about how nature changed according to these assumptions could still be made but were they always reliable enough? There was always the unexpected. Could determinism therefore, be nothing more than our own way of trying to make sense of a world that had no sense, or simply our own way of recognising order in disorder? The model that the Sun rotated round the Earth had made sense at one time, whereas now we think the converse is true, so perhaps our search for deterministic laws was an erroneous pursuit, since the closer we looked, the less ordered the World appeared to be.

An alternative to the deterministic view of nature, at least with respect to life on Earth, was postulated in 1859 by Darwin's theory of evolution, which took the less rigid form: 'if cause, then an effect, probably similar to that cause' would follow from it, generation after generation. This might explain how, by chance variation alone, the great diversity of all plant and animal life had come about. Although Gregor Mendel's experiments on the heredity of plants were not known by Darwin at that time, he noticed that the physical characteristics of all forms of life appeared to vary from their antecedents, even if only slightly, and if these variances proved to be less suited to their environment, the probability that they would survive and reproduce would be diminished. On the other hand, if they turned out to be better suited, they would be more likely to survive and, through the generations, pass on further variances of those inherited variances to their descendants. In this way, characteristics that did not suit their environment would gradually become extinct, whereas those more suited would tend to adapt to the niche environment within which they found themselves, and Darwin called this 'natural selection'.

Chance variations over time, like the growth in different directions of the branches of trees, would be enough to explain how the great diversity of all life-forms that inhabited different environments throughout the World had come about. Darwin referred to it as 'the principle of divergence'. Those species that survived were able to adapt to their environment, whereas the fossil records of those that were extinct had not been so lucky. Survival in the natural world appeared to be very much a hit-and-miss affair after all, and if the number of extinct species, compared with those that survived was anything to go by, more miss than hit.

By the end of the nineteenth century, determinism, as a model of change, was beginning to look less plausible than indeterminism, at least as far as species were concerned. On the face of it however, the predictive laws of science, based on 'cause and effect' still seem to suggest 'intelligent design', if not an 'intelligent designer'. Nevertheless, on closer inspection, any laws that predicted a perfectly reliable match between cause and effect still remained tantalising illusive. If there was any 'intelligent design' it appeared to have occurred in the wishful-minds of the observers than in what they were observing. Scientific enquiry had become an ongoing quest to construct increasingly accurate causal laws that appeared to match changes in nature, on the assumption that they already exist. Unfortunately though, with further investigation and experiment, these laws needed to be continually revised or replaced by better ones in order to improve their predictability. This continual adaptation of scientific enquiry to nature was rather reminiscent of evolution itself, so perhaps the concept that nature was perfectly ordered was more in the scientists' minds than in nature.

Another doubt about determinism was that, if cause really did equal effect, then the effect would have to equal the cause, implying a static, unchanging world, or even a reversible one. But this was evidently not the case, as everything seemed to be changing irreversibly all the time. A fallen tree could never re-assemble itself, for example and clouds change their shapes irreversibly all the time. Even the use of differential equations, in weather forecasting, quickly became increasingly subject to deterministic error and, in longer-term forecasting, totally unreliable.

Following on from James Clerk Maxwell's work on electromagnetism, Ludwig Boltzmann, one of the founding fathers of modern physics, was able to show how sub-microscopic phenomena always appeared to change indeterminately to become increasingly disordered, and his pioneering work on entropy contained the first 'time-irreversible' equation in the history of science.[2] This probabilistic interpretation of change showed that the cosmological arrow of time always seemed to point, from past order to future chaos. In other words, any so-called 'effect' was always going to be more disordered than any so-called 'cause' that preceded it. In fact, more than fifty years before anything was known of the Expanding Universe or the Big Bang, this idea had led Boltzmann to speculate, quite correctly as it turned out, that its distant origins must have taken the form of some sort of more ordered primordial atom. His micro-studies of molecules, along with his theoretical work on atoms, even before they had been officially recognised, gave support to Darwin's macro-studies of plants and animal. As Boltzmann expressed it, "the law-like character of the process of nature is a basic prerequisite for all cognition; it requires us to always ask for the cause. In fact, our curiosity is so irresistible that it urges us to ask the cause for everything having a cause".[3]

These questions highlighted perhaps, the most fundamental question of all; namely, whether the universe was determinate, with underlying laws governing its changing states, or indeterminate and driven by chance alone. As these terms are mutually exclusive, how could it be a bit of both? More recent ideas, such as 'morphogenesis', which is the study of changes in organic forms, suggested these so-called laws of nature were more like customs that changed probabilistically over time. "The regularities of nature are not imposed on nature ... what

---

[2] Boltzmann, L.: *Probabilistic Foundations of Heat Theory*, 1877. His concept of entropy had already appeared as a mathematical measure of 'disorder' in 1872.

[3] Cercignani, C: *Ludwig Boltzmann, The Man Who Trusted Atoms*, 1998, 179, 2007 reprint.

happens depends on what has happened before. Memory is inherent in nature. It is transmitted by a process that has been called 'morphic resonance;' things are as they are because they were as they were."[4]

We can recognise this happening sometimes, with respect to our own thoughts and actions. When we make a mistake, in order to correct our future actions, we try to remember not to make that same mistake again. So, although this process is indeterminate, it is often within such narrow parameters of variance, the difference between the observed and actual effect of change is rarely noticed. It has been suggested that: "the re-conceptualisation of physics going on today, has changed from deterministic, reversible processes, to stochastic, irreversible ones".[5] First-order logical programming needed to be revised to include probabilistic reasoning and inference, in an attempt to identify underlying principles, or laws of nature for predicting the future.

One of the problems associated with the concept of 'law' is that it has different meanings and applies in different contexts. There are laws that we invent and comply with when playing board, or sports games, for example. They are irrefutable and independent of nature, so are *a priori*. Then there are laws of science, such as Boyle's Law, or Charles' Law, that, again we invent but they are only temporarily *a priori* because they approximate to the way nature behaves. They may superficially appear to be embedded in nature but are really *a posteriori* because they were derived from hypotheses based on observation and experiment and are changing all the time in a never-ending attempt to describe reality accurately. And finally, there are spiritual and secular laws that seem to fall somewhere between the two. In an attempt to underwrite the authority of those who administer them, they are

[4] Sheldrake, R: *A New Science of Life*, 2009 revised edn., 4.
[5] Prigogine, I et al: *Order out of Chaos*, 1985, 232

claimed to be *a priori*, but they too are *a posteriori* because they are not based on inviolate principles of universality and in practice are subject to changing experiences all the time. Indeed, none of our ideas can ever touch the essential character of reality.[6] It is said: 'one swallow doesn't make a summer', so who or what determines how many do make a summer? Perhaps all our attempts to find these laws are of our own making, not natures' and reveal an often unrecognised weakness in the premise upon which the rational mind begins making judgments and evaluations to find them.

All those various facts, values, opinions, ideas and beliefs we have accumulated, in our attempted understanding of reality over the millennia, undermine the determinist belief that cause really does equalled effect. As Popper claimed, "only one instance of falsification would be sufficient to prove a law was not true, whereas an infinite number would be required to prove that it was true." Although this statement now seems obvious, his subsequent claim that it was only "through the falsification of our suppositions that we actually get in touch with reality",[7] is less obvious because if nature was fundamentally indeterminate, then there was not going to be any way of understanding how we could get in touch with it, other than by means of our own limited description of it.

But the final nail in the determinists' coffin was struck by quantum mechanics, which, had to be premised upon a principle that Werner Heisenberg called 'imprecision', but which later became known as the 'uncertainty principle'. Because aggregated colonies of atoms, such as those that formed planets and stars appeared to behave fairly deterministically, it was hard to believe that the fundamental properties of nature did not behave in the

---

[6] Boltzman's inaugural lecture, Leipzig, 1900. outlined first in Popper, K: *Logik der Forschung.* 1934

[7] Popper, K: *Objective Knowledge, an evolutionary approach*, 1979 edn., 360.

same way. Even Einstein was convinced that 'God did not play dice with the Universe'. After thousands of years of traditional thinking, the concept that nature was fundamentally indeterminate was hard to accept, but was now becoming even harder to resist. As Popper noted, "whenever a theory appears to you as the only possible one, take this as a sign that you have neither understood the theory, nor the problem that it was intended to solve."[8]

The 'cause-and-effect' model was turning out to be no more relevant to the aggregated world of our experiences than it was to the subatomic world of particle physics; it was only that we hadn't noticed it wasn't because we hadn't looked closely enough. In our hitherto unrecognised desire to turn chaos into order, and turn chance into certainty, the 'confirmation bias' of determinism had motivated scientific enquiry into believing there still had to be immutable laws and fundamental constants[9] buried somewhere within nature, so the rational mind has continued to try and find them. The 'thinking' mind is premised on questions, such as 'what causes this or that to happen?' But these are leading questions that presuppose answers. They don't generally ask: 'what causes us to even ask why this or that happened', or whether agency existed at all?

Relationships between variables are expressed in the form of mathematical equations but they don't explain nature, they merely prescribe how it would function under controlled conditions, in the form of observed levels of correspondence between 'causes' on the left hand side of the equation, and 'effects' on the right. Furthermore, they could only be equated to each other if the so-called 'causes', on the left and the so-called 'effect' on the right were to swap places, which would strait-jacket our

---

[8] Ibid, Appx.
[9] Sheldrake, R *The Science Delusion*, 2012, 92 sites the practical difficulties and unreliability in defining the speed of light, for example, and their effect on other constants.

perception of a static world into a number of meaningless tautologies.

There is, however, a far more parochial explanation as to why we even bothered to think the Universe behaved in the way it appeared to, and it's premised on the assumption that rational enquiry itself is an *a priori* concept that doesn't need to justify itself in thinking the way it does about the natural world. The rational, more objective mind's quest to understand the Universe has to be premised on the belief that it can be explained. On the other hand, the irrational, more subjective mind accepts its ignorance of something that it can only experience sensually. No wonder there is an un-resolvable incompatibility between these two levels of consciousness and we're permanently burdened with the neurological consequences of coping with their differences.

> If we wish to draw philosophical conclusions about our own existence, or significance, and the significance of the universe itself, our conclusions should be based on empirical knowledge. A truly open mind means forcing our imaginations to conform to the evidence of reality and not *vice versa*, whether or not we like the implications.[10]

Much, so far, has been said about the relationship between cause and effect with respect to external reality, but what is its relevance, if any, to that of our own thoughts and actions? We are still faced with deciding whether the way we process our thoughts and actions is either determinate, in which case how we think about reality is premised upon the assumption that it can be conceptually understood, or is actually indeterminate, in which case how we feel about it is premised on the

---

[10] Krauss, L.: *A Universe from Nothing: Why there is Something rather than Nothing*, 2012

assumption that it does not need to be understood. The uncomfortable feeling of dissonance, between order and the absence of order, that this dilemma generated must have encouraged 'compatibilists'[11] to search for ways of reconciling the two. At first, David Hume did not seem to think it could be done: "tis impossible to admit of any medium betwixt chance and an absolute necessity" but then he offered what he thought was a solution. "Responsible or morally free actions are caused by our own willings, whereas unfree actions are brought about by causes external to the agent."[12]

Yet, if we accepted that our own 'willings' might also have been 'brought about by causes external to the agent', then this distinction disappeared. Although we may feel that our own 'willings' allow us the freedom to do what we want, "maybe ...", as Voltaire succinctly put it, 'we can't help wanting to do what we want'. And if what we want turns out to be a mistake, we could only learn from the mistake after it had already occurred, so the effect could only influence subsequent causes. We might try to be more rational and plan what we do, but this process has the same retrospective origin for all species. As Darwin put it: "an inward monitor would tell the animal [or human] that it would have been better to follow the one impulse rather than the other",[13] but this implied the 'inward monitor' must have also acted retrospectively, so had made its judgement in hindsight, as referred to perhaps by Darwin as 'adoption'.

Even Popper claimed that "what we need for understanding rational human behaviour is ... something intermediate between what he called 'perfect clouds' and

---

[11] Kane, R (Ed.): *The Oxford Handbook of Free Will*, 2002, Part IV, 181-277 summarises the arguments.

[12] Hume, D: *A Treatise of Human Nature*, 2.3.2. 1/407.

[13] Darwin, C: *The Descent of Man ...* , 1871, Ch. 4.

'perfect clocks'[14] and, although this metaphor nicely illustrates the difference between the indeterminacy of clouds and the determinacy of clocks, it also demonstrates how mutually exclusive they are. Clouds are natural phenomena; clocks are man-made and not natural. However, once the man-made 'clock' leaves the drawing board, the workshop or the laboratory and is used to measure the indeterminate world of nature, it loses its accuracy because it can never take into account all the unknown and unstable variables contained therein. Its design is based on what its designer recognises as regularities in nature, so remains inescapably *a posteriori*.

The rational mind looks for these regularities but can never be sure how regular they really are, unless it can measure their precision against something outside the nature it intends to measure. However, Popper went on to suggest those more 'rational controls', we impose upon our own behaviour, such as: 'deliberations', 'plans', 'intentions', 'values', 'aims', 'purposes', 'rules', 'agreements' and 'promises' that define the parameters within which our thinking, allows us to find a target between objective determinism on the one hand, and subjective indeterminism on the other. None of these 'rational controls', however, can transform the way we think about reality into deterministic algorithms; they merely define the boundaries within which our thoughts continue to be processed less determinately. That is, because they are almost certainly pre-empted by those less rational influences, such as 'excitement', 'curiosity', 'surprise', 'fear', 'pleasure', 'disappointment' and so on. In our search for agency, it is short sighted to believe 'the buck stops with us'. "At any given time, the organism [which includes ourselves] is confronted with an infinite number of potential stimuli and, subsequently, an infinite number of

---

[14] Popper, K: *Objective knowledge. An Evolutionary Approach*, revised 1979 edn., 228.

potential outcomes ... there's no way of sorting accurately through this chaos to identify useful patterns. And yet what's the defining feature of associative learning? It is the absence of *a priori* theory."[15]

At best, we are no more than the forwarding agents of those experiences that, almost certainly, we begin to process subjectively, even if they subsequently appear to be otherwise. That's why no artist, nor scientist for that matter, can ever adequately explain where their creative ideas comes from, other than, at best, from some external influential experience, or force of circumstance over which they had had no independent control. If and when creativity comes, it comes unpredictably rather than because of our own freedom of choice. A child, aimlessly fooling about on the piano, might eventually learn to play well and might one day become a concert pianist but may never have had any original intention of doing so until after its experiences had already begun to sow the seed of the idea in the child's mind, or in that of its mentor's mind somewhere along the way.

Accordingly, Popper suggested that we actually interact continually with our environment by 'trial-and-error elimination' but, when faced with an unknown future, what does this actually mean? We are like the rat in the maze, wildly guessing which route might allow us to escape. Only with the experience of our previously failed guesses are we able to refine them by reducing our chances of making future errors. All our attempts to escape the maze become increasingly limiting guesses, because we can only remember how to avoid our failures. The number of guesses we are confronted with in an indeterminate reality are grossly outnumbered by those that are defined within the deterministic walls of a maze, for, as the mathematician Georg Cantor pointed out: "The fear of infinity is a form

[15] Curry, O. S: *Associationism*, This Idea must Die, Ed. Brockman, J, 2015, 200-1

of myopia that destroys the possibility of seeing the actual infinite, even though it has, in its highest form, created and sustained us, and in its secondary transfinite form occurs all around us and even inhabits our minds".[16] In reality, our so-called decisions are reduced to restricted guesses. For 'as soon as questions of will, decision, or reason or choice of action arise, human science is at a loss.' [Chomsky]

This guessing-game corresponds to the multi-dimensional activities of neural networking during problem solving.[17] At the level of our neurotransmitters, synapses and microtubules, perhaps even our nanotubes, there must be an almost infinite number of possible networking routes to follow before our thoughts are turned into actions. Even the humble travelling-salesman, who decides to visit the same ten customers by a different networking route each day, would need to live for nearly ten-thousand years, [viz: 10!] before covering every possible sequence. The same guessing-game that the spider employed to produce its web millions of years ago is no different in principle from the one we humans employed more recently to produce the World-Wide Web. Only retrospectively do we congratulate ourselves on our successes by conveniently ignoring all our failures, which usually grossly outnumber the successes. This is an example of our ego's desperate attempt to try and claim its means of understanding reality is not merely guess-work.

Most of our so-called decisions however, are only conditioned habits, acquired from memories of our experiences that didn't appear to fail us in the past and of avoiding those that did. In a turbulent world however, past successes can become future failures and past failures can become future successes, so our memories are never entirely reliable. We may call them choices but they are

---

[16] Rucker, R: *Infinity and the* Mind, 1995
[17] Babloyantz, A & Lourenço, C: *Computation with Chaos: a Paradigm for Cortical Activity,* Proc. National. Academic Series, 91, 9027-31, 1994.

never better than informed guesses, bound only by the parameters of variance that our on-going experiences impose upon them. Admittedly, the more we know about the environment, the more focused our guesses usually become, but they still remain indeterminate because we cannot know, until, as Robert Frost expressed it: "somewhere ages and ages hence" where they might lead us. "Two roads diverged in a wood, and I, I took the one less travelled by, and that has made all the difference". In this same way, a face across a crowded room may be enough to change the whole course of the observer's life. At that moment though, neither he nor she could ever know whether it might eventually lead to heaven or to hell.

All attempts to improve our chances of survival, no matter how rational they may appear to be, are aimed at converting external chaos into internal order. We do this by searching in our memory for correlations between so-called effects and so-called causes but, 'correlations' are not the same as 'causations', they are merely measures of probable correspondence. Furthermore, what we call 'causes' and what we call 'effects' are actually arbitrary points of proximity in an indeterminate continuum of experiences in 'the now'.

No event necessitates agency, any more than, say, the falling apple, was thought to be the agent that triggered the formulation of gravity. In fact, Newton's diaries showed he had been struggling with the problem for some time, and the apple symbolised an arbitrary event in a long process of trial-and-error elimination that happened to point him in the right direction. In fact, it probably wasn't the apple, but his tracking of comets as they changed direction after passing behind the Sun that triggered the idea. And, as he, himself, conceded: 'while the great ocean of truth lay all undiscovered', he had been able to see further, only 'by standing on the shoulders of giants', just as others after him would have to concede how their own discoveries came about. Those incidents in time, to which we ascribe causal words such as 'choice' or 'decision', have become correlated in our minds with effective actions, to which we ascribe consequential words, such as 'answer' or 'solution'. They are not, however, events that can be viewed autonomously because they are embedded in the on-going process called 'time' and can only be described in terms of what little we know about their ancestry and progeny.

In any event, the whole history of scientific enquiry is based on the 'empiricist principle', in which hypotheses are derived from thoughts, which in turn are derived from feelings about experiences, which in turn offer us further thoughts and hypotheses. Prior to public exposure, all the emotional turmoil and abortive effort that pre-empts most scientific insights, is swept under the carpet and conveniently forgotten about. It has been described as "an after-the-fact attempt to make an intuitive process appear methodological", since "no experiment or observation is possible without a relevant theoretical framework".[18] It's an inescapable conundrum that we have to construct an assumed truth in the hope of finding a valid truth. It is believed even "Einstein made eight attempts at finding a proof for $E=mc^2$. It took him nearly half a century and not once did he manage it without inserting a fudge."[19] And as Darwin argued, it is: "Often difficult to distinguish between the powers of reason and instinct [and because instinct is usually inherited habit] much of the intelligent work done by man is due to imitation and not by reason".[20]

In fact, there may not be any fundamental difference, other than in degree, between instinct and reason, as they both appear to have their origins, no matter how distant, in chance alone. Like evolution, science is very much a hit-

[18] Kothari, D: *Some Thoughts on Truth*, 1975, 5.
[19] Brooks, M: *Free Radicals: the Secret Anarchy of Science*, 2011, 60-1.
[20] Wallace, A: *Contributions to the Theory of Natural Selection*, 1870, 221.

and-miss affair; it "is not a monolithic truth-gathering method but rather a motley assortment of tools designed to safeguard us against bias".[21] No one would be human, not even scientists, if they weren't affected in some way by 'conformation bias', no matter how insignificant it may appear to be at the time. The more objective, rational mind is programmed against conceding to the more subjective nature of its source data.

In 1859 Darwin showed how species evolved by chance variances in inherited characteristics; in 1872 Boltzmann showed how molecules and atoms changed stochastically over time; in 1925 Heisenberg discovered the 'uncertainty principle' of sub-atomic particles, and in 1953 Crick and Watson discovered DNA, which led to the understanding of chance mutations of genes. Crick even admitted: 'that by blundering about we stumbled on gold'. Despite the fact that all these findings demonstrated the significance of chance and were, themselves, also discovered by chance, we still find it hard to accept that this same chance-based process undermines all our reasoning-power as well.

It is often claimed that forward planning and decision-making, has provided us with the unique ability to turn 'causes' into 'effects', and accordingly allowed us the freedom to decide on the future we want, despite the fact that we can never be sure it will be the future we like when we get it. If Robert Oppenheimer had been able to anticipate the consequences of the atomic bombs that were dropped on Hiroshima and Nagasaki, would he have accepted directorship of the Los Alamos project, where it was first developed? After witnessing its first explosion in the New Mexico desert, he recalled that phrase in the Bhagavad-Gita: 'Now I am become Death, the Destroyer of Worlds'.

Although those parts of our brain concerned with

---

[21] Lilienfeld, S: *Fudge Factor*, Scientific American, Nov. 2010, 8

judgment and evaluation developed much later than those concerned with unconscious non-judgmental experiences, they were both still products of evolution, so must be subject to the same indeterminate forces of nature. We think we have the ability to translate sensual experiences into rational thoughts, but we can only check whether this process makes sense retrospectively. Hindsight is all we have for deciding whether our so-called decisions were wise ones or not, but then of course it's too late, they have already been made for us; so who's in charge?

The *a priori* model of reality, whereby we conceive of a thought as the 'cause', and an action as the 'effect', is a misguided reconstruction of the way we process our experiences of reality subjectively all the time. Over millions of years we must have unconsciously recognised levels of correspondence between things and adjusted our behaviour accordingly, without having to think rationally about it first. Only subsequently did we think they had to be related by a 'cause' and 'effect' model of reality.

Not long ago, for example, it was assumed that alcoholism caused throat cancer. Then it was thought smoking might have had something to do with it too. Further investigation suggested poor diet was a relevant factor, then perhaps, an unhealthy life-style, possibly related to low levels of hygiene, low social status, even a poor education and the person's whole history. Attempts to translate all these variables into cause-and-effect relationships quickly became a thankless task. Perhaps, by seeing reality in terms of cause-and-effect, has inhibited, more than helped our sensual experiences of it.

7. HOW CAN MATTER BECOME MIND?

All living things are aware of their environment in different ways. Plants are aware of sunlight, animals are aware of danger, and a few social species, including *Homo sapiens*, are aware of themselves being aware. The development of this introspective form of awareness in human though, has gave rise to a more conceptual sense of consciousness and might have been the consequence of a neurological mutation upon which all our acquired information and knowledge of the world was gained and expressed, at first by word-of-mouth and then in writing.

By thinking about those less conscious experiences that our bodies feel for their environment externally, we have learnt to know it internally in a very different sort of way. This more conscious form of processing has developed over the millennia and has allowed us to define the world in terms of facts, values, ideas, opinions and beliefs. We might subjectively experience a sense of elation while observing a sunset, for example but, when we try to make sense of the experience, this feeling of elation seems to disappear, or at least is put on hold. This suggests a fundamental difference between subjectively feeling our experiences throughout our bodies and objectively thinking about them more in our minds. Our bodies are responding to our environment sensually all the time, but only sometimes do we become conceptually aware of these responses by trying to translate them into identifiable thoughts. As Jean-Jacques Rousseau said: "I felt before I thought: 'tis the common lot of humanity. I had conceived nothing, but felt everything. These conferred emotions, which I felt, one after another, certainly did not warp the reasoning powers that I did not yet possess but shaped them in me".[1]

Rather like his contemporary, David Hume, he realised that our more conscious thoughts must have originated from our less conscious feelings or emotions, except that Hume called them 'passions' instead. However, our thoughts about our experiences, along with our use of language to express them, probably developed much later in our evolutionary history. Some may say animals have a kind of language too but, as far as we know, their language is a way of expressing only their feelings, such as fear, excitement or anger and so on, by means of sounds such as screams, or whoops or growls, without any recognisable form of grammar or syntax. In pre-linguistic times our feelings were probably expressed in a similar way too, but now we express what we think more than what we feel about them, by means of words and sentences.

Perhaps the origin of this change, from feeling to thinking, can be traced back to a time when we began to recognise our own identities and reflect upon what we felt, thus triggering the first glimmer of judgment and evaluation of them. Hence expressions of emotion, by means of sounds, gradually became converted into

---

[1] Rousseau, J: *Confessions*, 1782, 435 which, contrary to common consensus at the time, implied 'reasoning power' was not *a priori* but dependent on 'conferred emotions'.

thoughts, as expressed in words about the things that triggered these emotions and a gradual schism occurred between 'knowing' things by experiencing them subjectively, and 'knowing' things by thinking about what they represented objectively. And although we still sometimes use words to express how we feel, we used them more frequently to express how we think.

So the thoughts within a person's 'head' must have had their more visceral origins in the emotions of the 'heart' and even earlier in their evolutionary history, from biological sensations in the 'gut'. This idea has been described as the Triune brain hypothesis,[2] which suggested our neurology probably evolved, from 'gut' to 'heart' to 'head'. Although it's a model that is now considered too simplistic, its chronology is still believed to be roughly correct.

How, though, did we humans become consciously aware of our more subliminal feelings in the first place? One suggestion is that the evolution of conscious thoughts about how we felt might have been enhanced by our ancestors' discovery of hallucinogenic plants that stimulate neuronal pathways, reinforced with the common practice of shamanism among band communities everywhere,[3] may have contributed at least in part, to our sense of self-awareness. Be that as it may, the evolution of more introspective processing might have been what first gave rise to our sense of self-awareness and the recognition that other's feelings were being mirrored in our own feelings.

This increasing recognition of the self is reflected in Greek mythology about Narcissus, who fell in love with his own reflection in a pool of water and became so intoxicated with it that he eventually died in solitary admiration of himself and forgot, or even came to despise everyone else. Like most mythological ideas, it probably

---

[2] MacLean P: *The Triune Brain in Evolution* ... , 1990
[3] McKenna, T: *Food of the Gods,* 1993

described what was happening to our developing sense of the ego at the time, which Freud recognised as a personality disorder and called 'narcissism'.[4] Apart from extreme cases though, this increasing recognition of the self gave rise to inner reflection and thought, which necessarily inhibited the outward feeling of sharing one's emotional experiences with others. In fact, this simple allegory contains all the ingredients of our ego's present need for detachment from the world of emotional experiences, particularly of each other, when it thinks, leading to solipsism and the belief that rationalising everything is our only means of survival. The Narcissus allegory might be the first cryptic reference to the ego's neglect of altruism and the widening gap that has arisen between egoism and altruism ever since.

This gap was also represented in Greece mythology, as personified by the emotional and chaotic experiences of Dionysus, as compared with those of the more focus and ration thoughts of his brother Apollo. Nietzsche explored these differences[5] and suggested Dionysus's consciousness corresponded to Schopenhauer's more natural concept of the 'will' to survive, whereas Apollo's was more like his *principium individuationis*, or what has here be described as the more inward-looking, objectively focused need to survive on one's own.

Before this division occurred though, our gregarious natures probably had their distant origins in the simple fact that those who lived together were more likely to survive together. This necessitated the amalgamation of different skills, such as hunting and gathering, infant-rearing, along with food-sharing and tool-making, all of which would have been impossible to do effectively on one's own. Understandably therefore, the division of such skills, each contributing to the common good, seem to have

---

[4] Freud, S: *On Narcissism, an Introduction*, 1914

[5] Nietzsche, F: *The Birth of Tragedy*, 1872

necessitated living in small bands together so as to improve their communal chances of survival, and this would have necessitated the ability to personally recognising each other's more emotional needs and respond to them appropriately, without the need to think more objectively about what they meant.

And, sure enough, brain-scanning techniques have discovered what are called 'mirror neurons' in the pre-motor and inferior-parietal cortex parts of our brains.[6] We may never know precisely how this process came about but without them it's doubtful whether we could have ever developed any real sense of emotional awareness of one another and of ourselves as separate identities. "This probably happened during the mental phase transition we underwent just a couple of hundred millennia ago, and would have been the dawn of full-fledged self awareness."[7] Although these 'mirror neurons' mimic the feelings of others, they pre-empt any conceptually conscious thoughts about them. Both the recognition and acceptance of other people's feelings occur almost simultaneously between them and, if there is any conscious recognition of this process, it's probably only by subsequent inference.

It's sometimes referred to as the 'theory of mind' but with the exception of those with certain personality disorders, such as Autism Spectrum Disorder or extreme forms of narcissism, people don't normally need to think about how others are feeling, they just 'know' instinctively because their feelings are somehow contagiously mirrored by their own. When a mother smiles at an infant, the infant smiles back; when people laugh or yawn, others in their company might find themselves laughing or yawning too.

---

[6] Pellegrino, G di, et al: *Understanding Motor Events: a neurophysiological study*, 1992, 91, 176-180 contains the first reference to mirror neurons, originally found in the macaque monkey, but subsequently in other social species, including humans.

[7] Ramachandran, V: *The Tell-Tale Brain*, 2011, 144

This 'mirroring' process is certainly an important feature of our gregarious natures and particularly in bonding partnerships, as was expressed, metaphysically, for example by John Donne: "My face in thine eye and thine in mine appears, and true plain hearts do in the faces rest ...".

Ironically though, these mirror neurons probably also gave rise to our increasing sense of 'self' and perhaps to the subsequent idea that this 'self' was capable of consciously choosing between alternative courses action in favour of itself. Thus began an almost irreversible attempt on the part of the ego, to gain increasingly objective knowledge of the world for its own advantage. This process was premised on the assumption that reality had to be ordered, even though the sensual experiences upon which this assumption had been based assumed no such order. This assumption of order can be recognised in the way parents teach their children to behave more objectively according to rules and regulations, at the expense of their children's more subjective impulses and intuitions and it has worked its way up through the educational system, into the way we try to conform to them throughout our adult lives. In smaller, less structured band communities though, children learn by example than by teaching from their parents.

Such thoughts gave rise in William James's mind to the idea that there were two selves [8], the 'I self', which experienced things subjectively in the 'now', and the 'me self' that was incapable of living in the 'now' because it was preoccupied in processing past experiences in order to plan for future ones. Although he did not specifically categorise these different selves in terms of levels of consciousness, it is suggested that 'sensual-consciousness', which experiences things non-judgmentally in the 'now', corresponds to the 'I self', whereas 'conceptual-

---

[8] James, W: *The Principles of Psychology*, 1890, Ch.3.

consciousness', which involves judging the past to evaluate the future, corresponds to the 'me self'. And although these two selves are fundamentally different, they are inescapably linked, because, objective 'concepts' are premised upon subjective 'precepts'. In other words, all our conceptionally conscious thoughts must have been derived, at some stage, from our sensually conscious feelings, so still remain entirely dependent upon them. Anyone bereft from birth of touch, taste, smell, sound or sight would surely be incapable of knowing anything conceptionally at all.

Although we're inclined to assume we're less likely to make mistakes when we think objectively before acting upon them than simply feeling subjectively about them, it's an essentially self-orientated process that neglects the possibility that others might see things differently. Consider the case of a written will, for example, which states the oldest male has power of attorney, and can distribute the family's inheritance among all the siblings as he chooses but, unless there is full agreement between them about how this is done, the whole lot goes to charity. We know instinctively the fairest distribution is equality all round but, with the power of attorney the oldest might think he deserves a larger share, which, even if accepted by the others for fear of losing everything, would almost certainly result in resentment against him for the remainder of all their lives.

This illustrates how intuitively, we know without question that 'fairness' means 'equality', but which has since become blurred and overrule by objective thoughts that focus on personal self-interest. In fact, the way society has become hierarchically structured has completely reversed this deeply held pre-moral belief that fairness was synonymous with equality and balance socially. One study, for example, has led researchers to "speculate that the controversy surrounding utilitarian moral philosophy reflects an underlying tension between competing subsystems in the brain".[9]

So there appears to be an irreconcilable split between the emotional mind that thrives on empathy for others, and the rational mind that thrives on its own more self-centred, and objective interpretation of these feelings. And because our more social needs, such as sharing and care-giving, are gradually being eroded by our more solitary needs, such as personal promotion and greed, cooperation is being replaced by competition.[10] Long ago, evolution had ordained that group survival was more successful than solitary survival, which is why we are, by our natures, still a basically gregarious species. At one time we instinctively aimed at maintaining balance and cohesion in order to survive together, which necessitated recognising each other's feelings and emotions and responding to them empathically. In fact, there is evidence that sensual feelings of compassion and kindness probably developed in our non-human primate ancestors before conscious thought and language developed in our own species.[11] But the modern idea that "we are all innately selfish ... has had a strong influence on how we interpret archaeological finds [even though] ... aggressive or selfish behaviour would have been very risky."[12]

Only subsequently did we unwittingly begin to be more consciously aware of our own needs at the expense of everyone else's, and:

> The 20th century is often said to be the bloodiest century in recorded history. In addition to wars,

---

[9] Greene, J et al: *The neural bases of cognitive conflict and control in moral judgment*, 2004, Abstract.

[10] Alexander, R: *The Biology of Moral Systems*, 1987; Vehrencamp, S: *A model for the evolution of despotic versus egalitarian societies*, Animal Behaviour, 31, 667-82.

[11] Spikins, P et al, A: *From Hominidity to Human Compassion*, Time and Mind, the Journal of Archaeology, Consciousness & Culture, 2010, V3, I£, 303-26.

[12] Spikins, P: *How Compassion Made us Human*, 2015.

the century witnessed many grave and widespread human-rights abuses. But what stands out in historical accounts of those abuses, perhaps even more than cruelty of their perpetration, is the inaction of bystanders.[13]

So how did this more objective and self-centred interpretation of the world arise in the first place? After all, no matter how much we might think we 'know' about it, there had always been another way of 'knowing' how to experience and respond to it. George Boole's little-studied work on the laws of thought[14] points us in the right direction when he asks: "how, from particular facts ... do we arrive at general propositions?" And suggests that: "it is the ability inherent in our nature to appreciate 'order' and the concurrent presumption, however founded, that the phenomena of Nature are connected by a principle of Order."

Perhaps it is not surprising then, that the 'me' self's survival had to make the assumption that 'order' was not just an acceptable precept, but could become a measurable concept. If, however, the world wasn't really ordered and didn't change according to underlying laws of nature, then there wasn't going to be any other way of understanding it conceptually. However, long before the 'me self' began this process of trying to define reality, the 'I self' already 'knew' how to cope with it intuitively by processing millions of bits of information every second without presuming anything: digesting food, fighting off infection, regulating body temperature, pressure, humidity, heart-rate, oxygen levels and so on, to say nothing of how it had been able to interacted and responded in balance with its environment and each other for so long.

This way of 'knowing' anything at all has been called

---

[13] Slovic, P et al: *Psychic Numbing and Mass Atrocity*, The behavioural foundations of public policy, Ed. Shafir, E, 2013, Abstract.

[14] Boole, G: *An Investigation into the Laws of Thought ...*, 1854, Ch. XXII

'system one'[15] and it functions at an emotional level, entirely below the level of conceptual awareness. Although it has been suggested that 'reason' is "emotionally engaging" because it is "shaped by the body",[16] it is more generally believed to have a more detached connotation. In any event, *Homo sapiens* was quite capable of solving most of its problems sensually, without thinking about, and trying to analyse them rationally at all. When we consider how this conscious-awareness came about, we might begin to appreciate the significance of those more ineffable experiences that triggered them in the first place. We can drive a car without having to think consciously about it, for example, but if we make a slight mistake an immediate rush of adrenalin tells us we should be more carefully about what we're doing. Most of the time though, we respond to our ever-changing circumstances instinctively and only when we realise they are in error do we begin making judgments about them and asking ourselves why. So our thoughts serve as a kind of objective controller of our subjective feelings after they have already occurred. Evidently Darwin recognised this when he said: "consciousness looks backwards, and serves as a guide for the future".[17]

In support of this idea, a number of important experiments have shown, counter-intuitively perhaps, that our intentions may have been generated before we were consciously aware of them. Or, to put it another way, we only become consciously aware of our intentions after their volition. In fact, our senses are responding instinctively to all sorts of environmental signals before we are consciously aware of them doing so. Apparently there

---

[15] Kahneman, D: *Thinking, Fast and Slow*, 2011: in which 'system one' has been described as not requiring any conscious effort because it is instantaneous.

[16] Lakoff G & Johnson, M: *Metaphors We Live By*, 1980, 5

[17] Darwin, C: *The Descent of Man* ..., 1871, V1

is a very small interval of time[18], usually only about 100-200 milliseconds, although some studies have indicated longer[19], for the more conscious thinking part of our mind to approve or veto an unconscious intention, if it so desires. In this heightened state of neural activity, it is believed we can selectively hold onto, and focus in on particular thoughts in our memory and then try to rationalise their implications before allowing their volition if we approve of them, or vetoing them before they turn into actions if we don't approve of them.

However, consciously thinking about, and trying to rationalise whether or not to have another drink at the party before driving home, for example, doesn't necessarily mean that by approving or vetoing our intentions we actually carry them out. Doing so implies freedom of choice, despite the fact that we may be quite unaware of what made us approve or veto our intentions before carrying them out. Put bluntly, we can never be independently free from the feelings that produce the thoughts that cause us to approve or veto our actions until after they have already occurred. "Men are mistaken in thinking themselves free; their opinions are made up of consciousness of their own actions, and ignorance of the causes by which they are determined."[20]

The whole processing-sequence, involved in dealing with real-life situations usually takes place quickly but almost certainly not in any straightforward algorithmic, or more rational way. It involves trying to cope with a whole mixture of relevant factors, many of which we may be quite unaware of at the time, so they cannot possibly be

---

[18] Libet, B et al: *Volitional Brain: towards a Neuroscience of Free Will*, 1999 edn.

[19] Soon, C et al: *Unconscious Determinants of Free Decisions in the Human Brain*, 2008 Nature Neuroscience 11, 543-5: "the outcome of a decision can be encoded in brain activity of prefrontal and parietal cortex up to 10 seconds before it enters awareness".

[20] Curley, E: *A Spinoza reader: The Ethics and other Works*, 1994.

solved rationally. We like to believe we are capable of making wise and thoughtful decisions but this is only 'confirmation bias' congratulating itself when our so-called decisions turn out well, and denial of them when they don't. It's hard for the 'me self' to accept how insignificant rational thoughts often are in this process and even harder to know what part if any, they play in the decision-making process. In the end, we might simply have to accept the fact that we didn't feel like trying to rationalise the situation and that it was probably more how we felt at the time that caused us to have another drink at the party before driving home, for example.

So what is actually going on in our heads while making these sorts of so-called decisions? The main thing to note is that, probably no real-life problem can ever be solved rationally, no matter how much thought is given to it in advance. Take the question of where to go for a holiday, for example: our choice might depend on the cost, the weather, the location and so on. Yet none of these factors can ever be compared objectively and evaluated against each other, any more than we can compare chalk with cheese. Even ranking different factors in order of importance to us is subjective; to rank the sun or sea above services or entertainment doesn't mean they are quantitatively better, just different. All we're doing is ranking one qualitative factor above another, according to our own personal preferences at the time, and these invariably have a more emotional than rational origin. We may simply feel we need peace and quiet, and are prepared to pay for it, or we might crave the sun because we're fed up with the dull weather back home. Without realising it, it's even possible our bodies are telling us we need an extra dose of vitamin D from the sunlight.

Even decisions of a more quantitative nature, such as those concerned with capital investments for example, usually turn out to be far less rational than they first appear to be. We might be cautious by nature and go for a fixed interest rate, or prefer the thrill of a more speculative investment, or perhaps we'd been tipped-off by someone who worked in the city and seemed to know what they were taking about, or because we simply felt the economy appeared buoyant or risky, according to what we had read in the papers that morning. Even childhood feelings of confidence or insecurity may have turned out to have a far greater influence on our level of risk-taking in later life than we realised. How we feel about real-life problems is bound to be subjective by its nature, because the reality of any situation usually contains far more degrees of freedom then we could possibly recognise, let alone evaluate quantitatively to find solutions to.[21] In short, we simply can't help being biased in one way or another about whatever we do in practise.

So how are our so-called decisions actually made? Consider, a simple choice between, say 'X' and 'Y'. Based on past experience we may feel like choosing 'X' rather than 'Y' because we remember, either the 'successful' consequences of having done something like 'X' before, or the 'unsuccessful' consequences of having done something like 'Y' before. And what we interpret as being 'successful' or 'unsuccessful' is usually more to do with whether we subjectively liked or disliked the outcome at the time, rather than because of some quantifiable gain or loss. And ultimately, even quantifiable gains or losses usually have had a qualitative pleasurable or un-pleasurable origin.

In any event, the pleasure we might gain from, say, having another cigarette isn't necessarily a very good reason for having one. And when we experience positive feelings of, say trust or empathy from others, it makes us feel we're worthwhile to them so respond in kind, whereas when we experience negative feelings of, say suspicion or distrust, it makes us we've not worthwhile to them and

---

[21] Even the 'Three Body Problem' in classical physics, which simplifies reality to three variables in space, is notoriously hard to solve.

respond in kind. David Hume evidently recognised this innate ability to mirror each other's feelings, when he said, "there seems a necessity for confessing that the happiness and misery of others are not spectacles altogether indifferent to us, but that the view of the former ... communicates a secret joy; [while] the appearance of the latter ... throws a melancholy damp over the imagination".[22] So what caused us to have these positive or negative emotions in our relationships with each other? They might have originated long ago from simply needing each other's company, or at least not wanting their avoidance, as both had a sound evolutionary basis for group-survival strategy.

Pioneering work on rats' brains, and subsequently on humans,[23] showed that the excitation or inhibition of the chemical dopamine had a lot to do with the regulation of these emotions. Although it was initially found that dopamine levels could be controlled artificially by inserting electrodes into a certain region of the brain, it was realised these levels were affected by natural social encounters all the time, even in humans. For example, the recognition of a friend would immediately trigger an increase in dopamine, whereas that of an enemy might decrease it. But not only do our social experiences influence our emotions electro-chemically to create an appropriate behavioural response; if we think more rationally about our experiences, the process becomes altogether more objectively impersonal and it has been found this secondary stage, involving separate cortical regions of the brain that can override the emotions. It is claimed by some however, that: "the advantage of such a separation is that the 'objective evidence' can be recombined with newly

---

[22] Hume, D: *A Enquiry Concerning the Principles of Morals*, 1751, 132

[23] Olds, J: *Pleasure centers in the brain.* Scientific American, 1956, 105-116; Delgado, J, et al *Intracerebral Radio Stimulation and recording in Completely Free Patients*, Journal of Nervous and Mental Disease, Vol 147(4), 1968, 329-340.

acquired knowledge when reinterpretation of the evidence is called for."[24]

Further work has been done on trying to understand the interplay between our ability to feel emotions sensually and our ability to translate them into more objective thoughts. If there is any genuine compatibility between them for examination though, its 'combined neurological mechanism remains unknown'. Any more, so-called 'objective evidence' must surely have had its origins, at some stage, in less objective experiences and those from even earlier ones, until it's usually quite impossible to pinpoint how they came about or why we ever thought they were 'objective' in the first place. Repeated experiences of, for example, night always following day, may have been the sorts of experiences that made us assume subjective evidence was actually objective fact. So we continually learnt by modifying future expectations in the light of our past experiences,[25] but this could be described more as conditioning rather than learning.

Unfortunately though, this on-going loop-feedback process is fraught with difficulties, of which the following are just a few. First, present experiences are never quite the same as remembered ones, so all such comparisons are error-prone. Our experience of every day is different in some way from our experience of every other day, so categorising them as if they were identical is unreliable. In any event, the sensations we feel when recalling similar experiences can change, which is why the second cup of tea on a hot summer's day may not seems quite as welcoming as the first. Also, our memories are not frozen in time like photographs or facts in history books; they are disaggregated and posted to different parts of the brain

[24] Schultz, W: *The Human Brain Encodes Event Frequencies while Forming Subjective Beliefs.* "The human brain encodes event frequencies while forming subjective beliefs." J. Neurosci 33(26):10887-97, a Bayesian approach involving combining probabilities is here assumed.
[25] Schank, R: *Dynamic Memory Revisited*, 1999

and, when recalled, re-assembled imperfectly according to our disposition at the time.

Anyway, most memories are less about objective facts, than about the subjective feelings associated with what we call the facts, and some of these may evoke memories below the level of consciousness awareness. As memories are mainly processed in the limbic brain, emotions evoked by sights, sounds, smells, touch or tastes are very impressionable and can remain in the memory long after the basic facts are forgotten. Even though men may not realise it, it is said that many of them are attracted to women who unwittingly remind them of their emotional experiences of their mothers, perhaps because of some embryonic or early imprinting. And even the way memories are continually re-interpreted can affect our recall of them. Those occasions that seemed positive or happy ones at the time, can, with repeated recall, become golden memories, whereas those that were negative or unhappy ones can play on our minds and evoke a nagging sense of regret, shame or guilt. And in old age, when thinking about the past is inclined to occupy more time than thinking about the future, they can become magnified out of all proportion. Could such effects be driven by a desire to want to re-live our successes and compensate for our failures? And the process of evaluating these memories in terms of pleasure or regret might explain why spiritual and secular lawmakers first felt it was necessary to transcribe them into objectively prescribed rules or laws of behaviour for all to follow.

Unfortunately though, these rules or laws of behaviour that have subsequently helped to define our cultural values and beliefs are not fixed constructs; they are changing unpredictably all the time. No matter how hard we might try to rigidly define, and live more objective lives according to them, they are imposed upon us by the society within which we find ourselves in its attempt to maintain order and discipline. In effect, the retributive justice system that reinforces their imposition by force of law, attempts to transpose its citizens' feelings about how they personally feel they 'ought' to behave into laws that define how society thinks they 'should' behave.[26]

So when we start thinking more objectively about our experiences, it involves trying to judge and evaluate the way we felt emotionally about them in the hope that we might then be able to validate them rationally. As I write this essay though, I'm aware that I'm trying to construct meaningful thoughts that represent my feelings about the subject. But, in attempting to do so, I might need to modify or revise my words and sentences from time to time. I can't be sure whether, what I am thinking represents what I am really feeling until after I've already thought it through and written it down. This retrospective trial-and-error correction-process takes place more in the pre-frontal cortex part of the brain, whereas those things that I instinctively feel comfortable or uncomfortable about seem to be milling about in a rather ill-defined way in the limbic region of the brain and this involves a back-and-forth process between the two.

At that more subjective level though, the molecules throughout our bodies are responding all the time to internal and external stimuli by means of 'perception switches' in their cell membranes.[27] Only sometimes, when we become aware of the signals these molecules are sending to each other and to the brain, can we begin trying to translate them into meaningful thoughts. If, for example, my body feels the need for sustenance, I might only become aware that I'm hungry after finding myself raiding the larder and consciously realise I've spoilt my

---

[26] 'Ought' is used here to express personal council, as compared with 'should', which implies legal obligation.

[27] Lipton, B: *The Biology of* Belief, 2005, 128, and in 1985 Candice Pert [Journal of Immunology] had suggested that molecules, neuropeptides and their receptors represented the 'biochemical substrata of the emotions'.

next meal.

In order to make judgments and find rational solutions to real-life problems, the 'me self' remains emotionally sterile and has to rely instead on reason and logic, which in effect, is all its got as a means of processing the data it receives. By its nature, it is neurologically trapped in a state of solipsism, cut off from actually experiencing anything at all. It originated perhaps from a neurological mutation that could only recognise these experiences conceptually. Like a parasite, the 'me self' feeds instead off subjective data from its host: the 'I self'. This reveals a curious paradox, because, when we are conceptually-conscious of what we think is reality, we embark on a never-ending *a priori* search to try and understand our sensually-conscious *a posteriori* experiences of reality.

No doubt Descartes was correct in claiming all sense-data experiences were subjective, but he was surely incorrect in assuming, that by establishing 'facts' derived from reason, it would be a more reliable way of knowing reality as there are different ways of knowing. Although many people believe facts exist before we have any need to sensually experience them, Nietzsche came to the contrary conclusion, namely: "there are no facts, only interpretations of facts". So, the unanswered question, 'how could matter become mind?' is a leading question. It presupposes that we already know what both 'matter' and 'mind' are and that they are different in some way that needs explanation. Although 'mind' is thought to be some kind of neuro-chemical process but, we still don't really know what 'matter' is, and although it is commonly thought to be some form of solid substance, George Berkeley preferred to deny its existence altogether.[28] We 'know' from our feelings, that something we call 'matter' must exist because, whatever it is stimulates us into having real emotional experiences about it, but what exactly gives

[28] Berkeley, G: *A Treatise Concerning the Principles of Human Knowledge*, 1710

us these experiences still remained unknown. Admittedly, our scientific understanding of what is conceived of as 'matter' has developed considerably over the last few hundred years, but the closer we look the more difficult it has become to define it and, at the quantum level, it has led us into a very strange world indeed.

> Quantum fluctuations are not the result of human limitations or hidden degrees of freedom; they are inherent in the workings of nature on an atomic scale. For example, the exact moment of decay of a particular radioactive nucleus is intrinsically uncertain. An element of genuine unpredictability is thus injected into nature.[29]

And the fundamental world of this thing, which, in ignorance we still call 'matter', gets even more mysterious with what has been called 'quantum entanglement':

> Entanglement is an unnerving kind of link that can develop between two or more photons, electrons or atoms, even if they inhabit distant parts of the universe. Consider, for example, a pion, a subatomic particle, which can decay into an electron and its antiparticle, a positron. When this happens, the particles fly off in opposite directions. But according to quantum theory, no matter how far apart the particles get, they remain mysteriously connected.[30]

Admittedly, sensually-conscious 'precepts' are subject to 'the delusion of dreams' as Descartes called them, but so too are our conceptually-conscious attempts to mould and shape them into 'concepts'. All thoughts, ideas, opinions,

---

[29] Davis, P: *The Uncertain Future,,* 'Chance', New Scientist, 2015, 148.

[30] Buchanan, M: *God Plays Dice* ..., 'Chance', New Scientist, 2015, 154.

values and beliefs, in fact our whole acquired library of conceptually-conscious knowledge of reality has still only been assembled from the building blocks of our sense-data experiences of it. Even though much of this conscious knowledge has now become so embedded in our thinking, and may even have become genetically inherited to mould and shape the way we can't help thinking, it is still remains a conceptually-conscious interpretation of reality, acquired from our sensually conscious experiences of it.

George Berkeley seemed to have recognised the two selves within us when he wrote "I know I am conscious of my own being and that I myself am not my ideas, but somewhat else, a thinking active principle that perceives, knows, wills and operates about ideas."[31] The translation of a sensually reality into a conceptual one therefore, is premised upon reason and involves questioning, sorting, organising, and verbally labelling sense data, for the purpose of establishing a more objective knowledge of reality; but it is still only the recognition of the self and our egocentric reflection of it that allowed this process to come about in the first place.

It was believed to have began about two million years ago with simple binary choices between, say: 'friend' or 'foe', 'fight' or 'flight', 'edible' or 'inedible', 'acceptance' or 'rejection' and so on, along with the gradual separation, no matter how insignificant, between qualitative and quantitative processing. This would have allowed *Homo habilis* to start making and using primitive tools, resulting in the conscious evaluation about their worth in doing so, followed, about a million years later, by *Homo erectus* who started making hand-axes and spears. But the birth of consciously recognising ourselves making these things perhaps began only a couple of hundred thousand years ago, since a great increase in the diversity of human

---

[31] Berkeley, G: *A Treatise Concerning the Principles of Human Knowledge,* 1710, 3rd. dialogue.

artefacts has been un-earthed, dating from about that period onwards. In this context therefore, it is important to distinguish sequentially between simply 'doing things', and 'thinking about doing things'.

One study found that during the Middle to Upper Palaeolithic transition, about a hundred thousand years ago, there was a significant increase in old-to-young people, or in their OY ration, from which it was claimed more knowledge, acquired by old people over their lifetimes could be handed down and conveyed to young people.

> Increased adult survivorship strengthens those relationships and information transmission by extending the time over which people can learn from older individuals and by the increase in the number of older people, which promotes the acquisition and transmission of specialized knowledge ... The large OY ratio we observe may therefore be a significant factor in the evolution of modernity not only through its importance for trans-generational information transfer but also because of its demographic impact. Recent models suggest demographic factors are responsible for the cultural innovations associated with modernity. Population expansion may have provided social pressures that led to extensive trade networks, increased mobility, and more complex systems of cooperation and competition between groups, resulting in increased personal ornamentation and other material expressions of individual and group identity.[32]

Certainly language would have facilitated the transfer of

---

[32] Caspari, R & Lee, S: *Older Age becomes Common Late in Human Evolution*, 2004.

this information in story-telling, no matter how fantastic, acquired by grandparents and passed on as knowledge to their grandchildren not 'simply about doing things', but also 'thinking first about doing things'. Such conjectures corresponded to a change of emphasis in the way we process information, from fantasising to conceptualising more about reality in terms of facts, which gave an impetus to ideas and the construction of more objective images of reality. This conceptually-conscious attempt to make everything seem more intelligible involved the activation of different cortical regions of the brain that enabled us to construct ever-more elaborate images of a materialistic world. And, from the Neolithic era onwards, was followed with the gradual imposition of laws of behaviour, followed by laws of nature, all of which has greatly facilitated the mind's objective conception of the body's phenomenological experiences of reality.

With the development of language, this more formal transition of experiences into ideas has also been facilitated by means of earth, and sand-drawings, cave paintings, the use of rhythm, song and dance routines and a variety of folkloric practices and beliefs that became transcribed into ideologies. These would have resulted in the transition of habits into customs, of feelings into opinions, of beliefs into ideas, of conjectures into testable hypotheses, of judgments into rules, and finally, of repeatable *a posteriori* experiences into what are now conceive of as *a priori* facts and laws of nature. And this gradual transition of ineffable feelings into conceptual thoughts about the nature of reality is what has most distinguished *Homo sapiens* from other primate species.[33] It has given rise to the feeling that we must be in charge of our emotions because we believe

---

[33] Semendeferel, K, et al: *Prefrontal Cortex in Humans and Apes*, American Journal of Physical Anthropology, 2001, Table 5, 238, indicates "higher cogitative functions such as undertaking of initiatives and planning of future action" exists in other social primates such as bonobos, chimps, gorillas and orang-utans.

we have acquired the knowledge and understanding to determine our futures.

It is thought that science is a more reliable approach to determining the truth, because it relies on reason and logic to define it, whereas all cultural practices from which they were derived, were simply emotional expressions of people's sensual experiences of reality. It is even claimed that "in theory, cultural relativism emphatically denies reason and objectivity [and that] in practice it sanctions the worst manifestations of violence and oppression".[34] There is however, a fundamental difference between cultural practices that unite people in communal empathy and gregariousness, and those that have subsequently been monopolised and transposed into formalised ideologies to unite people under spiritual and secular leadership. Relative cultural practices do not 'deny reason and objectivity'; they simply have not need of it. It is only when they are transposed into ideological beliefs, whose proponents emphatically deny the validity of cultural relativism that 'the worst manifestations of violence and oppression' follow from them.

> The brain has provided us with a wide variety of subjective feelings of reward ranging from hunches, gut feelings, intuitions and suspicions that we are on the right track to a profound sense of certainty and utter conviction. And yes, these feelings are qualitatively as powerful as those involved in sex and gambling. One need only look at the self-satisfied smugness of a 'know it all' to suspect that feelings of certainty can approach the power of addiction.[35]

---

[34] Kanarek, J: *Critiquing Cultural Relativism*, 2013

[35] Burton, R: *The Certainty Bias: a potentially dangerous mental Flaw*, 2008. Even, so called 'experts' are often 'no better than the rest of us at prognostication', see Tetlock, P: *Expert Political Judgment* ..., 1984.

And it is the addiction of 'certainty and utter conviction' of the few 'know it alls' who impose their addiction upon the many. Sensually-conscious experiences do not need to be validated; they make us what we are, whereas the conceptually-conscious processing of these experiences, does need to be validated. This is when the search for certainty and the need for utter conviction begins, but without repeated trial-and-error experimentation *ad infinitum* truth, in an indeterminate world the truth remains inordinately mystical and can never be known.

After all, the history of science itself is an on-going and never ending process of self-correction, so it's a safer bet assuming things that are commonly assumed to be true, actually aren't true, on the grounds that we can never be certain about anything except uncertainty. Although scientists may congratulate themselves that science has given us, for example, the "power to slingshot rockets around Jupiter to reach Saturn",[36] it could only have gained that power by means of a long and tortured history of trial-and-error elimination, almost certainly involving far more failures than successes. It's the same neurological process involving 'hunches, gut feelings, intuitions and suspicions' by which our ancient ancestors learnt how to successfully sling-shot spears at wild animals, in other words by guesswork. Although many of these guesses are tried out and tested in practice, they are almost certainly pre-empted by far more 'tried out' theoretical attempts within the mind, before any one of them ever becomes selected for testing in practice.

Perhaps the ego's bias, in favour of remembering its successes and overlooking its failures, is because it's so isolate from the feelings of empathy of others, so it needs to justify its claim to understanding reality, even though all its rational attempts to do so still depend on random

---

[36] Dawkins, R: *A Devil's Chaplain*, What is Truth, 2004 edn., 18

processing. This, of course, does not mean they are entirely arbitrary but are, nevertheless, always probabilistically random, within parameters of variance ranging from 'highly likely' or almost 'one', to 'highly unlikely' or almost 'zero'.

In the 'me' self's attempt to understand the 'I' self's experiences of reality, it will never find absolute truths about its experiences of nature, so why not start with the 'null hypothesis', namely that reality is fundamentally unknowable in any rational sense of the word, at least until such time as it can be proved otherwise and, to reject such a hypothesis would be to reject the fundamental principles of Darwinian evolution, for example. There is indeed 'more to truth than meets the eye', and indeed meets the all too limited boundaries of the human eye, which ultimately, is premised upon, not only the all-too-limited boundaries of our sense experiences, and yes indeed, also upon the all too limited boundaries of scientific enquiry.

Experiencing the world pre-empts any form of judgment of it, whereas thinking about, and trying to understand it, can only begin with judgment and unfortunately this eclipses the significance of simply experiencing it. It has made many of us so objectively dependent upon a virtual-reality, constructed out of words and numbers that it has separated us from experiencing the joy of life directly through our senses, and from this much illness has followed. For example: "Loneliness, a sense of disengagement, a loss of natural vitality and of innocent pleasure in the given-ness of the world, and a feeling of burden because reality has no meaning other than what a person chooses to impart to it."[37]

> [It] bypasses hardware and absolute concepts in favour of precepts, that is, a 'direct, non-

---

[37] Tuan, Y: *Segmented Worlds and Self: Group Life and Individual Consciousness,* 1982, 139

intellectual experience of reality' ... one could almost say the essence of it, is the awareness of the unity and mutual interrelation of all things and events, the experience of all phenomena in the world as manifestations of a basic oneness. All things are seen as interdependent and inseparable parts of this cosmic whole, as different manifestations of the same ultimate reality.[38]

No wonder we have become so isolated from each other, locked in inner contemplation, judgment and evaluation about how best to cope with a threatening environment and, more generally, with all the more practical problems we have discovered and surrounded ourselves with. At one time, true friendship and love occurred only between equals, or at least between those who did not judge each other as un-equals, because they instinctively knew whether they were kindred spirits or not. Judgment and evaluation came later and only inhibit these instincts. Perhaps that's why children, who at first tend to pre-empt judgment, are able to form friendships so much more easily than adults who have learnt by objectifying experience to be so much more cautious.

---

[38] Hwa Yol Jung: *Transversal Rationality and Intercultural Text*: Essay in Phenomenology and Comparative Philosophy, 2011

8. COOPERATION OR COMPETITION?

In his 'Treatise Concerning Human Nature', David Hume outlined "the difference betwixt impressions ... which first appeared in our mind" and "ideas ... which made their way into our thoughts". His great insight summarises the sequence of our so-called decision-making, from less-conscious feelings to more-conscious thoughts, but it also reflects the whole chronology of our neurological evolution.

At one time our distant ancestors solved their problems by making unconscious adjustments to their ever-changing circumstances all the time. Evolution had shown them how to do this instinctively; they would surely never have survived otherwise. And with respect to their social environment, they were able to make adjustments to each other's facial expressions, body language and behaviour, without having to think about it. All those impressions that first appeared in their minds were usually sufficient to enable them to maintain an acceptable level of social stability within their communities without ever having to consciously think about why they did so. Our ancestors were unconscious mind-readers, "monitoring one another's behaviour and drawing subtle inferences about each other's mental state without having the slightest idea that [they were] doing this."[1]

Although we still tend to rely on non-verbal signals more than verbal ones[2], we have become increasingly inhibited by all those more consciously constructed 'ideas ... which made their way into our thoughts', usually expressed in the form of words and sentences. Our feelings about each other are usually recognised instinctively from first impressions, whereas our thoughts are constructed more consciously and are usually recognised and defined by means of the words we use to express them, even though they probably represent only an echo of how we felt at the time.

Contrary to the American President's 'read my lips' speech in 1988, it's often safer to read people's facial expressions and body language. It all depends on how much we feel we can trust each other before trying to express our feelings. There is now however, a conspicuous conflict of interest between our personal needs and social needs. For reasons of self-preservation, everyone is primarily concerned about their own needs but, being a gregarious species, we can't help being concerned about the needs of others too. It's been described as a choice between egoism and altruism or, in more practical language, between competing against each other or cooperating with them, but how we make this choice depends largely on how much or how little we feel we can trust each other. If they seem empathic, it triggers feelings of affinity, if they don't we immediately become guarded. The level of trust between people is unconsciously being

[1] Smith, D: *Why we Lie*, 2004, 5.

[2] Argyle, M, et al: *The Communication of friendly and hostile attitudes by verbal and non-verbal signals*: European Journal of Social Psychology, V1, I3, 385-402, 1971.

tried and tested all the time, so whatever transpires from these encounters rests on a knife-edge and can go either way.

When Newton conceived of his Third Law of Motion, which states that 'every action has an equal and opposite reaction', he probably wasn't thinking about its social implications at all, nevertheless this idea has had a profound effect on the course of human history. Any relationship that develops from an embryo of mutual trust is usually fruitful and might even turn into a life-long friendship. On the other hand, initial misunderstandings can easily mushroom into 'neighbours from hell' and, in the case of whole societies or nation states, into wars and hell for millions. Most wars are premised on feelings of suspicion and distrust, for how rarely, if ever, do political leaders pre-empt their plans for war by questioning their own values and beliefs, or attempt to understand those of their enemies'? As surely as night follows day, cooperation follows from trust and competition from distrust. Adam Smith put it like this: "When we consider the character of any individual, we naturally view it under two different aspects; first, as it may affect his own happiness; and secondly, as it may affect that of other people."[3]

Long ago, evolution had shown our ancestors that cooperating with one another helped them to iron out their differences and maintain a reasonable level of social stability within their communities, so naturally, was encouraged, whereas competition only seemed to hinder it, so was avoided whenever possible. Hunter-gatherers and small band communities everywhere, were and still are: "Highly variable in their social organisation and subsistence patterns but, so long as they remained mobile, rather than sedentary, they were remarkably uniform in their social, moral, and political make-up."[4] This was

[3] Smith, A: *The Theory of Moral Sentiment* 1759, Pt. VI.
[4] Ember, C: *Myths about hunter-gatherers.* Ethnology 17, 439-48; Kelly, R: *The Foraging Spectrum: Diversity in Hunter-Gatherer Lifeways*, 1995

evident in their sharing of food, as "anatomically modern humans obtained an important part of their diet from larger-game hunting which [by sharing] provided a practical reason to outlaw [the dominance of] alpha males."[5]

Attempts to balance our own needs with those of others is still relevant to all our social encounters, and can only be dealt with by every individual trying to make allowances for the ever-changing needs and feelings of each other. "I wouldn't love [him] unless he love me back, exactly as much, absolute fairness. And, as he didn't, neither did I."[6] And, to quote David Hume's analogy: when "two men pull on the oars of a boat", they do so "without any promise or contract".[7] Only by recognising the needs of each other could they avoid any "inconveniences of transgression" and arrive at their mutually acceptable destination. This instinctive need for balance must have been the basis of morality, before it became so disastrously abused by the administration of so-called justice in favour of those who administered it. Although it's still often assumed we think before we act, this thinking is acquired only retrospectively from feelings of fairness in trying to avoid our mistakes. Without instinctively learning how to deal with our social problems iteratively in this way, we would surely never have enjoyed social intercourse and would have ended up as a solitary species like the bears, tigers or foxes.

Before our ancestors developed any formal language though, they seemed to cope well enough by means of those feelings or 'impressions ... which first appeared in [their] minds' based on a wide variety of facial expressions, body language and behaviour, just as our closest non-human primates still do. The subsequent development of

---

[5] Erdal, D & Whiten, A: *Egalitarianims and Machiavellian intelligence in human evolution,* Modelling the Early Human Mind, 1997, 139-50.

[6] Von Arnim, E: *Enchanted April*, 1920, Ch 11.

[7] Hume, D: *Enquiry concerning the Principles of Morals*, 1751, Appx. III.

language though, with all those more consciously constructed "ideas, which made their way into our thoughts"[8] tends to expose only the tip of an iceberg, beneath which all our more sensually conscious feelings, representing our real emotions, usually still lie hidden.

Exactly why this change of focus in the way people relate to one another came about must surely have had something to do with a general shift away from common feelings of trust and cooperation within smaller egalitarian communities, and more towards common thoughts of distrust and competition within larger hierarchically structured societies. There must also have been a corresponding change of emphasis, from living and responding intuitively and flexibly according to each other's emotional needs in 'the now' at a personal level, to living and responding more inflexibly according to our own more egocentric needs for the future. When certain individuals favour their own needs more than those of others, it emphasised their differences and, unless kept in check by others, can easily develop into exploitation and bullying. Such a self-centred attitude might be just temporary selfishness but, if persistent, causes others to react against it.

It's not certain whether those with little or no empathy for anyone but themselves are born or made, but 'neglect' or 'overly controlling parenting' are inclined to inhibit a child's ability to feel trust for others so, if the child's going to survive, it quickly learns to put itself first.[9] Caring parents may create a greater sense of morality than authoritarian parents[10] but those who persistently tell their

---

[8] The origin Homo sapiens is thought to be less than 200,000 years ago and as much as 2 million for earlier Homo species but when language gradually became more formal with grammar and syntax is unknown.

[9] Gullhangen, A & Nøttestad, J: *Looking for the Hannibal behind the Cannibal* ...: International Journal of Order Therapy ...5/2011, 55, 350-69.

[10] Baumrind, D: *Are Authoritative families really harmonious?* Psychological Bulletin, 1983, 94, 133-42.

children to 'try harder' can mean trying harder to do what they want the child to do irrespective of the child's needs. And: "Until very recently, it was held that, if a boy could not learn his lessons, the proper cure was caning or flogging. This view is nearly extinct in the treatment of children but it [still] survives in the criminal law".[11] Caning or flogging may be less prevalent these days but the threat of punishment for not obeying the law, is still the basis of all retributive justice systems, and, quite apart from in employment, even pervades the home and schools. Developing an appreciation of others' feelings is usually acquired in infancy by example,[12] and later more consciously reinforced by explanation, but when fear of punishment is exercised as a way of controlling society, it's unlikely to create much empathic understanding of social leadership at all.

At one time small egalitarian communities depended on leadership too but that usually meant group acceptance of the oldest, and therefore often the most experienced, with everyone participating in the decision-making process anyway. But when societies grew larger and more hierarchical, leadership was enforced by reference to written laws under threat of punishment when they weren't obeyed. Unfortunately though, this was, and still is, a painfully shallow interpretation of human nature because those who simply went along with it tended to wallow in feelings of pride, vanity and self-aggrandisement, while those who didn't either buried their heads in shame or guilt, or it promoted resentment and revenge. Even worse: enforced control of the law deprives people of their own personal responsibility and inhibits them from facing how they might instinctively feel they ought to behave.

---

[11] Russell, B: *Why I am not a Christian*, The Doctrine of Free-Will, Ch. 2, 1967, but first pub. 1930

[12] Hamlin, K: *Moral Blank Staleism*, 2015. *This Idea Must Die*, Brockman, J Ed. 2015, 197 claims "toddlers are internally rather than externally motivated to be pro-social".

While discussing personal problems with their clients, therapists are advised to be non-judgemental because it helps to create a mutually empathic atmosphere of trust and open-minded enquiry, bereft of any stigma of guilt, shame or blame, whereby they find it easier to solve their own problems than be told how to do so. When self-control is replaced by authorised control, people become litigiously conditioned to attribute credit or blame to each other and to themselves, according to the laws administered by spiritual and secular leaders. Research suggests this change in the way we relate to one another has been brought about by a shift away from intuition in one another based on emotional expectation,[13] and more towards imposition according to authorised moral judgment.[14] In any event, administering rewards and punishments under any punitive system of justice inhibits instinctive feelings of empathic and trust between the giver and receiver.

If we are accountable for our actions, we ought to be capable of realising whether we approve of them or not. This vetting process, however, cannot be done in advance of its occurrence because it only becomes consciously recognisable after it has already been formed from 'impressions ... which first appeared in our minds'. Our feelings can influence our thoughts but conscious consideration of them can influence our feelings too. In effect, both influence each other but feelings came first in our neurological evolution. The idea that they were nurtured, primarily by our experiences, was recognised by William James, who used, as an example, the feeling of 'fear', when he said: "we do not run away because we feel afraid, we feel afraid because we run away". He asked: "What kind of emotion of fear would be left, if the feelings

[13] Rotter, J: *Generalized expectancies of internal versus external control reinforcements*, Psychology Monographs, 80, 609, 1966.
[14] Green, J, et al: *An fMRI investigation of emotional engagement in moral Judgment*, Science, 293, 2001, 2105-8.

neither of quickened heart-beats nor of shallow breathing, neither of trembling lips nor of weakened limbs, neither of goose-flesh nor of visceral stirrings, were present, is quite impossible to think".[15]

So we might take a step even further back, in our search for agency, in that it must be our biological reactions to our experiences that create our feelings about them. In James's example, it is the dangerous experiences that trigger these biological responses that make us run away, which then give rise to the concept of fear associated with those experiences. Then later in our evolutionary development, the concept of fear gave rise to our thoughts about what had induced it. Consequently, it is our physiology that determines how we feel about our experiences, not the other way round. But then, of course, our inherited genes provide the foundations for our physiology. No matter how instantaneously we might react to our experiences, we do so only after we have both biologically and neurologically been conditioned by them[16] and our genetic inheritance, for better or for worse, is being 'imprinted' by these experiences all the time. We can never know for certain, whether our decisions are wise ones or not, nor whether they are morally faulty in some way; if necessary we can only learn from them after we have made them by trying to correct future decisions.

As far as altruism was concerned, that great evolutionary biologist, J B S Haldaine, claimed he would be prepared to 'sacrifice his own life for two of his siblings or eight of his cousins'. What he meant was that it was the survival of our genes, reproduced in kinship relationships that determined these feelings of altruism towards one another. And, in attempting to give altruism a purely

[15] Redding, P: *Feeling, thought and orientation: William James and the Idealist anti-Cartesian tradition*, 2011, 41
[16] Kornhuber, H & Deecke, D: *Hirnpotentialänderungen* ..., 1965; Libet, B: *Unconscious cerebral initiative*, Behaviour & Brain Sciences, 1985, 529-66.

quantifiable foundation, others went even further[17] by also considering those more general feelings of empathy for friends and neighbours over and above evolutionary determinism. "Our altruism is not unbounded; it is parochial. In support of this phenomenon, the hormone oxytocin, long considered to play a key role in forming social bonds, has been show to facilitate affiliation towards one's in-group but can increase defence and aggression towards one's out-group."[18]

With the birth of the city-state however, equality gave way to hierarchy, as a result of which ideas about 'good' and 'bad' behaviour gradually began to 'make their way into our thoughts' and became transcribed into consciously constructed rules, regulations and laws, which had to be enforced by state control. In practice this meant impressions, which made people feel how they ought to behave, began to be overruled by regulations and laws about how authority thought they should behave, with the word 'ought' being the motif for sensually-conscious feelings, acquired instinctively from personal council, and the word 'should' being the motif for conceptually-conscious thoughts, imposed by authorised obligation. Those instinctive feelings of self-regulatory control, therefore, became increasingly influenced by consciously constructed spiritual and secular lawmakers, as defined by those who claimed the authority to impose them upon societies.

The way such impositions gained recognition, acceptance and respectability[19] however, was not necessarily by means of any intrinsic merit based on

---

[17] Most notably William D. Hamilton's rule in 'kin selection', John Maynard Smith's evolutionarily 'stable strategy' in game theory and George R Price's 'frequency equation' in evolutionary genetic traits.

[18] Waytz, A: *Humans are by Nature Social Animals*, This Idea Must Die, 2015, 218

[19] Service, E: *Origin of the State and Civilization*, 1975; Vehrencamp. S: *A Model of the Evolution of Despotic versus Egalitarian Societies*, Animal Behaviour 31, 667-82.

reason, but primarily from fear of condemnation if they weren't obeyed, reinforced with commendation if they were. This transference in self-fulfilling social behaviour, from 'tradition' to 'imposition', encouraged people to focus less upon their own instinctive feelings of approval or disapproval of each other and of themselves, and more upon authority's conceived of ideas of approval or disapproval, as prescribed by their rules, regulations and laws.[20]

Perhaps the first leaders of church and state might have tried to influence their citizens' behaviour according to principles of mutual trust and cooperation, but the ever-increasing size of those organisations would soon have had to make them reinforce these principles by more control-centred considerations, thus enhancing their own conceived-of positions of authority. By so doing, however, all those more cooperative feelings of sympathy, kindness, compassion, friendship and trust, which had fairly successfully aided people's more altruistic need for group survival over hundreds of thousands of years, began to be replaced by all those more competitive feelings of fear, suspicion, pretence, envy, hatred, pride, shame, anger, and revenge, which now aid our leaders more self-centred need for their own survival and the survival of the society they claim to represent. Thus, when moral behaviour became defined in writing and enforced by written law, it must have been assumed people were incapable of intuitively knowing the differences between what became known as 'right' and 'wrong' behaviour anyway. In fact, "the moral institutions that drive many of our judgments often conflict with our own [non-judgmental] intuitions".[21]

---

[20] These are extremes of the Gini Coefficient [Gini, C: *Voviabilita*, 1912] which is a statistical measure of dispersion, usually applied to income but could also apply to power and control. For example, a probability of 'zero' would apply to a completely egalitarian society, whereas a probability of 'one' would apply to a strictly authoritarian society.
[21] Hauser, M: *Moral Minds*, 2009 edn., 459

Even today, authorities that advocated the Golden Rule, for example, which is premised upon the personally-biased belief that 'one should treat others as one would like others to treat oneself', became their self-centred way of claiming: 'what's good for me must be good for you too'. And, in its negative form, namely that 'one should not treat others in ways that one would not like to be treated one's self', became equivalent to saying: 'what's bad for me must be bad for you too'. No wonder most religions of the world revered this rule as it has become to mean, in effect: 'whom-so-ever is not with me is against me' [Mark 9:40]. Since then it has been increasingly replaced by 'you'll do as I say, not what you say'. Confucius had already recognised this danger by questioning the absence of any need for reciprocity contained within the Golden Rule. It might win votes amongst the less discerning members of society, but careful consideration reveals it to be a cryptic recipe for conflict between one person's egocentric need to promote a following and another's, not only within societies but between them too. And ever since such superficially appealing maxims gained loyalty for those who promoted them, this conflict has led to violence, bloodshed and war.

As George Bernard Shaw conclusively put it, "the Golden Rule is that there are no golden rules". If there were any moral imperatives underlying ethical behaviour, they could surely never be claimed by such self-centred bias, but rather by an underlying empathic desire to maintain a balance between the conflicting needs of egoism and altruism in each other and in ourselves. After all, empathy implies the mutual acceptance that others often have quite justifiable feelings, thoughts and beliefs that differ from our own, and sometimes they can even be complementary. Most harmonious partnerships, for example, are sustained in balance and flourish, not because they try to treat each other as they themselves would want to be treated, but more because they try to treat their partner in ways they feel their partner might want to be treated. This implies a respect for each other's differences; gender perhaps being the most significant, yet possibly the least appreciated case in question.

At one time, people did not think consciously about how they should, or should not behave towards one another in terms of moral imperatives, let alone of how these had been defined and ossified in writing; they did so out of trust in one another. This sub-cortical processing derived from a deep-seated feeling that empathy was all that was required to maintain this balance. At least it was until it began to be overruled by the imposition of what became defined as moral imperatives for all to follow. Surely though, such ideas were born within the minds of those egocentric individuals, whose own thoughts overruled their feelings for others. Yet, "when people confront certain kinds of moral dilemmas, they activate a vast network of brain regions, including areas involved in emotion, decision-making, conflict, social relations, and memory"[22] and none of these can possibly be standardised rationally by overriding imperative, defined in writing and imposed by law. There is a world of difference between feelings of being appreciated or not among fellow members of egalitarian communities, and thoughts of being approved of or not, among hierarchically structured societies controlled by force of law.

Ironically though, as people gradually began to think more consciously about their behaviour in terms of imperatives defined by state law, they became less trusting of each other and even of themselves. The seven heavenly virtues[23], for example, have their roots in cooperation and trust, whereas the seven deadly sins[24] originated from competition and distrust. Perhaps they were called 'deadly

---

[22] Ibid., 241

[23] Chastity, temperance, charity, diligence, patience, kindness & humility.

[24] Anger, greed, sloth, pride, lust, envy & gluttony.

sins', because conflict, violence and bloodshed often followed from them. Without continuously trying to adjust to each other's feelings at a personal level, it would have been difficult enough to maintain social stability and survive for long in those smaller, close-knit band communities, whereas in all those much larger and more consciously constructed hierarchical societies, it was going to be virtually impossible, at least, that is, without the strict enforcement of the law.

Charles Darwin must have recognised the origin of this when he wrote:

> Primitive man, at a very remote period, would have been influenced by the praise and blame of his fellows. It is obvious, that members of the same tribe would have approved of behaviour, which appeared to them to be for the general good, and would reprobate behaviour which appeared evil. ... It is therefore, hardly possible to exaggerate the importance during rude times of the love of praise and the dread of blame.[25]

But there is all the world of difference between the 'love of praise and dread of blame' conveyed both ways, at a personal level, horizontally between 'primitive man at that very remote period' and when it became conveyed one way vertically downwards at a much later period. At those 'rude times', it kept everyone in balance with one another because the survival of the whole community was at stake, whereas, at a much later period it kept everyone in obedience to centralised control because the survival of authority was at stake.

When deviation from egalitarian balance occurred, it could usually be restored by focusing on making good the loss to victims, rather than by punishing offenders. Later

---

[25] Darwin, C *The Descent of Man*, Ch 5, 165, 1871

though, when deviation for hierarchical imbalance occurred, conformity was maintained more by punishing the offenders, rather than by compensating the victims and the greater the inequality in social status between those who authorised the law, and those who broke it, "the more penal and moralistic the handling of the conflict [was] likely to be".[26] Cultural traditions were originally maintained by an equal balance of power, as they drifted and flowed, with everyone drifting in unison with one another as they changed unpredictably over time, but conformity to these traditions became replaced by an unequal balance of power by the imposition and maintenance of the law.[27]

A spectacular example of this change in social structure, from equality to inequality, occurred when William the Conqueror seemed to believe that the completion of his Doomsday Book in 1086 consolidated his right to the ownership of most of the land and possessions throughout England, along with the right to rule over its people. Despite his claimed, and many like it before and since, becoming the accepted way of controlling society, the idea that anyone had the right to rule over and control anyone else, just because they had the power to do so, still remains groundless.

In practice, any organisation that creates: "social competition, with a limited number of positions at the top [along with] substantial legitimate authority or coercive force at their disposal [will always tend towards] a social order that the ethnologist would call despotic".[28] Even a

---

[26] Black, D: *The Social Structure of Right and Wrong*, 1993, 144-9.

[27] This was determined by the Gini coefficient: Gini, C: *Voviabilità e mutabilità*, 1912] which measured levels of dispersion in social factors such as income, that ranges, theoretically from 'zero' in a perfectly egalitarian society where everyone's income was the same, to 'one', under perfect totalitarianism, where everything was owned by its ruler.

[28] Boehm, C: *Conflict and the Evolution of Social Control*, Evolutionary Origins of Morality, Katz, I (Ed.), 2000, 83; Service, E: *Origin of the State and Civilization*, 1975.

democratic vote for a leader, no matter how apparently trustworthy, amounts to little more than the blind acceptance that someone can force you, under threat of punishment, to behave in ways you might subsequently find abhorrent. Any attempt to aggregate and control the feelings of whole populations about how they should, or should not behave, defined by state legislation, seriously inhibits how they might otherwise have done so by trial-and-error and on-going personal responsibility.

Authorised laws therefore could only have been adhered to from fear of punishment, rather than as a consequence of personal conviction, to say nothing of fear from the lynch-mob mentality that might also have been conditioned from fear of punishment to adhere to these laws and ensure everyone else did likewise. Authority implied laws should be complied with blindly, more like algorithms, on the assumption that they would thereby lead to behaviour that no one could disagree with. So people became compelled to accept such imperatives for no reason, other than that they should trust in the wisdom of those with the power to authorise them to do so.

This demarcation between cooperation within smaller egalitarian communities and competition within larger, more hierarchically structured ones, unfortunately has become somewhat blurred because some research at least suggests that "cooperation, enforced by retribution can lead to the evolution of cooperation".[29] Certainly commercial organisations involved in the production of goods and services, is able to enforce cooperation under threat of dismissal, but only in competition against other rival organisations. And enforced cooperation among people in the armed forces can unite them, but only on the pretext of their unity in destroying, or being destroyed by opposing armed forces. So there is still a fundamental

---

[29] Boyd, R & Richardson, P: *Punishment allows the Evolution of Cooperation*, Ethology & Sociobiology, Vol.13, Issue 3, 171-95, 1992.

difference between cooperating instinctively to attain unilateral balance, and cooperating under threat of punishment to maintain hierarchical control.

Not everyone who acquires this control abuses that privilege of course; many simply have natural leadership skills. These may include an ability to evaluate alternative courses of action in organising and planning ahead, along with a natural charm or charisma that can inspire others to follow such people. Nevertheless, any assumption that having these skills implies others are obliged to obey them is vacuous. On the plus side, those who can help and guide others will naturally feel good about themselves, it raises their dopamine levels. So far so good, but any guidance they give might make those they have helped feel indebted towards them, and could make their leaders interpret this as a sign of their sublimation and vulnerability.[30] As dopamine is addictive, leaders can easily be tempted to exploit this perceived imbalance in favour of themselves by excessive use of power and control,[31] and, as Edmund Burke realised, it can act like an addiction: "Those who have been once intoxicated with power, and have derived any kind of emolument from it, even though but for one year, can never willingly abandon it."[32]

A more recent study within capital organisations found that: "It is easy for leaders to get caught up in their own worlds as there are many systems in place that make it all about them. These leaders identify so strongly with their leadership roles that instead of remembering the only reason they're there is to serve others, they start thinking, it's my world and we'll do things my way."[33] And for many

---

[30] The Master-slave relationship, intrinsic to all hierarchical societies, has never been stable for long, ref. Hegel's: *Phenomenology of Spirit*, 1807 or Nietzsche's *Beyond Good and Evil*, 1886

[31] Moran, M: '*Dopamine serves a positive reinforcer for aggression*', Psychopharmacology, 14.1.2013.

[32] A letter to a Noble Lord, 1796

[33] Kiel, F: *Return of Character*, 2015

leaders this power of control is such an aphrodisiac that it "changes the chemistry of the brain, making [them sometimes] more ... aggressive",[34] thus giving them the illusion of authority. In common parlance, 'power corrupts and absolute power corrupts absolutely'. A further study indicated that:

> Many dishonest acts are speculatively traced back to a sequence of smaller transgressions that gradually escalated. From financial fraud to plagiarism, online scams and scientific misconduct, deceivers retrospectively describe how minor dishonest decisions snowballed into significant ones over time. Despite the dramatic impact of these acts on economics, policy and education, we do not have a clear understanding of how and why small transgressions may gradually lead to larger ones.[35]

Leadership and authority often go hand-in-hand, but they are fundamentally different. Leadership inspires others to follow; authority compels them to do so, and the transition, from voluntary guidance to compulsory control in the minds of those with leadership skills, and hence in the minds of those who come under this control, could easily occur unwittingly. Although we still tend to accept authority as necessary for maintaining order in society, its mythical status has developed and spread throughout the world like a pandemic, only as a consequence of its enforced promotion by those more self-centred individuals who claimed it for themselves in the first place. Not only

---

[34] Robertson, I: *The Winner Effect*, 2012; Wrangham, R et al: *Demonic Males: Apes and the Origins of Human Violence*, 1996; Masters, R: *The Nature of Politics*, 1989

[35] Garret, N et al: *The Brain Adapts to Dishonesty*, Natural Neuroscience, 2016, abstract.

is it ill conceived, it can become extremely destructive,[36] as witnessed by the cruelty inflicted on innocent populations under more extreme forms of authoritarian control all over the world. And those with narcissistic tendencies or psychotic personality disorders[37] who have no feelings for anyone but themselves, tend to take control of crime organisations or cult religions, or gravitate to the upper echelons of business, commerce or politics. It's quite possible the myth of authority has infiltrated and abused the true meaning of leadership by infiltrating many of the most influential positions throughout history. In fact, the maintenance of all hierarchically structured societies depends on people at every level being enforced to comply with the needs of those above them, while ensuring their own needs are complied with by those below them. It's primarily a self-centred system throughout. In order to do this effectively though, self-interest, manipulation, cunning and deceit often need to be covertly employed at every level, which was probably why Shakespeare asked: 'Cannot a plain man live and think no harm, but that his simple truth must be abus'd by silken, sly, insinuating Jacks?'

We may never know exactly how the illusory status of authority took over from leadership to become so widespread throughout the world, but certainly it rests entirely upon the deference, sublimation and obedience of those who allowed it to happen in the first place. And early signs of authority turning into narcissism or psychosis are best nipped in the bud before they gain too much support to be resisted. These 'sly, insinuating Jacks' are not always easy to spot because they often present themselves as the most admirable and lovable characters imaginable. If Hitler's early ranting and raving had been ignored or

---

[36] Milgram, S: *Behavioural Study of Obedience*, Journal of Abnormal and Social Psychology, Vol 67(4), Oct 1963, 371-378; Zimbardo, P: *The Lucifer Effect*, 2007 et al.

[37] Hare, R: *Psychopathy Checklist, revised technical manual*, 2003

laughed to scorn from the start, whatever followed would surely have been a far less horrific story.

From conception onwards, our brains attempt to make thousands of links in neural connectivity,[38] particularly with respect to our relationships with one another. One might speculate that the degree of control parents and teachers exercise over their children, for example, might inhibit or enhance their neural connectivity, and in the same way the degree of control authorities exercise over their citizens must surely influence them in similar ways.[39] The intoxicating power of control might encourage leaders to become authorities at the expense of those they control but it can have either a positive or negative effect on performance, depending on whose performance is being fulfilled: the controller's, those they control, or both in genuine unison with one another.

Understandably, all hierarchically structured societies depend upon such people but that's probably because they were the one's that created them in the first place. Even if people with more self-centred personalities did once exist within those smaller egalitarian communities, in which everyone depended on everyone else and knew each other almost as well as they knew themselves, their behaviour would surely have been kept in check or ostracised, because the survival of the whole community was always going to be more important than any individual within it.

The concept of sublimation and idolatry though, probably had its genesis in a simple, and probably very understandable respect for the powers of nature, but which subsequently became mythologized with folkloric tales about spirits and gods. But the apotheosis of man gaining divine power can be traced back to long before the

---

[38] Greenough, W & Black, J: *Induction of Brain Structures by Experience:* Minnesota Symposium on Child Psychology, V. 24, Development behaviour Neuroscience, 1992, 155-201.

[39] Popper, K: *The Open Society and its Enemies*, 1945, contrasts scepticism with dogmatism within the social context.

birth of Christ, when 'the word of God became flesh' [John 1:14]. In any event, many of the first leaders of church and state claimed divine guidance in formulating their own ideologies and belief-systems, so demanded unquestioning obedience to their authority.

Despite the fact that these different ideologies and belief-systems inevitably followed, Immanuel Kant believed these differences would eventually be overcome by applying what he called his 'categorical imperative', viz. "act only according to that maxim whereby you can, at the same time, will that it should become a universal law".[40] Yet the different ways communities experienced their environments subjectively represented their different ways of living and, as Herodotus had already shown, cultural relativism ruled supreme over all moral imperatives. When he asked the Greeks if they were prepared to eat their deceased, even though it was their custom to burn them, they were horrified by the idea, and when he asked 'Indians' if they would burn their deceased, even though it was their custom to eat them, they were equally horrified. These different practices had evidently become accepted and practiced long before they were ever consciously thought about and rationally defined as 'acceptable' or 'unacceptable' in law.

Nevertheless, Kant still insisted reason was the only way of standardising moral behaviour and establishing universal laws. To this day though, the closest we've ever got to achieve this is defined by the United Nations' Universal Declaration of Human Rights. Article 5, for example, states: "No one shall be subject to torture or to cruel, inhuman or degrading treatment or punishment", yet, many of the retributive 'justice' systems that still prevail throughout the world today clearly interpret this in very different ways, so Kant's believe in universal reason

---

[40] Kant, I: *The Metaphysics of Morals*, 1785, the first formulation of his 'Categorical Imperative'.

still remains a dream.

As a result of their acceptance of authority, most people still find themselves embroiled in competing against each other for status, power and control. It's a system that at every level necessitates co-dependency between the controller and those they control. Under such circumstances, people unwittingly seem to harbour the ancient acceptance of the 'divine right of kings' and that their own survival depends on participating in ascending the stairway to acquiring the divine right to become kings. When Ludwig Boltzmann, one of the founders of modern physics, received unrestrained adulation for his ground-breaking work on entropy, he immediately saw through the fallacy of this mythical belief by announcing to his audience:

> I asked myself; can any individual deserve being honoured in this way? Surely all of us are just collaborators in a great enterprise, and everyone who does his duty deserves equal praise. If therefore an individual is singled out from the community, this can in my view never be aimed at him as a person but at the idea that he represents.[41]

This was no false modesty, such as is often expressed in embarrassment for the award of Oscars, Gold Medals and Nobel Prizes; it represented his deep-seated conviction that agency belonged to the fate of a person's inherited attributes, applied to the circumstances they found themselves involved in, yet which their mutant egos instinctively tried to claim credit for. Over the millennia, the rise of these mutant egos depended entirely upon their ability to transform the experiences that fed them and in

---

[41] Boltzmann, L.: *Populäre Schriften*, 1905, as confirmed from his philosophical notes.

competing to achieve its more status-orientated life-style at the expense of a more covertly spiritually one, it has created an imbalance of the regulatory hormone cortisol, along with all its detrimental consequences.[42]

Unfortunately though, competition usually involves robbing Peter to pay Paul, so is self-defeating, because Peter is either left with nothing worth robbing, or tries to survive by robbing Paul in response, which is why the growth of societies, nation-states and empires throughout history have invariably been followed by their decline, and why economies regularly fluctuate between boom and bust. During a bull-market everyone wins; until, that is, the bubble bursts and then everyone loses. But even the actions of successful investors influence the reactions of unsuccessful ones, so second-guessing is required to compete against first guessing, and so on, *ad infinitum*.

This competitive need to win has inevitably resulted in worldwide feelings of suspicion, distrust and a fear of losing. In order to survive and promote ourselves within such a climate, we are compelled to try and find out what others are planning for their own promotion. This requires personal, commercial and industrial espionage, which evokes counter-espionage, along with political and military 'intelligence', which evokes counter-intelligence. Within such a climate 'Big Brother' is watching us; surveillances is everywhere with CCTV cameras and spies-in-the-skies, while the tentacles of the CIA, MI5 and the KGB spread out and infiltrate the computer highways through locked doors, security-codes and secret off-shore bank accounts behind all those overt displays of title, rank and honour, behind which our paranoid egos desperately seeks to protect their vulnerability.

---

[42] These might include Alzheimer's, arthritis, atherosclerosis, asthma, certain kinds of cancer, cirrhosis, pulmonary disease, type 2 diabetes, heart disease, metabolic syndrome, chronic renal failure, osteoporosis, strokes, depression, obesity, along with alcohol, smoking and drug addition. [Wikipedia]

After the defeat of Nazism in 1945, both East and West began stock-piling weapons for their own defences, because they believed each other's stock-piles were really for their offences instead; yet the greater the offences became, the greater the defences became. Only the nightmare of Hiroshima and Nagasaki prevented this lunacy from tipping over into 'Mutually Assured Destruction', or MAD for short. The terrifying consequence of this global brinkmanship then became transferred into a one-upmanship space-race, and a renewed interest in Game Theory, which aimed at optimising the decision-making processes involved in every form of competitive encounter.

In order to treat this theory rationally though, it had to be assumed that participants were free to decide whether to cooperate or compete with one another; also that they had equal chances of guessing what each other's decisions were going to be, and that all gains and losses could be measured quantitatively. Under this 'curse of symmetry' it soon become obvious that the outcomes, whether for just two people or groups of people, or even randomly distributed populations of people, either cooperating or competing and reproducing themselves over time, would always end in stalemate. So participants were eventually forced to accept the fact that they could no longer improve upon their own positions without their competitors trying to improve upon theirs' in response, and hence producing permanent instability. This became known as the Nash Equilibrium[43] and its reluctant acceptance appeared to be the only way of avoiding on-going competition, conflict and, ultimately, 'mutually assured destruction'. And, even by attempting to hide one's real intentions, by using 'mixed strategies' to convey unpredictability as a means of preventing others from anticipating one's own intentions,

---

[43] Nash, J: *Equilibrium Points in n-person Games*, National Academy of Sciences, 1950, 36(1), 48-9.

evoked a similar response, so also became counter-productive. There is however, a fundamental difference between Rational-choice Game Theory, which aims at trying to win at other's expense of loosing, as compared with Evolutionary Game Theory, which aims at trying to maintain equality at no one's expense. And it has been said that, in the end, "dynamical models of cultural evolution and social learning hold more promise of success than models based on rational choice".[44]

Only when everyone continuously tried to make cooperative adjustments to each other's facial expressions, body language and behaviour were they going to avoid on-going competition, instability and conflict. This process has been described as 'reciprocal altruism',[45] and was solved at a sensual level, evolutionarily, long before our egos began trying to promote themselves rationally at the expense of everyone else's. This must have been what first upset that long-held balance between egoism and altruism in favour of egoism. Such egocentric bias gave rise to social inequalities and the emergence of a 'master-slave' morality, which could only survive by imposing upon society a self-fulfilling system of rewards for those who accepted the idea, and punishments for those who didn't.

The fact that this punitive control mechanism had to be administered under the guise of so-called 'justice' is quite an irony though, because any genuine meaning of the word connotes trust, harmony and balance between individuals, whereas, in practice it promoted precisely the opposite effect, namely distrust, discord and imbalance. And since its inception, it has not simply amplified our differences; it has created a widening gap, wherein "the [richest] one per cent are not simply at the pinnacle of material wealth, they are on the outermost edges of a

[44] Skyrms, B: *Game Theory, Rational and Evolution of the Social Contract*, Evolutionary Origins of Morality, Ed. Katz, L, 2000, 282

[45] Trivers, R: *The Evolution of reciprocal altruism*, Quarterly Review of Biology, 46, 35-57, 1971

widening chasm"[46] that is unsustainable.

Under the ego's mythical belief in its power of control, not only of each other but of evolution itself, it has created a materialistic environment that is a far cry from those rare occasions when we can still occasionally experience a sense of being at one with each other and with the whole of nature. Alas, though, these moments are a distant echoes of a time when all "men lived in sameness with the birds and animals, side by side as fellow clansmen with the myriad creatures"[47] of the earth. It was a time when they shared: "A deep and complex relationship within the natural world: one which presumed no superiority over land, the plants, and the animals ... and land was understood in terms of stewardship and responsibility, rather than ownership."[48]

Before the rise of the mutant ego, such feelings were fundamental to our inheritance, and had been passed on through the generations to those few remaining indigenous minorities who still manage to escape exploitation by living in the more remote and unspoilt regions of the world, much as they had always done according to their belief that 'united they stood, divided they fell'. Now though, such people are the exception, and, as they say, for the rest of us who have become predatory, not only on each other and the whole of nature, the exception proves the rule, which is: 'divided we stand, united we fall'.

---

[46] Else, L: *The Age of Inequality*, New Scientist, 28 July, 1012, 38.

[47] Zhuangzi: c 400 BC

[48] Coates, K: *A Global History of Indigenous Peoples* 2004, 47-50.

9. WHAT A PIECE OF WORK IS MAN?

'What a piece of work is man?' proclaimed Hamlet. 'How noble in reason, how infinite in faculty, how expressive and admirable in action... and yet', as many of us have asked of ourselves, 'what is this quintessence of dust?'

In his second Meditation, Descartes claimed it was his ability to think that defined him. He believed thinking was the agency for his own identity upon which he could begin to gain knowledge of himself and of the world around him, but then conceded his thoughts had been derived from his senses, which he described as the 'delusion of dreams'. In other words, this process began by experiencing the world subjectively through our senses, so our experiences must be the agents of our senses, which then product the thoughts about these sense experiences. This is a contrary view to Descartes' but actually, it's not quite one way or the other because, like all species, we are influenced by our environmental experiences and they are influenced by us too.

To separate mind from matter became known as

Cartesian Dualism and divided philosophical enquiry into 'empiricists' and 'rationalists'. Although we may feel we know reality empirically by experiencing it subjectively through our senses, we believe we can know it more objectively by thinking about it conceptually. This gives rise to the idea that there are two entirely different ways of knowing things. Without thinking, a toddler 'knows' instinctively how to walk; it will stumble and fall a few times but, without actually trying, it will never 'know' how to do so. On the other hand, we 'know' how to play games like Scrabble or Monopoly by simply reading the rules provided for us because they were thought up by us and had nothing to do with reality. Nature teaches us intuitively how to know reality subjectively by trial and error, but the only way we can attempt to know it objectively is by forming in our minds facts, opinions, ideas and beliefs about what we think it is. The distinction between 'heart' and 'head', or what is sometimes referred to as that between the more subjectively emotional arts and the more objectively rational sciences, has been described as follows:

> Science provides an outer picture of the scaffolding of emotions, constructed from universal, measurable and reproducible facts, whereas our direct experience of emotions is much akin to living inside the building behind the scaffolding. It is the fruit of our consciousness of what is otherwise known as phenomenology and is not entirely amenable to the scrutiny of science.[1]

Long ago though, Eastern philosophers realised we were an integral part of the reality we sought to know. Whatever we believed depended as much on the nature of the 'observer' as on what the 'observer' thought he or she

---

[1] Frazzetto, G: *How We Feel*, 2013, 130

was observing, or indeed touching, tasting, smelling or hearing too.

This self-centred bias, however, led us to believe at one time that the Sun rotated around the Earth; until Copernicus side-stepped the issue and showed that it was the other way round. And here is a more recent humiliating example: people reluctantly had to conclude that hurricanes with female names were more dangerous than those with male names, because the carefully recorded number of deaths they categorised by gender over a number of years appeared to prove it. This puzzle was eventually solved when it was realised that people had not been as cautious about protecting themselves against hurricanes with female names as they had against ones with male names. By assuming the damage a hurricane could do related to the gender we gave it was the real cause of the problem.

So we do not always interpret our environment quite as rationally as we think we do. Socrates' claim, that 'the unexamined life wasn't worth living' might very well be extended to include the claim that 'our unexamined thinking self wasn't worth living' either. Without having to think about it very much at all, our ancient ancestors probably just accepted the way things were and 'knew' instinctively how to respond to changes in their environment by trying to remain in balance with its changes, as and when they occurred. They simply responded to nature and to each other instinctively, in much the same way most other species still do; namely by means of their senses alone. Evolution had taught their senses what to do and, without the recognition of our selves and the emergence of our conceptually conscious thoughts, it would have been a result of our senses too.

A pet dog might respond to its owner's feelings and mood swings even before its owner recognises them; without thinking it just 'knows' instinctively how its owner feels. And the way all social species experience each other's feelings don't appear to require conscious thought either. Like our closest non-human primates, we once communicated with each other by means of our facial expressions, body language and overt displays of behaviour, sometimes accompanied by audible expressions of emotions, perhaps also by the smell of each other's pheromones, indicating feelings of fear or happiness, and so on. At those time, no kind of conceptual knowledge was required to communicate how we felt. The way we learnt how to understand and respond to each other's feelings emotionally was usually instantaneous.

Mirror neurons, which are the building-blocks of bonding amongst all social species, must have allowed our ancestors to recognise, not only the feelings of others but their own feelings mirrored in theirs as well, and this must have been what gradually gave rise to our more conscious sense of self-awareness.

> The mirror neuron system evolved initially to create an internal model of other people's actions and intentions, in humans it may have evolved further, turning inwards to represent or re-present one's own mind to itself. A theory of mind is not only useful for intuiting what is happening in the minds of friends, strangers and enemies; but in the unique case of *Homo sapiens*, it may also have dramatically increased the insight we have into our own mind's workings.[2]

Many social species, such as whales, dolphins and some of our closest non-human primates, communicate their feelings to one another in this way, so must have some sense of self-awareness, even though, they don't appear to have developed any formal language like ours, with its own grammar and syntax. One of these non-human primates

[2] Ramachandran, V: *The Tell-Tale Brain*, 2011, 144

that does this very well is the Gelada Baboon, which lives in large herds in the Ethiopian Highlands and has a wide range of vocal expressions for "communicating recognition, friendship, aggression, defence, appeasement, ambivalence, reassurance, and so on".[3] But, as far as we know, none of these have been translated into conscious thoughts. The development of our spoken and written language probably occurred in conjunction with that of thinking about our experiences, expressed as sounds, and eventually as words and sentences. It has been suggested that:

> The first tracts of language could have appeared as early as ... the human-chimp split 5 to 7 million years ago ... [However] modern *Homo sapiens*, which appeared about 200,000 years ago ... had skulls like ours. It is hard to believe that they lacked language, given that biologically, they were us, and all biologically modern humans have language.[4]

With the development of speech in humans however, biological changes in the larynx, tongue and lips were necessary, along with corresponding neurological changes to do with auditory processing in the left region of the cerebral cortex.

Like our closest non-human primates, the recognition of each other's emotional states of mind were picked up instinctively by their mirror neurons, but what made us humans so different from all other social species must have been an increased conceptually-conscious sense of awareness of these emotions and the accompanying development of word-sounds in our attempt to define the experiences they represented. The recognition that this was

---

[3] Richman, B: *Some vocal distinctive features used by Gelada monkeys*, Journal of Acoustical Society of America, 60 (3), 1976, 718-24.

[4] Pinker, S: *The Language Instinct*, 1994, 352-3

what we ourselves were doing must have given rise to a mutant sense of an independent 'me self', which needed to express itself in the form of words and sentences. Living for so long together in such a co-dependent manner must have necessitated the gradual identification and classification of our own and each others' experiences as an aid to group survival. And this repeated sharing gradually took the form of commonly used sounds representing habit-forming words, which when linked together, began to form sentences.

The dependence on feedback from our experience came to apply as much, or even more to the way we thought about and expressed them verbally as it did to the way we felt about and expressed them emotionally. Only with the development of speech and language did our inarticulate emotions about our experiences begin to be recognised conceptually and translated into more cogent, and articulately expressed thoughts.

Speech may have originally helped to define the way we felt, but it may also have help to control it too. The way we originally felt influenced the way we thought, but the way we subsequently began to think also influenced the way we felt. Today, we can sometimes recognise the direction of influence in our conversations. They are either more about the 'me self' trying to convince others that they should think likewise, in the hope of promoting the 'me self', or otherwise more about the 'I self' trying to communicate feelings it believes it shares with others, in the hope of promoting empathy between the 'I selves'. And most conversations involve an iterative process that fluctuates between the two; unless, that is, there is an imbalance of egoism or altruism between them.

Although feelings and thoughts are fundamentally different, an inescapable symbiosis still exists between them. They've sometimes been compared to analogue and digital data respectively, but thoughts, and the words we use to represent them, are not digital; their meanings change all the time according to context, tone of voice and so on. In fact, ultimately, they still remain premised upon, not only our emotional states of mind at the time when we use them but how we memorise them. So, no matter how abstracted from their roots they may appear to have become, they are still ultimately dependent upon our emotions. Many of our conversations with one another, for example, are peppered with sentences that begin with 'I think ...', whereas, what we often mean is 'I feel ...'. Rarely do we think about, and try to accurately define what we are going to say before saying it and, even when we do try, its meaning usually depends on context and the personal experience of both parties concerned.

Careful consideration of what we actually said after saying it, often tells us it had a more subjective origin and demonstrates how ineffectual language, as a means of communicating thoughts, can be. Jacques Derrida deconstructed it to the level of meaninglessness, with his frequent references to context, ambiguity, pun, metaphor and indeterminacy. He said: "A text remains forever imperceptible. Its laws and rules are not, however, harboured in the inaccessibility of a secret; it is simply that they can never be booked in the present into anything that could rigorously be called perception."[5] And, although he did not explain his attempt to undermine the whole of structuralism in quite the following way, his argument boiled down to the fact that the meaning of words were merely second-order derivatives of first-order experiences.

This explains why our emotions and our thoughts are processed differently. An fMRI scan shows greater activity in the limbic system when our experiences are being processed emotionally and greater activity in other parts, including the prefrontal cortex, when our thoughts about these experiences are being processed conceptually. It is suggested that thoughts, and the words we use to represent

---

[5] Derrida, J: *Dissemination*, 1981.

them, originated from an assumption that the world had some rational meaning, so had to be objectified in order to be understood. This assumption may seem obvious but, in sensing our experiences emotionally, we don't actually assume anything about its meaning, nor indeed whether it has any. Its effect on us is direct and pre-empts judgment, we don't need to conceptually evaluate it, whereas thinking about its effect begins with judgment about these conceptions and is soon followed by evaluation and the meaning we attach to it.

This slowly evolving recognition of what William James called the 'me self' and its need to express itself by means of verbal, or even symbolic language, must have given rise to the idea that, by thinking about the world and trying to understand it, this 'me self' would gain some sort of objective control over it. This suggests a marked distinction between the two levels of consciousness; sensual-consciousness which reacts subjectively to *a posteriori* experiences almost as soon as they occur, whereas conceptual-consciousness can only react to these *a posteriori* experiences by converting them into *a priori* concepts because it is incapable of feeling them, so has to try and use reason in order to gain some sort of control over them.

Although language has helped the 'me self' communicate its thoughts about what it thinks its experiences are to others, all these experiences were first felt emotionally, so could never be expressed accurately by means of words and sentences. Because the 'me self' is incapable of seeing, touching, tasting, smelling or hearing what the 'I self' experiences, it can only develop an emotionally sterile language of its own to define what it thinks these experiences actually are, in its forlorn hope of promoting its understanding of them. Yet "no one can make clear to another who has never had a certain feeling

... the quality or worth of [what] it consists"[6]

The way two people feel when they look at the same daisy, for example, will always be slightly different, as the exact nature of their respective experiences can only be felt directly by them individually. What they think they experience, can be communicated and shared by noun-words that categorise it, along with adjectival words that describe it and conjunctions that link them. In this particular case, their 'me selves' can at least agree that what they are talking about is a thing that is commonly categorised as a flower, that can be sub-categorised as a daisy, that can be described as a common European species of the genus *Bellis perennis*, which is of a certain colour or smell, and so on. Yet, what they each feel at the time, rather than subsequently think about and try to agree upon remains uniquely personal.

Wittgenstein would have called the recognition of the genus 'a fact'[7], from which the use of language has allowed us to accumulate a vast body of commonly accepted knowledge by linking these 'facts', that together he called the "sum total of our reality of the world".[8] This enabled us moreover, to construct ideas about these 'facts', which he called 'states of affairs', but these could only be 'determined by the facts', which he thought could only be 'induced' by means of reason and logic, so were always more remote from reality than had been assumed.

Even though the 'me self' creates a world of 'facts', because it believes it is the thoughts about its experiences that count, the 'I self' can't recognise 'facts', it simply experiences things more holistically. Buddha evidently recognised this by favouring the heart rather than the head and Apollinaire would have agreed, in claiming 'people would forget what you said but would never forget how

---

[6] Rae, M & Pojman, L: *Philosophy of Religion, An anthology*, 2015 edn. 400

[7] Wittgenstein, L. *Tractatus Logico-philosophicus* 1919. Proposition 2: 'a logical picture of facts is a thought'.

[8] Ibid. Proposition 2.063

you made them feel'. Before the development of language, our ancestors responded sensually to their environment and to each other's mood-swings directly in 'the now' all the time, with little conscious conception of the past or future. Since then though, our increasing knowledge of 'facts' and 'states of affairs' about 'facts' stored in our memories about our experiences, have allowed the 'me self' to think carefully and analytically about them in order to plan its future, which might have been what gave rise to its concept of 'time'.[9]

In an intrinsically unstable world though; the past isn't necessarily a reliable guide for planning the future. Using the past for our future advantage my very well turn out to be abusing it to our disadvantage. Self-awareness and conscious knowledge are not essential pre-requisites for planning ahead anyway because, at one time, we didn't consciously plan our futures at all. Evolution had showed us how to respond to changing patterns in nature instinctively. It allowed us, and indeed all species, to do so without having to think consciously abut the past or the future. In the same way our distant ancestors' behaviour accommodated to the seasons, animals such as squirrels store nuts for the winter, swallows fly south in late summer, and flowers blossom in the Spring when they are ready to be pollinated.

Since the emergence of the 'me self' and its self-centred ability to think, it has made us become increasingly committed to plan for our futures, on its assumption that it can do a better job than evolution has. Georg Hegel saw 'the whole history of the world' as 'none other than the progress of the consciousness of freedom', and even prophesied it would "bring about an objective understanding of our natures and a complete

---

[9] There is a fundamental divide between the right-brain, which lives in 'the now' and the left-brain, which is focused on making use of past experiences to plan for future ones. It has been described by Tolle, E: as *The Power of the Now,* 1999

rationalisation of the world".[10] In other words, by learning to understand our natures, we would be able to overcome our subjective experiences and progress towards a more rational future. But wasn't he putting the cart before the horse?

Descartes' *cogito* turns out to be a secondary stage in our on-going neurological processing-sequence: beginning with experiencing the world; then only after feeling these experiences, can judgment and evaluation of them begin. These different levels of consciousness are an integral part of the whole processing sequence, so are more complex than Hegel had imagined. In fact, it's not surprising there is still no consensus of agreement as to the meaning of 'consciousness'. To say we are 'conscious' immediately begs the question: conscious of what, an experience, an emotion, a feeling, a fact, an opinion, belief or idea about a fact, or simply 'the sum total of our reality of the world'? More recently, it has been suggested that: "Non-conscious processes are, in substantial part and in varied ways, under conscious guidance [and that] consciousness came of age by first restraining part of the non-conscious executives and then exploring them mercilessly to carry out pre-planned, pre-decided actions".[11]

This interpretation is consistent with Hegel's, in so far as it suggests that consciousness has a strong controlling influence over non-consciousness. On the other hand, this controlling influence might operate the other way. There appears to be an on-going struggle between rational thoughts, consciously trying to influence feelings and irrational feelings unconsciously influencing thoughts, but without trying. For example, "one of the qualities of information flow is that it can be unconscious, occurring below the level of awareness; we see it in operation at the

---

[10] Hegel , G: *Lectures on the Philosophy of World History*, 1770-1831, introduction.
[11] Damasio, A: *Self comes to Mind*, 2010, 269-270

automatic, or involuntary level of our physiology".[12] In fact, much, perhaps all of our behaviour, for better or for worse, begins to be processed by the 'I self', before the 'me self' is even aware that this processing has already been set in motion. It has been suggested, for example:

> That consciousness does not emerge from a single level of biological organization ... but is a consequence of interdependent modelling activated by networks at different levels of organization including the molecular, organelle, and cellular levels, in some way entrained to produce consciousness.[13]

When, for example, the sun shines and the temperature increases, the molecules in our skin signal their agitation to our sweat-glands, so they must be conscious of this change of temperature, even though we might still not have a clue this is going on. Only subsequently might the more conscious 'me self' begin to sense this agitation and think, 'it feels hot' and begin to act on this thought by making us seek the shade or take off our coats. This suggests there is a difference, at least sequentially between how the body responds biologically to environmental changes, and how the mind responds neurologically to them, with how we feel perhaps linking the two in some rather ill-defined way.

Electro-chemical changes might evoke emotions and, when the nerve-fibres send signals associated with these emotions to the brain, they become identified as feelings that promote various thoughts about the changes, which then trigger ideas about how to act. By then though, those electro-chemical changes would have already begun to trigger our sweat-glands to cool us down. Although the 'non-conscious processes' are said to be 'under conscious

---

[12] Pert, C: *Molecules of Emotion*, 1997, 185
[13] Dryden, R: *Fractal Networks for Consciousness and Awareness*, 1996, Abstract.

guidance' in order to 'carry out pre-planned, pre-decided actions', our 'I selves' might not be quite so easily persuaded. How often, for example, are people's 'pre-planned', 'pre-decided' New Year's resolutions conveniently ignored or forgotten about by the end of January?

There appears to be an on-going conflict of view-points between these two selves, since the nature of the circumstances we are confronted with at the time must affect the nature of the way we subsequently respond to them. We appear to have evolved two quite distinct ways of 'knowing' reality. If we bump into an old friend at a party we instinctively shake their hand or give them a hug without thinking about it; on the other hand, if our car unexpectedly breaks down, we begin to think why and take a more rational approach by checking the petrol gauge or battery leads, and so on.

> People often use the word 'consciousness' loosely to refer to two different things: one is qualia, the immediate experiential qualities of sensation, such as the redness of red, or the pungency of curry, and the second is the self who experiences these sensations. Qualia are vexing to philosophers and scientists alike because even though they are palpably real and seem to lie at the very core of mental experience, physical and computational theories about brain functioning are utterly silent on the question of how they might arise and how they might exist.[14]

As our feelings seem to be more directly 'in touch', literally as well as metaphorically, with reality, we might say their sensual knowledge of it is 'first-hand', whereas our thoughts can only get in 'in touch' with reality, 'second-

---

[14] Ramachandran, V: *The Tell-Tale Brain*, 2011, 248

hand' through our senses by trying to translate them into rational concepts. Emotional experiences in themselves are therefore beyond rationalisation, whereas thoughts about them are emotionally sterile. They might recognise, and try to rationalise our emotions; they might even be able to describe the feelings these emotions generated and know conceptually how they affect us, but, in themselves, they are quite incapable of actually experiencing them. On the other hand, our sensually-conscious emotions are conceptually sterile because, as soon as we start thinking about them in any conceptually-conscious way, the emotional experience simply vanishes. It is difficult to see these as exclusive alternatives because they often seem to appear simultaneously, but this is because we are usually just switching back and forth, from one to the other almost instantaneously.

So how does conscious awareness apply to this process of transmitting the body's bio-sensual experiences about the world, into the mind's neurological thoughts about them? For convenience we might call the body's responses to environmental stimuli as being in a state of 'biological-consciousness'; the emotions that these responses evoke, as being in a state of 'sensual-consciousness', and the brain's rational evaluation of them, as being in a state of 'conceptual-consciousness'.

Whether these different types of consciousness are discrete links, or continuous parts of the same processing sequence is not clear but, since the whole body is wired up by nerve-fibres that send electro-chemical signals to and from the brain all the time, they must be at least partially dependent on each other to make up the person's coordinated behaviour, from feeling to thinking to acting. At the biological end of the spectrum, the signals are entirely instantaneous and therefore subjective, non-judgmental and non-evaluative; at the other end they are rational translations of them, so are objective, judgmental, and evaluative.

Over millions of years, our bodies have evolved from vast colonies of molecules and cells to form various specialised functions that could only have survived symbiotically together in human form by communication in some kind of neuro-chemically coordinated way. Even our molecules could be said to experience emotions, as it has been discovered they sense environmental changes and influence one another by means of "information-processing receptors on their nerve-cell membranes, thus establishing a bio-molecular basis for our emotions."[15] First and foremost therefore, we experience our environment biologically, (i), then we might begin to experience sense-induced changes emotionally, (ii), and sometimes, as a consequence, the more rational parts of our mind recognise these changes as feelings and begin to try and judge and evaluate them by translating them into conceptually-conscious thoughts, (iii), which can then be remembered and analysed for planning purposes, (iv).

The sensually-conscious mind, which corresponds to James's 'I self', just experiences circumstances in the 'now', whereas the conceptually-conscious mind, which corresponds to James's 'me self', can only evaluate them after they have occurred, in order to plan for the future, so cannot experience them in 'the now'. Not all the stages identified above need necessarily be involved in this process though: usually just (i), or (i) & (ii) seem to be involved; only occasionally does (iii), or, when (iii) is followed by (iv) occur, do all four stages become involved. Much of the time though, these stages might be signalling back and forth to each other many times a second. A continual stream of experiential data is being received biologically but at first it is neither sensually experienced nor conceptually recognised. Only sometimes are these experiences subsequently felt by the 'I self', whereas the 'me self' has continual access to data after it has been

---

[15] Pert, C: *Molecules of Emotion*, 1997, 179

received, so can evaluate them conceptually at any time when we're not experiencing them sensually.

It is however an ongoing relationship of action and interaction with an ever-changing external reality, without any obvious beginning or end. We are rather like iterative processing machines, but there is far more going on in how we experience the world subjectively than we can possibly think about and try to rationalise objectively. It has been estimated that: "The body processes about 14 million bits of information a second. The bandwidth of [conceptual] consciousness is about 18 bits. This means we have conscious access to about a millionth of the information we daily process [sensually] to survive."[16]

So, has either our subjective experiences or our more objective understanding of them, brought about weapons for not just hunting and self-protection but for killing and mass destruction? And have our sensual experiences, or our more objective understanding of them, brought about the wheel for not only easier transportation but for traffic-jams and carbon monoxide poisoning? And have subjective experiences, or our more objective understanding of them, brought about settled farming for not only food production but also for factory farming and obesity? Both sensual and conceptual consciousness seem to have contributed to the world within which we find ourselves immersed but the so-called law of 'unseen consequences' reminds us that today's successes might very well bring about tomorrow's failures.

The 'self' appears to comprise two quite distinct characteristics, which Descartes categorised as 'the immaterial mind' and the 'material body'. From birth to death we are processing data in biological and sensually-conscious ways practically all time; only sometimes though, in a more conceptually-conscious way too. All forms of processing might be regarded as types of 'learning' but

---

[16] Gray, J: *Straw Dogs*, 2002, 66.

there is an unresolved demarcation between them. Sensually-conscious 'learning' is more like evolutionary conditioning, but conceptually-conscious 'learning' can only follow from it, so is perhaps just conditioning too. It has been described as:

> The beauty and delight of becoming absorbed, seeing the world in different ways with different possibilities. It is about challenge, surprise, desire, joy, expectation and mystery: the thrill of discovering oneself in relation to new ideas and contexts. When we teach we invite students into the beauty of our worlds, 'to embrace what we have found so alluring'[17] to understand the promise, mystery and intrigue associated with a subject that has occupied our hearts and minds for so long.[18]

This description however, need not necessarily involve any formal education, as emotions such as 'surprise', 'desire', 'joy' and so on, can just as easily be induced through quiet meditation in 'the now' when we are not caught up in self-imposed thoughts about wanting to be doing things. Even though this demarcation problem has not been adequately resolved, you can still: "discard your thirst for books, so that you won't die in bitterness, but in cheerfulness and truth, grateful to the gods from the bottom of your heart." [Marcus Aurelius, *Meditations*]

---

[17] Liston, D: *The allure of beauty and the pain of injustice ...,* 2004, 101
[18] Alsop, S (Ed.): *Beyond Cartesian Dualism,* 2005, Introduction.

10. CAN WE KNOW BUT NOT EXPERIENCE?

The 'self' comprises both body and a mind but how do they relate to each other? How can physical things give rise to non-physical feelings, such as joy or sorrow, along with thoughts that induce opinions, beliefs and ideas? The body comprises a vast collection of molecules that make up our physiology, and the mind comprises a vast collection of neurons that send signals to each other that make up our feelings and thoughts.

Much of the time we respond to our experiences without having to think about them at all; at other times we reflect on them and sometimes they give rise to new ideas, without us knowing quite how they came about. Some recent research might give us a clue to this mystery though. It has been found, counter-intuitively perhaps, that when we are concentrating on problems in a more conceptually-conscious way, our brains are actually using less energy than when we appear to be just idling, or daydreaming. In other words, when we are more objectively focused on problem-solving tasks, such as crossword puzzles or how to budget the housekeeping money, we are actually using less energy than when we don't seem to be thinking about anything in particular at all and are in, what has been called, 'default mode'.[1]

During these apparently more relaxed states of consciousness, powerful interactions are going on between the right and left medial temporal lobes in trying to sort out the disorganised mass of data we have been unwittingly experiencing all the time. At these times our brains are actively trying to communicate with, not only the hippocampus, which is concerned with memories of recent experiences, but also with the medial prefrontal cortex, which tries to evaluate and integrate recently received data into our already acquired neurological map of reality.

In fact, these fundamentally different ways of processing data seem to correspond roughly to the two hemispheres of the human brain.[2] The right-hemisphere, including the right hippocampus with which William James might have associated the 'I self', is believed to sense data in a more holistic and indiscriminate way, whereas the left-hemisphere with which he might have associated the 'me self', is somewhat more detached from these experiences and tends to focus in on certain features of this data, which it then attempts to processes more objectively.

Although it is generally accepted that one hemisphere is activated before the other, some regard the distinction as a 'pseudoscience'[3] because, for most situations, the two hemispheres appear to work together. It is claimed: "The hemispheres are in constant communication with each other and it simply isn't possible for one hemisphere to

---

[1] Buckner, R et al: *The Brain's Default Network* ..., Annals N Y Academy of Science 1124, 1-38, 2008.

[2] McGilchrist, I: *The Master and his Emissary*, 2009, 17-22

[3] Blakemore, S & Frith, U: *The Learning Brain* ..., 2005

function without the other joining in."[4] Presumably this is based on the assumption that experiencing emotions and making judgments about them are integral parts of the same process.

However, consider your reaction to the news that a supermarket was going to be built next door to your house. Emotionally, you might be horrified by the idea. On reflection though, you might think it would be a convenience, but there's no way of reconciling these different reactions. Certainly, both your sensually-conscious and conceptually-conscious minds will be active in trying to process the news but, no matter how quickly you fluctuate between horror and convenience, you cannot experience the two reactions together. It depends which is more dominant in your mind at the time and, like most real-life situations, there's no right or wrong way of reconciling the two, either you accept the news willingly, or grit your teeth and bear it, and in the end perhaps just dismiss it as an unsolved problem.

The Solomon Asch 'Conformity Experiment'[5] nicely illustrates this problem. Unsuspecting participants are asked in front of others to answer a simple question, which most of the others have already been told to deliberately given the wrong answer to. If the unsuspecting participant gives the correct answer, their more rational left hemisphere was dominant because they ignored or overruled the majority of other incorrect answers. If they give the same incorrect answer as the majority, their more sensitive right hemispheres might have felt group conformity was more important.

This demonstrates the incompatibility between egoism and altruism. Egoism tries to rationalise situations objectively, so tends to bypass emotional experiences

[4] Blakemore, S: *Left-Brain/Right Brain*, This Idea Must Die, 2015, 299-300
[5] Asch, S: *Opinions and Social Pressures*, Scientific American, Vol. 193, No.5, 31-5. 1955

because they can't be rationalised, whereas altruism, which is more bound up in feelings, tries to remain in balance with the majority. There is a constant struggle going on via the corpus callosum between these irreconcilable needs in all of us. In real life we sometimes process data more rationally because we can see only an objective solution to the situation we are confronted with at the time, but sometimes we find ourselves more subjectively caught up in the whole experience. However, we can never be certain at the time how 'wisely' we have processed our experiences; that is, until after we have already processed them but by then it may be too late to take corrective action.

When we are in 'default mode' and not conceptually-conscious of anything in particular, our minds are engaged in a fairly random process of sifting through the vast quantity of data we receive more directly through our senses, in order that they might be assimilated harmoniously into our overall neural networking patterns. But when we are not conceptually aware of what's going on during these less inhibited ruminations, they surely cannot be the result of 'conscious guidance'; more likely they are the brain's intuitive way of trying to cope with the overwhelming amount of data it has amassed during our more recent experiences.

Before we became aware of our own egos, we weren't very conceptually-conscious of anything at all; nevertheless, processing data intuitively in this way provided us with a fairly reliable method of keeping in balance with our environment. And it has been suggested that the reason why this process consumes so much more energy, perhaps even as much as twenty times more than when we are processing data in a more conceptually-conscious way,[6] is because it necessitates making amino acids, which help to reinforce existing neural pathways, or

[6] Raichle, M: *The Brain's Dark Energy*, Scientific American, March 2010

in opening up new ones, across what we subjectively feel are compatible synapses. In other words, when our brains are in this 'default mode', they are iteratively engaged in a rather ill-defined kind of 'spring-cleaning' operation, which strengthens or weakens links between neural pathways that make up our overall cognition-webs of experience of the world. It has been claimed that:

> The right hemisphere alone attends to the peripheral field of vision from which new experiences tend to come, ... Novel experience induces changes in the right hippocampus, but not the left ... it is the right hemisphere that is attuned to the apprehension of anything new ... The left hemisphere deals with what is known and therefore prioritises the expected ... This makes it more efficient in routine situations where things are predictable ...[7]

'Default mode networking', which is therefore associated with right-brain activity, is essentially an inductive process,[8] so is believed to be more creative since it doesn't appear to conform to any of those more rigidly defined and accepted rules or laws, or logical forms of reasoning normally associated with left-brain processing. This may be why creative people sometimes say their moments of insight or inspiration, tend to occur unexpectedly when they don't seem to be consciously deliberating on anything in particular at all. In fact, true creativity is induced from 'without' and is inductive; we cannot make it come, it's a consequence of the way we experience the world through our senses. Only the ego credits itself with what it thinks are its creative deductions

---

[7] McGilchrist, I: *The Master and his Emissary*, 2009, 40; Goldberg, E et al: *Lateralization of Frontal Lobe* ...J. of Neuropsychiatry, V6, 4, 1994.

[8] Goel, V: *Anatomy of deductive reasoning*, Trends in Cognitive Science, 2007 435-41

from 'within' because it is closed off from experiencing the world sensually, so is incapable of recognising from where else it could have come.

Another reason why 'default mode' networking requires so much more energy might be because it involves an extremely large number of trial-and-error attempts to find subjectively satisfactory answers to open-ended, and multi-variable problems, even before any attempt to rationalise them begins. Although greatly speeded up, this inductive process is not dissimilar to the indeterminate principles involved in biological evolution because many of the patterns that we see have evolved in nature, such as in snowflakes, sea-shells, ferns, feathers, flowers, vegetables, even the branches of trees are comparable in appearance to those generated by fractal geometry, which involves the same sort of iterative process of induction.

This form of processing contrasts strongly with analytic left-brain thinking, which tends to focus in on well-defined problems that are more suitably handled algorithmically, in much the same way computers are usually programmed within defined boundaries, to solve goal-orientated problems. As a consequence of our 'split-brain' therefore, we are inclined to either see the world more rationally in terms of well established rules or laws, which we become conditioned to conform to, or in less inhibited and open-minded ways irrespective of this conditioning, and often we flip from one to the other almost instantaneously, rather like a spinning coin, whose heads and tails are incapable of recognising each other's ways of 'seeing' things.

But are these rules or laws actually externally embedded in nature, or have they become internal constructs in our own mind, in attempting to recognise order in an external reality? It would be rather distressing to think we had conditioned ourselves thus, to live our lives according to these deterministically constructed laws if they weren't really in nature but only in our heads; on the other hand, not taking anything for granted, nor even being guided by convention or tradition, would surely lead to instability, and perhaps even schizophrenia.

Within the vast neural network of the human brain, numerous attempts to make micro-tubular links across synaptic gaps for compatibility occur every second, but not so much because the neurons that fire and wire together actually are objectively compatible, but rather because they are subjectively felt to be so. All neurological processing of real-life data involves numerous unidentifiable variables, so cannot possibly be evaluated objectively at an individual synaptic level. Our opinions, beliefs and ideas are moulded and shaped subjectively at a more holistic level, yet we still like to think they can help us make rational choices. But how can we compare apples with oranges? Most of the time our decisions boil down to personal preferences, for or against what appear to be compatible models of the multi-variable problems we are confronted with all the time, so surely remain personal, temporal and subjective in nature. The mind is both 'player' and 'referee', the 'player' being the 'I self', which instinctively responds in a non-judgmentally way to sensual stimuli and, over millions of years had generally been able to keep in balance with its *a posteriori* experiences, whereas the 'referee' is like the 'me self' that tries to evaluates these responses retrospectively, and judge them according to what it conceives of as *a priori* rules or laws of nature.

In particular, when we try to communicate verbally with one another, we become embroiled in what Wittgenstein called 'language games'. These usually involve the instantaneous conversion of feelings into thoughts, represented by greatly simplified modes of speech, so "their essence is hidden from us".[9] Nevertheless, certain levels of agreement between people can be achieved in this way, which Wittgenstein referred to as 'customs' and

---

[9] Wittgenstein, L.: *Philosophical Investigations*, 1991 Brown Book 23.

sometimes these become established as rules, under the assumption that they represent universal and unchanging truths, and hence universal and unchanging laws to which we feel obliged to conform.

Immanuel Kant would have agreed with this conclusion, but not with how it was arrived at. He went to great lengths to show that these, so-called 'universal and unchanging truths' about the nature of reality were independent of experiences and derived instead from reason and logic alone. For example:

> If understanding in general is to be viewed as the faculty of rules, judgement will be the faculty of subsuming under rules; that is, of distinguishing whether something does or does not stand under a given rule [and that] everything that can be presented to our senses must be subject to laws which have their *a priori* origin in understanding alone. [10]

He went even further with yet another assumption; namely, that "there is only one possible concept which determines a thing as *a priori*, namely the concept of God", whose proof of existence went something like this: if anything existed, and Kant knew for certain he himself existed, it was absolutely necessary that there had to be an ultimate cause, an *ens realissimum*[11] as he called it, for that thing to exist, which was God. In the light of subsequent research however, it might now even be argued that the egocentric part of the mind that can only think more rationally, could itself believe it was the apotheosis of an *ens realissimum*. It certainly acts like that sometime.

In his second Critique,[12] Kant claimed that Aristotelian

---

[10] Kant, I: *Critique of Pure Reason*, 1781-7, A132, B171
[11] Kant, I: *The Critique of Practical Reason*, 1788, 'the cosmological proof'. A605 B633
[12] Kemp, J: *The Philosophy of Kant*, 1968, 126

logic, Euclid Geometry and Newtonian physics were in essence the last word on their respective subjects. From these premises he claimed universal *a priori* concepts, such as 'space' and 'time', 'identity', 'equality', 'categorisation', 'correlation' and 'causation'- 'enables us to think' but didn't seem to believe it was necessary to prove first that they were *a priori*. He appeared to be so committed to the groundwork of rational thought laid down by those forefathers that even the more sensual experiences which pre-empted rational thought, such as falling in love for example, also needed to be validated by rational thought.

At least, this appeared to have been the case in his personal life, since he waited until he was 57 years of age before coming to the conclusion that his long suspended love affair justified his proposal of marriage. However, before coming to this conclusion his intended partner, probably long since tired of waiting, had already left the district, fortunately for her because he was reputed to have defined marriage as 'the reciprocal use of each others' sexual organs'. Nor did he appear to re-consider his conviction, as he remained a bachelor for the remainder of his life. It has even been suggested he was so committed to reason that he needed to get drunk sometimes to escape from his reasonableness. For his rational mind to equate marriage with 'each others' sexual organs' and nothing else, as for example, similarly expressed by the Earl of Chesterfield's claim that 'the pleasure is momentary, the position ridiculous and the expense damnable', bypasses its real meaning altogether, as was expressed a whole lot more empathically by Elizabeth Barrett Browning, who wrote about Robert: 'I love you not only for what you are, but for what I am when I am with you'.

Be that as it may, let us now consider whether some of these other, so-called *a priori* concepts, upon which are built our conceptual understanding of the world, really are independent of experience. To start with, Kant's references to the concept of 'space' appear to contradict this assumption. Although he wrote, for example, that "space is not an empirical concept which has been derived from outer experience", elsewhere he also wrote that "it is the subjective condition of sensibility, under which alone outer intuition is possible for us",[13] without explaining what give rise to 'sensibility'. Moreover, he claimed, the concept of 'space' was grounded in Euclidian geometry, which, to him, appeared to have remained unaltered for 2,000 years, so had to be *a priori*. Evidently, he was unaware that Omar Khayyam had revised Euclid's postulates over 600 years earlier.[14] And unfortunately, Kant had died only a few years before Carl Gauss also exposed Euclid's limitations,[15] as a consequence of which it had to be re-evaluated empirically on several subsequent occasions.

Kant was equally certain 'time' was "not an empirical concept drawn from experience, for neither simultaneity nor succession would themselves come into perception if the representation of time did not ground them *a priori*." And although he insisted "time is a necessary representation, lying at the foundation of all our intuitions", its meaning too had to be revised in the light of subsequent experience, starting with Carnot's conjectures,[16] which, in turn, led to the Second Law of Thermodynamics and to General Relativity, both of which relied on experimentation and therefore, did have to be 'drawn from experience' after all.

In more practical usage though, the concept of 'time' had evolved from a discontinuous series of neurological jumps at irregular intervals, involving ruminating in the 'present' about experiences in the 'past' in order to decide what to do about them in the 'future'. Only changes in

---

[13] Pinhas Ben Zvi: *Kant on Space*, Philosophy Now, 110, 2015

[14] Amir-Móez, A: *Discussion of Difficulties in Euclid,* Scripta Mathematica 24, 275-303, 1959

[15] Klein, F: *Elementary Mathematics from an Advanced Standpoint*, 1948 English edn., 176

[16] Carnot, N: *Reflections on the Motive Power of Fire*, 1824

nature, which anyway often occur unexpectedly, could be conceived of rationally in terms of the concept of time, in the hope that they could be measured at precisely defined and predictable intervals. In any event, these can only be measured empirically in terms of what appear to be regularities within nature, rather than outside it, such as the rotation of the Earth or stars, or even the spin of caesium atoms for example, so its measurement still had to have some *a posteriori* foundation. And, although we impose these measurements of 'time' upon ourselves, in order to give meaning to our lives, it still remains subjective. To a 10 year-old, a year seems like an eternity because it represents 10% of its life, whereas the same period flashes past for a 50 year-old as it represents just 2%. It even changes subjectively according to which side of the bathroom door you're on in the morning. And, as Thomas Mann observed, 'time has no divisions to mark its passage, there is never a blast of trumpets to announce the beginning of the new month or year'.

Next, for convenience we attribute the autonomous concept of 'identity' to physical things, along with the related concept of 'equality', when they are assumed to be identical to each other. In reality of course, no single physical thing, or 'identity' can be precisely 'equal' to another in character, let alone in 'time' or 'space', so cannot be added to, or subtracted from any other with any degree of reliability. This is sometimes referred to as the 'fallacy of equivocation' and undermines yet another of Kant's so-called *a priori* concepts, namely that of 'categorisation' or classification. In fact, the often unrecognised 'problem of universals' applies to all forms of classification, particularly with respect to cultural relativism,[17] which, incidentally, Kant tried to rescue by means of, what he called, his

---

[17] Unsworth, S. et al: *Cultural Influences on Categorization Processes,* 2015. Chinese children, for example, are more likely to categorise objects based on shared relationships, whereas American children tend to categorise objects based on similarity.

'categorical imperatives'

But any categorical proposition concerning 'universals', such as 'all swans are white', only remains valid until such time as black swans are discovered. The fact that Carl Linnaeus, who only 50 years earlier had established a quantifiable method of classifying plants, may have helped to reinforced Kant's conviction that 'categorisation' was 'prior to experience'. However, had Kant still been alive when Darwin wrote: "I was much struck how entirely vague and arbitrary is the distinction between species and varieties",[18] he might have had to reconsider his belief that 'classification' was *a priori*. And, had he fully understood the implications of Darwinian evolution, he would have had to go back to square one.

Although 'categorisation' might help us recognise order in nature, in fact we would be ill-equipped to reason in mathematical logic without it, we're also sometimes ill-equipped to deal with it. The 'categorisation' of people, for example, according to race, religion, nationality or gender, has had a profoundly misleading effect upon the way we think about and treat one another.[19] Paradoxically, the more constrained we become by these so-called 'pure concepts of understanding', the more prejudiced we sometimes also become, as witnessed by the bigoted, hostile and cruel way we so frequently treat people we categorise as being different from ourselves.

Moreover, as Russell had pointed out,[20] there was a self-contradictory paradox in 'categorisation' or 'set theory' as the logicians call it, since there had to be a category of 'identities' that were united, only in so far as they all shared the same attribute of 'uniqueness', which actually meant they all belonged to that one universal category or set, which, by definition, over-ruled all categorical sub-sets.

---

[18] Darwin, C: On the Origin of Species 1859, 48
[19] Banaji, M et al: *Blind Spot: Hidden Biases of Good People,* 2013
[20] Known as 'Russell's Paradox', Russell, B: *The Principles of Mathematics,* 1903

And since nothing can be 'equal' to anything but itself, all apparent 'identities' turn out to be never more than approximations to one another. And, by extension, this paradox invalidated Kant's *a priori* reliance on all mathematical equations, which, by definition, rely on equality.

This same undermining conclusion was verified independently by the mathematician Kurt Gödel when, in 1931, he published his 'incompleteness theorem'.[21] This showed that, before one could validate any proposition in mathematical logic, one needed to rely on axioms that lay outside those from which its conclusions were derivatives. In other words, they relied on data that were not contained within the premises from which they had been derived. This meant all mathematical or logical forms of processing relied on some sort of *a posteriori* premise. Put simply, all deductive reasoning involved in our multifarious attempts to define reality logically must have had some inductive origin.

Next are the two concepts of 'correlation' and 'causation', which Kant described as "the relation of cause and effect".[22] If, for example, it was observed that an event, or variation in an event, subsequently occurred in close proximity to another event or variation in that event, then it had to be assumed there was some kind of 'correlation' between them, but, as we are so frequently reminded by statisticians, 'correlation does not mean causation'. Only statistical tests of significance can measure frequencies of 'correlation', ranging from 'very little significance', i.e. with a probability approaching, but never reaching, zero or near absolute uncertainty, to 'very highly significant', i.e. with a probability approaching, but never reaching, 'one' or near absolute certainty.

---

[21] Gödel, K: *Über formal unentscheidbare Sätze der Principia Mathematica ...* , Theorem VI, 1931

[22] Kant, I: *Critique of Pure Reason*, 1781-7, B232, [which has been discussed at length in Chapter 6.]

These measures of significance are entirely empirical, so do not rely on any *a priori* assumption about 'causation', and their measure of probable 'relatedness' could only be obtained empirically and defined as 'causal' if they were found to be precisely one, according to an infinite number of such tests. At best therefore, we could say only that there was 'constant conjunction', as Hume called it, between two events, or variations in events. In fact, the null hypothesis, which is consistent with Hume's empirical approach to philosophy, assumes 'causation', and hence 'cause and effect', offer us an entirely theoretical concept to our understanding of reality and, according to the 'classical square of oppositions', is in 'contradictory proposition' to Kant's uncompromising approach to understanding reality, whereby he claimed "all alterations take place in accordance with the law of cause and effect, and no alteration takes place without a cause".[23]

Evidently he thought he knew better than Hume, when he wrote: "A complete solution of Hume's problem rescues the *a priori* origin of the pure concepts of the understanding and the validity of the general laws of nature ... not in such a way that they are derived from experience, but that experience is derived from them."[24] And he persisted in claiming: "everything that happens presupposes that which it follows in accordance with a rule". These claims are repeated in different ways throughout his Critiques, for example: "everything in nature, as well in the inanimate as in the animate world, happens or is done according to rules, though we do not always know them ...".[25] This though, is a curious statement because if we don't always know the rules, how can we be sure they always are rules unless we assume they are?

---

[23] The second of Kant's 'Analogies of Experience'.
[24] Kant, I: *Prolegomena to Any Future Metaphysics*, 1783 & *Kant and Hume on Causality*, Stanford Encyclopaedia, 2013.
[25] Ruler, N: *Kant on Causality*, 2011.

For example, he insisted his 'categorical imperative', which related to moral law, should remain *a priori*, irrespective of our varied and ever changing interpretation of it. On recognising his single-minded commitment in this respect, Nietzsche dryly asked: "what does the assertion, that there is a categorical imperative in us ... indicate about him who makes it?" And suggested Kant might have answered narcissistically: "what is estimable in me is that I know how to obey, and with you it shall not be otherwise than in me."[26] Nevertheless, with respect to our behaviour, Kant still claimed:

> It is enough for me ... to couple the concept of 'causality' with that of 'freedom' and with what is inseparable from it: that is moral law as its determining ground. I have this right, by virtue of the pure non-empirical origin of the concept of 'cause', since I here make no other use of the concept than in relation to the moral law which determines its reality... [27]

And, again, by circular argument, he claimed moral law depended on yet another *a priori* concept, namely "freedom of the will", which he described as a "law of nature that sprang from man as *noumenon*",[28] i.e. a thinking, rather than a feeling being; not an object of the senses but as a 'thing-in-itself', even though it is now evident that *a priori* 'thinking' about anything at all derives, both chronologically and sequentially from *a posteriori* feelings about our experiences of anything at all.

---

[26] Nietzsche, F: *Beyond Good and Evil*, 1886, para. 187. He thought Kant had deceived himself in claiming he had discovered a new faculty in man, the faculty of synthetic *a priori* judgment. Kant's explanation as to why, was 'so circumstantially imposing and with such a display of German profundity and verbal flourish, that one altogether loses sight of the comical *niaiserie allemande* involved in such an answer.' Para. 11
[27] Kant, I: *Critique of Pure Reason*, 1787, KPV v56
[28] Ibid, A254/B310

As all of us, from the moment of conception onwards, begin to be blessed or cursed with these experiences throughout our lives, all our thinking is at least partially conditional upon them. This doesn't allow Kant much scope for any alternative validation that 'freedom of the will' is still an *a priori* concept. By relying on what he called 'pure reason' as the *a priori* premise from which to validate our understanding of reality, he traps his rational mind in solipsism by overlooking, or at least not accepting, the significance of Hume's concluding remark in his own *Philosophical Essays*, which reads:

> If we take in our hands any volume, of divinity or school of metaphysics, for example, let us ask: Does it contain any abstract reasoning concerning quantity or number? No. Does it contain any abstract reasoning concerning matter of fact or existence? No. Commit it then to the flames, for it can contain nothing more than sophistry and illusion.[29]

Indeed, if 'causation' was *a priori*, the event we call the 'cause' would have had to be the 'effect' of a previous event we call its 'cause', and so on, leading backwards by 'infinite regress' to the necessary abandonment of an *ens realissimum,* which is, in itself, somehow conveniently excluded from the need of a previous 'cause'. And likewise: an event we called the 'effect' would have had to be the 'cause' of a subsequent event we called its 'effect', and so on, leading forward by 'infinite progress' to what might objectively be thought to be 'a state of perfection', which would somehow be conveniently excluded from the need of any further 'cause'. Yet, both these conjectures about the meaning of 'causation' point to the same conclusion, namely that the Universe and everything in it

---

[29] Hume, D: *Inquiry concerning Human Understanding*, 1748, XII.iii

must be fundamentally deterministic. In other words, rigidly defined by an infinite causal chain from which nothing could deviate indeterminately, also, incidentally, including Kant's 'freedom of the will' that would make any attribution of credit or blame to us for our actions quite meaningless. By contrast, the empiricist view, one that is implicit in evolution, is only that certain regularities between things in nature can sometimes be observed, but which can never be certain or absolute.

From the previous excerpts alone, it should be evident that Kant judged himself a rational being, who lived by order and rules. It was even rumoured that people set their clocks by him when he passed their houses on his daily walks. Maybe his strict Lutheran childhood inhibited him from giving his more subjective feelings any serious credence, and why his unequivocal commitment to rules or laws rewarded him with such a following from like-minded people, whose needs perhaps, for order unwittingly steered them away from uncertainty. For others though, the ubiquitous rules of law were far too oppressive, especially if they felt they were being permanently judged according to their conformity to, or deviation from them.

Perhaps the most commonly used, yet least appraised *a priori* 'concept' though, is that of 'measurement', which always necessarily falls within the very limited boundaries of our five senses. It is an attempt to bridge the gap between order and disorder, by constructing a numerical system we can recognise and understand, upon a fundamentally chaotic one that by definition, is beyond recognition or understanding.

Although the stars we see in our mind's eye at night are single points of light, some are larger than our Sun and even represent whole galaxies of stars. At the other end of the scale, within the limits of the human eye, we cannot identify any object much smaller than a tenth of a millimetre across, and the limits of our hearing usually fall within the range of 20 to 20,000 Hz. Even the most sophisticated instruments for enhancing the effectiveness of our senses still severely restrict our ability to measure anything in nature precisely enough. Although we may think we can measure distances round coastlines accurately, for example, on closer inspection their convoluted and interminably changing contours become recognised as increasingly fragmented and, on a scale of one-to-one, become a dynamic confusion of sea, sand, pebbles and rocks.

> Nature has played a joke on the mathematicians; the same pathological structures ... turned out to be inherent in familiar objects all around us. Yet without mathematics we could never have conceived of nature's true intricacies. With greater and greater magnification, true density vanishes almost everywhere, except at an infinite number of isolated points, where it reaches an infinite value. Analogous considerations are applicable to properties such as velocity, pressure, or temperature. We find them growing more and more irregular as we increase the magnification of our necessarily imperfect image of the Universe.... Indeed, the conclusion we have reached above can also be arrived at by imagining a sphere that successively embraces planets, solar systems, stars and nebulae ....[30]

This was written in 1913 and pre-empts what is now known, or should I say what is unknown, about the quantum world concerning measurement, because it is considered to be "one of the most mysterious, and certainly the most argued about ... like doing two things at once, being able to pass through walls, or possessing spooky connections, only when one is looking. Once they

---

[30] Perrin, J: *Les Atomes*, 1913, Preface.

are observed, or measured in some way, they lose their weirdness and behave like the classical objects that we see around us."[31]

With the rational mind's insatiable desire to discover the 'fundamental laws of nature', more questions than answers are always revealed from our enquiries, no matter how far we scale up or down. The limits to magnification alone should be enough to point us unavoidably toward the null hypothesis that reality is ultimately unknowable and, our quest to find any truly reliable and universally accurate *a priori* laws embedded in it is an ill-conceived of illusion. It has been suggested that the *a priori* concept of certainty, in people's minds, is frequently associated with schizophrenia[32] and that schizophrenia and manic-depressive psychosis are 'the consequences of modernity'.[33]

Even the scientific method itself remains forever a fundamentally empirical *a posteriori* process in search of finding *a priori* truths, but which in practice only aims at describing, rather than defining, reality less inaccurately. It has been described as: 'a method of testing the validity of an hypothesis by means of systematic observation, measurement, and experiment' and, in order to guard against error or bias, these same steps need to be repeatable continually. The first problem with the scientific method though, is defining the hypothesis to be tested, whose genesis, at some stage, must have come from sense-data experiences and which, in any event could only be validated by 'observation' and 'measurement'.

In fact, all scientific-enquiry is subject to the 'problem of induction' highlighted by Hume, although it had a much earlier history, as Xenophanes claimed: 'only through seeking, may we learn and know things better ... for even if by chance a man were to utter the final truth, he would

[31] Al-Khalili, J: *Life on the Edge*, 2014, 32-3

[32] Barham, P: *Schizophrenia and Human Values*, 1984

[33] Greenfeld, L: *Mind, Modernity, Madness: The Impact of Culture on Human Experience*, 2013.

himself not know it: for all is but a woven web of guesses.' The probability of a particular 'effect' happening in consequence of a particular 'cause' could only be measured by comparing it with all the other 'effects' that might have happened in consequence of that same 'cause'. For example, the probability that a smiling face across a crowded room that sparked a sequence of events, which resulted in a particular sperm fertilising a particular egg to make you, the reader of this particular sentence at this particular moment in time, could only be calculated if we knew how many other possible 'effects' might have occurred in the intervening time as a consequence of that same smile. And 'given that we can live only a small part of what there is in us, what happens to the rest?' [Pascal Mercer]

If there is anything to be gained from a conceptual understanding of reality, it must surely be the recognition that the null hypothesis underwrites all our feelings and thoughts that generate this conceptual understanding, because it is only "through the falsification of our suppositions that we can actually get in touch with reality".[34] Doesn't this, therefore, imply 'reality' is ultimately unknowable because it would require an infinite number of 'falsifications' to find it?

In any event, it's a leading question to ask: how do subjective experiences give rise to objective thoughts because thoughts are never objective, they are merely less subjective than those we experience sensually all the time. After all, 'the world we see around us is like the fabric of a silken dream, whose fragile threads are woven out of all our fears and passions and expectations.' [Simon Pashoe] All we can say when we are thinking about the world, is that beneath the outline of apparent order, there must be unrecognised infinities within infinites of what we call

---

[34] Popper, K: *Objective Knowledge, an Evolutionary Approach*, revised edn. 1979, 360

'causes' that could have resulted in unrecognised infinities within infinites of what we call 'effects' within what must ultimately be disorder.

In conclusion therefore, there appear to be two quite distinct ways of 'knowing' reality. Either we can 'know' it directly by non-judgmentally experiencing it through our senses subjective: (i), or we can 'know' it indirectly by judging and evaluating these experiences objectively to make up the "sum total of our reality of the world"[35]: (ii). But there doesn't appear to be any way of reconciling (i), which pre-empts judgment and evaluation, and (ii), which is premised on judgment and evaluation. If reality is chaotic it is indeterminate and has no meaning, so (i) is the only way of knowing it. On the other hand, if it is not chaotic, it must have meaning and functions according to deterministic laws, so (ii) is the only way we can know it, and these two ways of knowing anything at all appear to be irreconcilable.

When we are sensually-conscious, we are in *a posteriori* harmony with nature but when it changes, we feel compelled to change with it so as to regain that harmony. When we are conceptually-conscious however, our egos are in a permanent state of restless enquiry about nature, in order to find *a priori* truths in it, in order to understand and change it to our advantage. Ironically, it seems, the ideological *a priori* fantasies of the 'me self' are so intoxicating that it is inclined to overrule the more *a posteriori* experiences of the 'I self' that simply goes with the flow. Consequently, the 'me self' seems to think 'the boy is now father of the man' from whom he has forgotten he was once conceived.

---

[35] Wittgenstein, L.: *Tractatus Logico-philosophicus* 1919. Propositions 2 & 2.063

11. DO WE LEARN OR ARE WE CONDITIONED?

From the moment of conception onwards, the physiology and neurology we inherit from our parents begins to be moulded and shaped by our environment, but our environment is being moulded and shaped by us too. So we immediately become bound up in a symbiotic relationship with the whole of nature and, being a social species, bound up in symbiotic relationships with each other too. Our natures are inescapably shaped by each other, they are not just all around us, they are in us too.

> There's never a period in the development of individuals, from their gamete stage to adulthood, when they are not being affected by their environment ... Their cells have been thoroughly bathed in their environment before their parents mated ... we currently have no basis for distinguishing environment from innate

predispositions or instincts.[1]

Even Darwin recognised how soon after birth children became influenced by the social habits of their caregivers. He realised they involved 'traditions', 'language', 'customs' and 'cultures'.[2] Studies of early folklore indicate how deeply our ancient ancestors felt themselves to be an intrinsic part of nature, and were far more empathically involved with each other and the whole of their environment than we do today. They tried to live in balance with nature and coordinated their own needs with the needs of others. This necessitated an ability to recognise the feelings of others and continually try to accommodate to them. The way they mirrored each other's emotions, however, gradually gave rise to a more reflective attitude towards their behaviour and the gradual emergence of thoughts about 'right' and 'wrong' ways of doing things. A change of emphasis, from automatic to more reflective thought though, implied a belief in agency about their behaviour and, following from the emergence of rules and laws came the idea of reward for conforming to them, along with punishment for not doing so. And although Descartes' *cogito* may have reinforced people's belief that they were the agents of their thoughts, Nietzsche posed the more penetrating questions:

> From whence did I get the notion of thinking? Why do I believe in cause and effect? What gives me the right to speak of an 'ego' as a cause, and finally of an 'ego' as a cause of thought? [He then went on to insist that] the hundred-times-refuted theory of 'free will' owes its persistence to its charm alone. I shall never tire of emphasizing ...

---

[1] Everett, D: *Instinct and Innate* - This idea must Die, Ed. Brockman, J. 2015, 208.

[2] Darwin, C: *A biographical Sketch of an Infant*, 1877. A Quarterly Review of Psychology and Philosophy 2 (7) (July): 285-294.

that a thought comes when 'it' wishes, and not when 'I' wish; so that it is a perversion of the facts of the case to say that the subject 'I' is the condition of the predicate 'think'.[3]

This insight undermines the whole status of the ego as the agent of its thoughts. By assuming the subject 'I' is the agent of the predicate 'think', we seem to forget, or conveniently ignore the fact that the way the person's environment moulds and shapes them is the real agent of the predicate 'think'. Consequently, the introspective way we have come to focus in on ourselves when we think tends to make us assume there is an direct cause-and-effect link between us as the cause and 'think' as the effect, and that we must be the agents of our thoughts, rather than the forwarding-agents of the way our environment causes us feel about our experiences that then causes us to think about them. Without us continually being sensually stimulated by our environmental experiences, we would be quite incapable of thinking about anything at all. Nietzsche put the link between having subjective experiences and having objective thoughts about them like this: "You know these things as thoughts, but your thoughts are not your experiences, they are an echo and an after-effect of your experiences, as when your room trembles when a carriage goes past".[4] Only then, when we begin translating these experiences more objectively into thoughts, do we become egocentrically focused in on what we think we can do about them, usually to our own advantage, rather than anyone else's.

Egoism and narcissism appear to be on the rise in our society, while empathy is on the decline. And yet, the ability to put ourselves in other people's

---

[3] Nietzsche, F: *Beyond Good and Evil*, 1886, paras. 16-7.
[4] Nietzsche, F: *Thus Spake Zarathustra*, 1883-5

shoes is extremely important for our coexistence. The research team, headed by Tania Singer from the Max Plank Institute of Human Cognitive and Brain Research, has discovered that our own feelings can distort our capacity for empathy. This emotionally driven egocentricity is recognised and corrected by the brain. When, however, the right supramarginal gyrus doesn't function properly or when we have to make particularly quick decisions our empathy is severely limited.[5]

The most extreme examples of this egocentricity though occur in people who have seriously defective personality disorders with 'zero [negative] degrees of empathy'.[6] They are incapable of emotionally experiencing other people's feelings themselves and, like parasites or viruses, are able to feed off their empathy and manipulate it to their own advantage. They usually believe that they are superior to others because they have the power to control them, which many have been the original *raison d'être* why egalitarian communities, that had survived on empathy for so long, began to be reorganized hierarchically according to such people's need for power and control.

There may not have been much disagreement about the way people's more emotional experiences were expressed subjectively, but as soon as they started to think about, and express them more objectively, according to words and sentences, ambiguity, confusion and disagreements began to rear their ugly heads. It's a deeply disturbing irony that, although we tend to assume spoken or written language is

[5] Silani, C: *I'm OK, You're Not OK: Right Supramarginal Gyrus Plays an Important Role in Empathy.* ScienceDaily, 9 Oct. 2013. Singer, T. *Are you egocentric? Check your right supramarginal gyrus,* 28 May 2014. Web. 3 July 2014

[6] Baron-Cohen, S: *Zero Degrees of Empathy,* 2012, in particular, 'Zero-Negative Type P 48-60

an aid to communication and understanding between people, it has frequently had quite the opposite effect. We use words and sentences to try and clarify our thoughts as an aid to expressing them to each other, yet continually have to modify and re-define them in order to do so, or become so committed to them they take control of our lives and have to be defended to the death sometimes.

In its infancy perhaps, language expressed only how we felt about each other and our environment but subsequently expressed how we thought about these things too. Early on in its development, it must have been an aid to story-telling and mythologizing, as a way of describing our environment, but subsequently about how we could control it, and by impressing our own thoughts upon others as an aid to influencing and controlling them. Thinking, expressed in the form of opinions, beliefs and ideas about reality, often followed by rules and laws about how to define them, appear to give reality meaning and our lives a sense of purpose but, before language, probably neither of these things were necessary. With the development of words and sentences therefore, people became increasingly committed to their own creeds or those that had been impressed upon them, often resulting in distrust, suspicion and sometimes even conflict and violence.

Comparisons between different creeds can have odious consequences because our own convictions are invariably derived only from our own experiences. As Nassim Taleb showed,[7] retrospective empirical evidence, which was all we had to go on anyway, was always unreliable, so needed continual modification and updating. Unexpected events, which he calls 'black swans', often force us to re-define our on-going attempts to understand reality, and although we might be able to cope well enough instinctively with minor

---

[7] Taleb, N: *The Black Swan*, 2007

unexpected events, at a subatomic level they occur all the time. We may think we can ignore minor changes but they can have a cumulative effect, such as 'aging' for example; until that is, one morning after the night before we look in the mirror and can't avoid its uncompromising effect.

Most changes are miniscule and occur within such narrow boundaries of variance, we tend to accommodate to them without realising we're doing so. At the other end of the scale, events such as earthquakes, economic crashes, or wars can undermine our whole perception of reality. Either way, 'black swans', no matter how insignificant they might appear to be, affect us all the time and can sometimes cause quantum changes in exactly the same way mutations have done throughout the course of evolutionary history.

Some think that the predictive powers of science can cope well enough with 'black swans' but only retrospectively, and it can take a long time before science catches up. In the following passage, Bertrand Russell suggests we redefine the universe as being 'irredeemable mystical', or put more prosaically 'fundamentally indeterminate':

> In its quest to discover how the patterns of reality are organised, the story of modern science hints at a picture of a set of Chinese puzzle boxes, each one more intricately structured and wondrous than the last. Every time the final box appears to have been reached, a key has been found which has opened up another, revealing a new universe even more breathtakingly improbable in its conception. We are now forced to suspect that, for human reason, there is no last box, that in some deeply mysterious, virtually unfathomable, self-reflective way, every time we open a still smaller box, we are actually being brought closer the box with which we started: the box which contains our own

conscious experience of the world. This is why no theory of knowledge, no epistemology, can ever escape being consumed by its own self-generated paradoxes. And this is why we must consider the universe to be irredeemably mystical.[8]

It is often assumed the process of acquiring knowledge about the world by thinking about it is how we get in touch with reality but we easily forget it's an inflexible and emotionally sterile process that always trails behind the way we feel about our experience of it. The notion of 'sensual-consciousness' corresponds roughly to what has been called 'phenomenal-consciousness', and that of 'conceptual-consciousness' to 'access-consciousness',[9] and although being 'sensually-conscious' may appear to involve what Daniel Kahneman calls 'fast thinking', and being 'conceptually-conscious' more with what he calls 'slow thinking',[10] certain semantic differences arise from this distinction. 'Fast thinking' has been described as an "automatic and intuitive process of the brain", and 'slow thinking' as a more "deliberate process that requires effort and attention", but, if 'thinking' of any kind involves 'judgment and evaluation, in order to arrive at a particular opinion, belief or idea', then 'fast thinking' can hardly be described as thinking at all.

Furthermore, 'slow thinking' has been "credited with self-control" but, if Nietzsche was right, and free will is a delusion, it's doubtful whether self-control applies even to 'slow thinking'. As William James pointed out, "many people think they are thinking when they are only rearranging their prejudices". The conceptually-conscious mind is permanently 'out of touch' with reality, both literally and metaphorically, yet, paradoxically, it believes

---

[8] Gibson, G: *Philosophical Topics*, 2009, 21
[9] Block, N: *Two Neural Correlates of Consciousness*, 2005 Trends in Cognitive Science, 9.2, 46-52.
[10] Kahneman, D: *Thinking Fast and Slow*, 2011

the towering monument of knowledge it has constructed
to define it is now so vast and penetrating that all those
sensually conscious experiences by which we got in touch
with it in the first place, can now be disregarded or at least
treated as insignificant.

Towards the end of the *Tractatus*, Wittgenstein bravely
admitted his own error in this respect. Although he
claimed the '*logico-philosophicus*' propositions he used to
define the world did not, in themselves, say anything false
about it, they didn't actually say anything worthwhile
either. He explained it this way:

> My propositions serve as elucidations in the
> following way: anyone who understands me
> eventually recognizes them as nonsensical, when
> he has used them, as steps, to climb up beyond
> them. He must, so to speak, throw away the ladder
> after he has climbed up it. He must transcend
> these propositions and then he will see the world
> aright. What we cannot speak about we must pass
> over in silence.[11]

Indeed, his subsequent *Philosophical Investigations* showed
he had indeed thrown away 'the ladder' after having
climbed up it. A similar sense of disillusionment about the
value of logical atomism and scientific inference in trying
to understand the world rationally, might have occurred to
Russell too, for, after completing his monumental *Principia
Mathematica* with Whitehead in 1913, he began focusing
more on humanitarian issues.

The 'ladder analogy' reveals a common oversight in our
attempt to get in touch with reality objectively, namely the
egocentric bias contained within the limited boundaries of
our conceptually conscious knowledge of it, since it
remains a second-order derivative of our sensual conscious

[11] Wittgenstein, L: *Tractatus Logico-philosophicus* 1921-2, ref. 6.54 & 7.

experience of it.[12] In defining, analysing and then utilising those *a priori* rules our egos have constructed about the nature of reality, they ignore their origin and delight in the self-congratulatory solipsism.

Kant had hoped to show that modern philosophy could be built upon judgment and evaluation, which he claimed revealed *synthetic a priori* truths that transcend the boundaries of sense experience; but this is a self-contrary paradox because any attempt to show they were still need to be validated empirically. Nietzsche invited us to ask ourselves: "Why is belief in such judgments necessary?"[13] "Granted that we want the truth: why not rather untruth and uncertainty, even ignorance?"[14] Popper would probably have agreed.

In fact, the evidence only demonstrates how singularly vacuous our egocentric bias in favour of establishing objective truths about the nature of reality actually is, because our egos have got nothing else but reason and logic to motivate them. Yet how singularly persuasive its ideological beliefs can still be by overlooking the possibility that "Someone had blundere'd". After all, in the words of Tennyson: "Theirs not to make reply, / Theirs not to reason why, / Theirs but to do and die. / Into the valley of Death / Rode the six hundred."

The Scientific Revolution that emerged out of the Renaissance movement in Europe began to favour rational thought and probably contributed to the Enlightenment and an increasing emphasis on materialism, which then brought about the Industrial Revolution. But what was all that rationalisation leading to? And why did we become so hell-bent on changing the world and our own lives in the

---

[12] Hacker, P: *Insight and Illusion*, 1986 however, rejects the unbridgeable gap between mind-body problems and the difference between having non-judgmental, *a posteriori* experiences and judging them to be *a priori* in order to evaluate them.

[13] Nietzsche, F: *Beyond Good and Evil*, 1886, Ch.1, 11.

[14] Ibid. Ch.1, 1

process? A shift of emphasis, from an intuitive sense of outward 'existence', to a more inwardly reflective one of 'essence', promoted a belief in the value of objective thoughts at the expense of subjective feelings, but how could 'existence' be transformed into 'essence'? Søren Kierkegaard was one of the first to explore these alternatives. In his book[15] he compared the aesthetic life of freedom, serenity and beauty, as expressed in poetry, drama and music, with that of the ethical and religious lives of those who felt obliged to contend with the rule of duty and moral responsibility. How these alternatives came about though is not fully explained, but they appear to roughly correspond to the primary and secondary forms of processing data outlined above.

Once our more conceptually-conscious thoughts become embedded in our minds we tend to be increasingly committed to them. They make us less concerned with how we acquired them in the past, and more with how we might make use of them for the future. Yet, by focusing on 'effects' of 'causes', rather than on 'causes' of 'effects', the ego becomes conditioned to try and change the present in favour of the future, rather than learn from the past to try and stabilise the present. By attempting to achieve future outcomes that are an improvement on the present ones, our egos suffer from an 'above-average' confidence. But it's "a misperception that can have a deleterious impact on health"[16] and has infiltrated all levels of society. Wittgenstein put it like this: "A man will be imprisoned within a door that's unlocked and opens inwards, so long as it does not occur to him to pull rather than push it".[17]

---

[15] Kierkegaard, S: *Either-Or*, 1843
[16] Larwood & Whittaker: *Managerial Myopia; Self-Serving Biases in Organisational Planning*, Journal of Applied Psychology, 1977, 62; & Dunning, D: *Flawed Self-Assessment. Implications for Health, Education and the Workplace*, Psychological Science, 2004, 5, 3.
[17] Wittgenstein, L: *Philosophical Investigations*, 1953, Culture and Value 1980, 42e

By evaluating all those experiences stored in our memory-bank rationally, our egos convince themselves they will gain enough knowledge of the world to create a 'better tomorrow' for themselves than 'today'. Unfortunately though, by thinking more about our future needs, rather than by focusing more on coping with our present ones, we might go on polluting and plundering the world's resources indefinitely and overlook the fact that we will still have to experience this so-called 'better tomorrow' sensually whenever it comes. Ecclesiastes evidently recognised this oversight more than 2,000 years ago, in claiming 'he that increaseth knowledge increaseth sorrow'.

Schopenhauer described it as a 'general will' in itself 'to live' but subsequently distinguished this 'general will' from our own 'inner will' to improve our lives, which required knowledge in order to try and understand 'the riddle of the world' by means of what he called 'principles of sufficient reason'. Like Kant, he saw it as search for *a priori* concepts, by assuming, like Laplace, that 'the effects of Nature were only mathematical results of a small number of immutable laws'[18] embedded in it.

Nietzsche, however, recognised this 'will to live', or 'survive' more specifically as a 'will to power' which necessitated some hierarchical kind of: "scaffolding by means of which a select class of beings were able to elevate themselves to their higher duties and in general to a higher existence".[19] By coming under the control of this 'select class of beings' however, others felt compelled to promote themselves to become select being themselves too, perhaps not pathalogically like psychopaths, whose ignorance of feelings for others makes them believe they must be 'select' anyway, but at least more narcisissistically out of necessity for their own survival under their influence.

---

[18] Laplace, P: *A Philosophical Essay*, New York, 1902, p. 177.
[19] Nietzsche, F: *Beyond Good and Evil*, 1886, para. 258.

Unfortunately, the inflated self-image of the psychopathic is rarely restrained by feelings of failure or guilt, so mercilessly tries to crush any threat to its own 'will to power'. Because psychopaths have often been so successful in doing this throughout recorded history, others have also had to put their own survival first, for fear of being left behind in the 'rat race'. It has been suggested however, that: "In order for your inflated self-image to serve you well, to have survival benefits, it must be inflated to just the right degree and no further. Psychologists describe this balance by saying that the resulting distortion must maintain the illusion of objectivity".[20] Surely though, this only continues to make us distrustful, suspicious or even paranoid about each other competing for their survival too, which is exactly what has happened and will continue to happen until we stop trying to inflate our self-image.

Such internal neurological turmoil is an inevitable consequence of what the conceptually-conscious brain's 'will-to-power' seems to be striving for. It's killing the goose that, before the dawn of civilization had laid the golden egg, when our gregarious natures ensured equality and balance was all that was required. Since then though, the rise of our egos has conditioned us to believe we simply "must not stop thinking" and need "to keep the world going"[21] both of which are typical features of schizophrenia brought about by an excessive will to promote ourselves.

Some still seem to think this has resulted in "an increasingly non-violent world" that has "allowed our 'better angels' to prevail".[22] But has there really been an improvement in our natures, as is claimed by, for example

[20] Mlodinow, L: *Subliminal*, 2012, (2014 edn. 206-7).
[21] Spitzer, M: *On Defining Delusion*, Comprehensive Psychiatry, 31 1990 393.
[22] Pinker, S: *The Better Angels of our Nature: The Decline of Violence in History and its Causes*, 2012

'abolition of slavery' and data showing fewer violent death rates per capita, particularly since the Enlightenment and throughout 'the Long' and 'New Peace' since World War II, or is this just wishful thinking? Slavery may be less conspicuous but it may also be far more widespread and 'death rates' is only one measure of violence, whereas psychological control, manipulation and dominance are other less conspicuous measures. Could a change in the nature of violence be a more realistic interpretation? An apparent lack of overt violence among the present population of North Korea, for example, could hardly have allowed their 'better angels to prevail'. Perhaps a decrease in overt violence, has been replaced by a corresponding increase in covert violence, as less easily measured by the amount of intimidation, bullying, imprisonment, torture and mass mind-bending conformity from fear of retribution, to say nothing of a possible increase in mental illness?

So have all our attempts to create a 'better tomorrow' been the result of more stringently imposed rules, regulations and laws, telling us how we should behave in response to authorised control; or have they simply been the result of chance opportunism, telling us how we ought to behave in response to circumstances, as was suggested in the opening sequence of that film: '2001: a Space Odyssey'? When one of those pre-hominid ancestors noticed a bone it had been idly playing with, broke some skeletal remains lying nearby, it provided it with the chance opportunity to make a useful weapon out of it, but a weapon for offence or defence?

In an indeterminate world, all we can do is conjecture randomly about what 'tomorrow' might bring, and, when our egos cherry-pick yesterday's experiences that turn out to be advantageous, we congratulate ourselves, while conveniently ignoring all those failed conjectures involved in the same process. This is a serious misappropriation of agency, as we can never know whether the long-term consequences of our conjectures are going to be for better or worse, and sometimes they have resulted in the worst violence in human history. "We cannot resort to the excuse that our violence is a product of our pre-hominid evolution; ... it is only since the emergence of the first agricultural civilizations that humans have accumulated wealth and surpluses which have led in turn to egocentric greed and competition. Capitalization and signs of prosperity are certain to trigger feelings of greed in the less well off,"[23] to say nothing of feelings of greater greed in the more well off.

As a social species though, probably the most fundamental dilemma that continues to face all our conjectures is how to resolve the conflicting needs of egoism and altruism. In other words, whether we should give greater credence to our own needs, or to the needs of the communities within which we find ourselves, since our survival depends on both. It's the age-old dilemma between cooperation and competition, and two of our genetically closest non-human primates, the chimpanzees and the bonobos have evolved very different ways of dealing with this problem.

Chimpanzees are omnivorous and compete with other primates for food, which is probably why they eat alone and generate high levels of testosterone that promotes aggression and helps ward off rivals. On the other hand, their smaller cousins, the bonobos, inhabit the fruit-bearing forests to the South of the Congo River where there's plenty of food and little competition from other species. Consequently, they are vegetarians, and, in generating far less testosterone, happily share their food and are more cooperative.

Chimpanzee-communities are organised hierarchically, which involves occasional skirmishes based on physical

---

[23] Guilaine, J & Zammit, J: *Origins of War Violence in Prehistory*, 2005 edn., 19

strength between alpha-males; the strongest emerge as pack leaders and have the pick of the females. But as Jane Goodall observed, "there were gang-attacks of extraordinary brutality. The male chimps pounded their victims and left them to die of awful injuries. They did things to their fellow chimps that they would never do within their community".[24] This aggressive behaviour, contrasts strongly with the less hierarchically organised bonobo-communities, which are far more playful and friendly, with the most cooperative females emerging instead as pack-leaders. And, although they are not as physically strong as the males, they can prevent any threat of dominance and bullying from them by means of even stronger social alliances with other females, who tend to prefer mating with the gentler and less aggressive males anyway.

Chimpanzee behaviour therefore, is more competitive, self-centred and status-orientated, with a pecking order usually established by means of occasional expressions of physical strength and aggression, whereas bonobo behaviour is more altruistic, cooperative and egalitarian, with plenty of food-sharing, tactile bonding and free sexual activity.[25] Since the two species are almost genetically identical to each other, perhaps it was not because of any inherited biology that caused their social behaviour to be so very different; but rather because the environments they inhabited pointed them in such different directions. Darwin would probably have called this 'the principle of divergence'. Since we humans have very similar genes to both chimpanzees and bonobos, perhaps it was not so much our inheritance, but more the way we diverged, from hunter-gathering to settled-farming, that changed our behaviour so much. Over-population in the more fertile

---

24 McKie R: *Chimps with everything: Jane Goodall's 50 years in the jungle*, 2010, even though Power, M: *The Egalitarians, Humans and Chimpanzees*, 1991 indicated Goodall's earlier studies showed an absence of violence.
25 Block, S: *The Bonobo Way: The Evolution of Peace Through Pleasure*, 2014

regions of the world, coupled with an accumulation of wealth and surpluses, brought about greed, competition and both overt and covert violence.

So perhaps any, so-called mass violence[26] could be traced to a reaction against the increasing divergence between egoism and altruism in favour of egoism. Although it might be somewhat fanciful to believe that before the agrarian revolution the earliest hunter-gatherers and band communities had been an entirely non-violent, peace-loving species, living in a Garden of Eden in harmony and balance with nature, but there may be very good reasons for believing this had some basis in reality. Certainly early folklore mythologized about it and during Palaeolithic times the widely dispersed populations of nomadic band communities throughout the world usually found an availability of food, which would not have favoured a need for competition or violence. Although it was commonly thought scarcity of resources during Palaeolithic times might: "Lead to goods and territory being seized from neighbouring groups, this theory is based on a somewhat impoverished view of prehistoric society, and research has indicated, with near certainty, that early societies were perfectly capable of meeting their nutritional requirements."[27]

Other studies of our pre-agricultural ancestry[28] also showed that, just like female bonobos, who cooperate together 'to prevent dominance and bullying', band communities tended to work together to ostracize and reject more self-centred individuals who forcibly tried to rule their group. Contrary to popular belief, many of these

---

[26] Wade, L.: *10,000 year-old Massacre*, 2016, showed the earliest dated evidence of a massacre of 27 people was at the beginning of agricultural farming, not before.

[27] Guilaine, J & Zammit, J: *Origins of War Violence in Prehisotry*, 2005 edn., 20.

[28] Hill, K & Hurtado, A: *Ache Life History*, 1996; Ellison, P: *On fertile Ground...*, 2003

early communities were matrilineal like bonobos, as distinct from matriarchal or patriarchical in structure, and tended to be more politically and sexually egalitarian.[29] And: "For female baboons, macaques, and vervets maternal kinship is an important axis of social networks, coalition-nary activity, and dominance relationships."[30]

Those occasional displays of 'alpha-male dominance' among chimpanzee communities in the virgin jungles of the Congo have been replaced by persistent displays of "authoritarian dominance"[31] among modern humans in the man-made jungles of the human zoo. And, in order to reinforce the idea of an essentially male hierarchy, cooperation has been eclipsed by competition. It begins with our educational system, which teaches us to compete under the guise of succeeding, even though success for the few means failure for the many. The same is true in sport, recreation, entertainment and just about every other conceivable activity, including of course all those associated with trade, commerce and profit-making, even though 'winning' for the few implies 'losing' for the many. So, are we 'educating' ourselves to be successful, or simply conditioning ourselves to be 'competitive'?

The inflated ego's thirst for power and control depends upon the surrender of power and control by those they exploit, or by exploiting the world's natural resources to attain it. Like a parasite, it feeds off and chokes its host. It creates a cut-throat environment in which:

> Mental illnesses are five times higher in the most unequal compared with the least unequal societies. Similarly, in more unequal societies people are five times as likely to be imprisoned, six times as likely

---

[29] Knauft, B: *Violence and Sociality in Human Evolution*, 1991, Current Anthropology 32/4, 391- 409.

[30] Silk, J: *Kinship Selection in Primate Groups*, Int. Journal of Prmatology, 2000, V23, 849-75

[31] Barfield, A: *Saving the Appearances: A Study of Idolatry*, 1957

to be clinically obese, and murder rates may be many times higher.[32]

Industrialisation, particularly over the last 300 years, has gradually brought about a general increase in urbanisation,[33] with now, more than half the world's population living in cities. This in turn has also brought about an increase in mental illness.

---

[32] Wilkinson, R & Pickett, K: *The Spirit Level*, 2010 edn. 176

[33] Alok Jha: *City living affects your brain,* 2011; Weich, S et al: *Rural/non-rural differences in rates of common mental disorder*, 2005; Gold, J & I: *Mental Illness*, 2015, illness increases with size of population.

12. ALL THE WORLD A STAGE

Having come to the conclusion that many of our social practices and beliefs were ill conceived or illusory, writing these essays has seen more like an 'un-learned' experience than a learned one. My curiosity probably began at school when I was punished for not conforming to 'normal' standards of behaviour and because I was so frequently punished, all I learned was that I wasn't 'normal'.[1] This sparked my curiosity about the 'retributive justice' system to which I had been subjected and which I later discovered was ill-conceived, even though it is still widely exercised at all levels of society and in diverse forms of severity all over the world.

One thing led to another and, rather like trying to identify and fit together bits of a jigsaw to make up a more complete picture, my curiosity drove me to consider a number of other inter-related and, what also appeared to be illusory concepts, such as: 'authority', 'hierarchy',

---

[1] ASD inhibits mirroring others' feelings and thoughts, and is an isolating disability that is sometimes inclined to make one feels as if : 'all the world's a stage'.

'democracy', 'justice', 'morality', 'decision-making' and 'progress', all of which, I felt, might perhaps have had their distant origins in a mutant ego of some kind. The overall picture, of course, is far from complete, but at least these essays offer the reader an alternative explanation as to how such concepts have come about and how they appear to have not only conditioned, but practically hard-wired most of us into complying with them because of what is generally believed to be our 'freedom of choice', yet another illusory concept. Indeed, thousands of years ago the concept of 'free fill' became so deeply embedded in our thinking that we began trying to evaluate ourselves hierarchically, which changed the way societies became re-structured, and we're still suffering from the consequences.

So, just to recap on some of the themes discussed in the foregoing essays, let's begin with the origin of Homo sapiens. Its earliest chronology is uncertain, but current research suggests it began in Ethiopia between 200 and 100 thousand years ago.[2] At that time our ancestors survived, primarily by living in balance with each other and with their largely un-judged and un-interfered with environment. Then, perhaps about 60,000 or more years ago, when they first started to recognise their own identities and did begin to judge and evaluate their environmental experiences, the great 'Out of Africa' migration started.[3] Before our ancestors began trying to understand and alter their environment to their own advantage, evolution had ordained they remained in balance with it. So this migration marked a change, from just accepting how things were to judging how they thought they ought to be.

Although we sometimes call this process 'learning from experience', there might be very good reasons that will be

---

[2] Stringer, C: *Human Evolution: out of Ethiopia*, Nature 423, 2003, 692-5
[3] The 'out of Africa' date is still contested. Lawlor, R: *Voices of the first Day* ..., 1991, claims more recent evidence indicates Aborigines might have reached Australia 150,000 years ago.

amplified later, for describing it as 'conditioning', not 'learning'. Those responses to changing circumstances that appeared advantageous become habitual, whereas those that don't become obsolete but, because they aren't always able to respond quickly enough, the whole process is very much a hit-and-miss affair. In those distant times, people lived principally in kinship bands of nomadic hunter-gatherer communities and the way their cultural practices drifted and flowed was beyond any consciously conceived-of or planned form of organised control. If we could have seen the way they responded to changing circumstances speeded up over time, they might very well have looked like murmurations, or to use Popper's analogy, like gnats that "fly quite irregularly in all directions, ... the cluster keeps together even though it has no leader ... it is the most egalitarian, free, and democratic society imaginable".[4]

Because these communities shared about half their parents' and siblings' genes, about a quarter of their uncles', aunts' and grandparents', and about an eighth of their cousins', they must have instinctively felt 'blood was thicker than water', which would have helped to keep them together. What this meant was that their biology, more than their neurology was the principle determinant of their altruism towards each other and allowed them to maintain a cohesive balance between the extremes of egoism and altruism within those communities.[5] Altruism though, which is defined as 'an unselfish concern for the welfare of others', might connote a more conscious sense of obligation, so perhaps 'empathy' would be a more appropriate word than 'altruism'.

Empathy, which has been defined as 'the ability to

---

[4] Popper, K: *Objective Knowledge*, revised edn. 1979, 208-9, and more recent studies of 'swarms' of insects, bats, birds, fish and some mammals show group-coordination without leaders.

[5] Adam Smith was probably the first to explore the difference between 'egoism' in *The Wealth of Nations*, 1776 and 'altruism' in *The Theory of Moral Sentiments*, 1759.

identify what someone else is thinking or feeling and to respond with an appropriate emotion', had helped to keep egoism in check, so for good reason has been described as "one of the most valuable resources in the world".[6] It alone allowed our ancestors to instinctively read each other's facial expressions and body language and adjust their own behaviour accordingly. In any event, this unconscious self-control mechanism provided a fairly stable means of ensuring they were able to survive cooperatively together like that for thousands of generations. So they evidently depended primarily on what they felt, rather than thought about each other. However, the gradual emergence of, what I've called a 'mutant ego' that began to think independently of others, changed all that.

Authority

Authority is understood to mean something like 'the exercise of power to enforce control over those with less power' but, to be effective, this became re-enforced by the use of rewards for those accepted being controlled and punishments for those that didn't. It is an obvious self-fulfilling prophecy that when behaviour that others approve of is rewarded with what have been called 'positive-reinforcers', that same behaviour is more likely to occur again, and when disapproved of is punished with what have been called 'negative-reinforcers' that same behaviour is less likely to occur again.[7] However, when people trust each other, approval and disapproval operate at a sensually conscious level and don't need to be enforced because they tend to respond to each other in kind.

At first, "ancient men acted without analysing their

---

[6] Baron-Cohen, S: *Zero Degrees of Empathy*, 2011, 130 & 12 respectively.

[7] Skinner, B. F: *Beyond Freedom & Dignity*, 1971, 27.

behaviour, presumably because they were less self-aware and so free from feelings of guilt and pride".[8] But during the late Palaeolithic, this newly conceived-of form of control began to be employed by more self-centred individuals, who, because of their inability to empathise with others, thought of themselves as authorities over them and used these 'reinforcers' to reward those who supported them and punish those who didn't. Hence, expressions of what Darwin called 'praise' and 'blame', based on 'pattern recognition' of group-conformity, began to be hijacked by egoists who started manipulating the behaviour of others in favour of themselves. Their controlling influence altered the long-held balance of trust in one another in favour of their own more single-minded distrust of others.

Consequently, those intuitive feeling of 'leadership', based more on age and experience, which, for millennia had inspired people to follow, became transposed into those more conceptually-conscious thoughts of 'authority' based on egoism, which enforced people to follow, and therein lay a quantum shift of feelings of trust to thoughts of distrust in the whole course of our social evolution. Various explanations, as to how this change came about have been proposed and here is one suggestion:

> The appearance of new ways of thinking and communicating, between 70,000 and 30,000 years ago, constitutes the Cognitive Revolution. What caused it? We're not sure. The most commonly believed theory argues that accidental genetic mutations changed the inner wiring of the brains of Sapiens, enabling them to think in unprecedented ways and to communicate using an

---

[8] Taylor, S: *The Fall*, 2005, 108 and several references to Heinberg, R: *Memories and Visions of Paradise*, 1989 amplify the point.

altogether new type of language.[9]

So, before the emergence of this 'Cognitive Revolution' and the first written laws that followed from it, our ancient ancestors probably had very little 'conceptual' understanding of the world at all, nor even of themselves. But with the gradual recognition of the self, along with the development of words and sentences to aid their understanding, people became more aware of their own behaviour, and began crediting or blaming one another and themselves, according to these consciously conceived-of rules and regulations and ethical practices, prescribed in law.

When these practices became monopolised by authority, in the form of ossified codes of conduct, they had to be obeyed by force of law. However: "There is also such a thing as verbal bullying; language can be used in deceitful and manipulative ways, and used to maintain hierarchy as easily as to pull it down. I am not at all persuaded that language shows an inherent bias to the good."[10]

So people's sensually-conscious experiences about how they felt they 'ought' to behave towards each other, gradually gave way to conceptually-conscious thoughts about how they thought they 'should' behave according to these authorised laws. The word 'ought' is used here to connote intuitive feelings of personal obligation, based on empathy and trust in treating each other equally, as distinct from the word 'should', which is intended to connote consciously conceived-of thoughts about enforced social imperatives. And this enforcement had to be administered by a centralised form of authority because it eventually

[9] Harari, Y: *Sapiens, A Brief History of Mankind*, 2014, 21, suggests 'it was a matter of pure chance', which is consistent with the idea of a mutation.
[10] Carling, A: *Equality and Consciousness in Early Human Society*, The Evolutionary Origins of Morality, 2000, 121

became accepted to be a more reliable and clearly defined method of controlling behaviour than every individual's own intuitive method of personal self-control. This involved a change of focus from one's own more subjective way of processing situations to authority's more objective way of making you process them.

The focus of attention in neurological processing, between the right and left hemispheres of the human brain has been loosely described as the difference between emotional intelligence and conceptual intelligence and, when our ancestors began trying to communicate with one another by words and sentences, more than simply by facial expressions and body language, they became increasingly biased in favour of conceptual intelligence. The fact that the faculty of speech, which is associated with the Broca and Wernika, both of which are situated in the left hemisphere, would seem to testify to this.

The earliest expressions of conceptual intelligence began to appear in mythology, and this was passed on, embellished and modified, down through the generations by word-of-mouth in story telling and folk-art. At first it took the form of witchcraft and sorcery, and as early as two millennia BC formed a significant part of Babylonian culture but probably had parallels in Eastern cultures too. These ideas took on spiritual connotations and later formed the basis of the major religions of the world. In support of them, numerous messiahs, apostles, missionaries and other holy men began promoting their different beliefs as widely as possible because they each represented their own self-centred solutions should be adopted by others.

This process however, might really have been less about the intrinsic validity of their different ideologies, but more about their egos trying to gain reassurance, power and control from support by those they were able to convince. Claims such as: "I am the way, the truth and the life ...", for example, encouraged ideas of absolute authority in the minds of those who promoted them. Moreover, written commandments, such as: "You shall have no other Gods before me" [Exodus 20:3] or even "the great gods have ordered my rule",[11] indicated a divine right to control the behaviour of their followers. Beneath the façade of guidance and care for others these written or verbal imperatives only encouraged bias towards egocentrism in the minds of such people. [12]

The first verse of the Gospel according to St. John, for example, starts with: "In the beginning was the Word ...", but perhaps it should have read: 'in the beginning of conceptually-conscious thought was the Word'.[13] In any event, this change in the structure of society, from a communal need for equality and balance, to a self-centred need by some for inequality and imbalance, might be illustrated by the difference between empathy, which is a kind of theory-of-mind ability to 'double-feel' at a personal level, and egoism, which is rather like what George Orwell called an ability to 'double-think' at an impersonal level. He described it as "having the power to hold two contradictory beliefs in one's mind simultaneously, and accept both of them". An example might be, calling 'armed forces' 'defence forces' when they are primarily employed for attack. "When they say peace they mean war, when they say love they mean hate, and when they say freedom they mean slavery".[14]

The ability of such egotistically minded people to 'double-think', therefore, began to overrule empathy to 'double feel' and, when insisted upon forcefully enough under the guise of authority, would have helped to impress

---

[11] Hamarabi's Code, c1700 BC

[12] Dénos, I: *Person Liberty and Political* Freedom, 2008; Triandis, H: *Collectivism v. Individualism*, 1988

[13] Beavers, A: *In the Beginning*, n.d. 'Spoken words at first must have been meaningful in some similar sense. But in time the word became flesh (corpus) and ...in time inaugurated the dawn of human history'.

[14] Orwell, G: *Nineteen Eighty-Four*, 1949, Pt. 1, Ch.9

obedience and conformity on others. Consequently, the meaning of what they said was less relevant to its validity than to the authoritative way they said it. Here is yet another way of describing how this quantum change in social evolution came about:

> The arrival of the Neolithic tolled the knell of this golden age as humans became slaves to work: there was a regression of sorts as servitude began in earnest, a gradual descent into Hell. ... They began to perceive their relationship with their environment differently, to fill their surroundings with symbolic significance, to change their behaviour towards others and to see their own role differently, having gained control over their environment, upon which they had previously been dependent. Thus, humans too underwent great changes on a cultural, ideological and psychological level. Yet when humans are already in control of the animal, plant and mineral worlds, what kind of relationship can they have with others of the same species? Did this progressive domestication lead certain individuals to go one step further on the road to hegemony? History has, unfortunately revealed such fears to be well founded and violence began to take on various different forms from the advent of farming onwards.[15]

So larger concentrations of populations, in fertile regions where settled farming began, would have helped to promote the idea of ownership of land and everything within it, since, before that time, it was generally felt nobody owned anything, and certainly not each other. Hence, empathy, which had helped to keep egoism in

---

[15] Guilaine J & Zammit, J: *The Origins of War*, 2005, 30 & 82.

check, was beginning to be threatened. Personal ownership began to mean power, influence and control, and gave those who claimed it the ability to enforce this self-centred idea on others. It even persuaded them to think likewise. Rousseau described the source of the problem with pinpoint accuracy, when he said: "The first man, who having enclosed a piece of land, bethought himself of saying 'this is mine' and found people simple enough to believe him, was the real founder of civil society".[16] After all, only those bereft of empathy for anyone but themselves would have contemplated the idea that they had the right to make such an outrageous claim.[17] 'Ownership' at that time was such a new idea no one would have believed them, unless of course, they had been force or bullied to do so, by preventing them from challenging their self-delusion in some way. If, such egocentrically minded people had had the power to harness the air we breathe, they would surely have claimed the right to its ownership and control that as well.

The thought that a person's labour was not part of their contribution to the community any more but belonged to themselves instead, might have been an early example of the concept of ownership but, when its meaning started to applied to other things, its meaning became altogether more tenuous. Perhaps this ownership of land and chattels, in the minds of a few such self-centred individuals, would have been enough to taint these instinctive feelings of openness and trust in one another with suspicion and distrust. Such an effect on communities seems to have necessitated an increasing emphasis on their own survival, more than everyone

---

[16] Rouseau, J: *Discourse on Inequality*, 1754.

[17] Paulhus, D & Williams, K: *The Dark Triad of Personality, narcissism, Machiavellianism, Psychopathy*, Journal of Research in Personality, v36, I6, 556-63, 2002, distinguishes these 3 little-understood and overlapping personality types

else's,[18] and sometimes at their expense too. Tom Paine put his finger on it when he said: "land ownership separated the majority of people from their rightful, natural inheritance and means of independent survival."[19]

In fact, land that didn't involve the personal labour of those that claimed it, seemed to have given more egocentrically minded individuals the illusory power to make others use their labour to cultivate their land to enhance their power even further, which might have been how all 'civic societies' began to reinforce their power of influence. It has been suggested that: "The first type of behaviour to be dubbed 'deviant', in some non-human primate species, could have been alpha-male type behaviour",[20] but when this became ownership of land in humans it must at first have amounted to little more than fleeting incidents of physical encounter before returning to peace and stability.

The reason why women subsequently began to be treated more like 'second-class citizens', from the beginning of the Neolithic era onwards, was perhaps when control by physical strength because more threatening, which is indicative of psychopathy and more commonly a male personality disorder.[21] Be that as it may, since then we have become almost hard-wired to believe that the degree of power and control people exercise over each other is the principle criterion by which we should respect them, but only because our own survival depends on it.

---

[18] Taylor, S: *The Fall*, 2005, claims about 4,200 BCE, 108, and quotes Eisler, R: *The Chalice and the Blade*, 1987, which claimed it was "a change so great, indeed, that nothing in all we know of human cultural evolution is comparable in magnitude".

[19] Paine, T: *Agrarian Justice, opposed to Agrarian Law, and to Agrarian Monopoly*, 1795

[20] Boehm, C: *Egalitarian behaviour and the evolution of political intelligence*, 1997

[21] Baefield, O: *Saving the Appearances*, 1957, 43; Lilenfeld, O: *What 'Psychopath' Means*: Scientific American, 2007; Norris, C: *Psychopathy and Gender ...*, 2011.

This era marked the emergence of an endless struggle for ownership, power and control over not only each other but of whole societies and nation states, along with the land and resources contained therein, often with little regard for the indigenous peoples who had lived on it since time immemorial, The Americas, Australia and New Zealand during colonialism being among the most blatant examples.

These days we tend to accept the concept of 'authority' without question because it has been an essential feature of society for so long, yet rarely, if ever, do we question whether it had any validity in the first place. Could its initial belief by a few mutant egos, have been enough to tip the long-held balance between egoism and altruism into a worldwide pandemic in favour of egoism? The irony about all this is though that 'authority', which is defined as 'the right to control the actions of others', could originally only have been surrendered in servitude from fear of punishment. The natural feelings for the wisdom of experience with age was what communities once called leadership, after which it became transposed into authority by physical strength or posturing, reinforced by the illusion of ownership and the power to control anyone who owned less or nothing at all. And for the person who owned most of all, it became transposed even further into 'the divine right of kings'. In our more recent history however, authority has 'grown out of the barrel of a gun'. [Mao Zedong]

Hierarchy

The degree of power and control therefore, became the principle criteria by which societies began ranking themselves hierarchically all over the world. The authoritative effect of being in hierarchical control however creates the subservient effect of being controlled. This contrived way of polarising people at all levels within societies may have had its distant origins in the concept of a divine creator, followed by the formation of many religious beliefs; Judo-Christian folklore perhaps having eventually become the most influential. It contained implications of reward and admiration for obedience to its divine laws, coupled with those of sin and suffering for disobeying them. These are reflected in some of the Old Testament manuscripts and more overtly in those of the New Testament. Evidence can be seen in quotations, such as: 'Every perfect gift is from above' [James 1:17]; 'Father, into thy hands I commend my spirit' [John 391:15]; 'Happy is the man who fears the Lord, who is only too willing to follow his orders' [Psalm 112:1]; 'Blessed are those who obey the word of God' [Luke 11:28]; 'God, be merciful to me a sinner' [Luke, 13]; and 'Blessed are the meek; for they shall inherit the earth' [Mathew, 5:3]; and so on.

Commitment to these ideas suggested entering into a kind of contractual master-slave relationship that involved authorisation and control on the part of the master and sublimation and acceptance of control on the part of the slave. Although they appear to have originated in the Middle East, they began to spread, at first by zealous evangelists throughout Europe, for example: 'Go ye out into the highways and hedges, and compel them to come in' [Luke, 23], and 'Go ye into the world and preach the gospel to every creature' [Luke 16:15]. Then in the fifteenth century, this master-slave relationship became more secular, as Spanish, Portuguese, English, French and Dutch colonialism began to spread throughout the World.

The power of ownership, particularly of land therefore, became the established way of enforcing control and social ranking, not only within societies and nation states but between them too. It amplified differences and evoked feelings of hubris, hypocrisy and posturing on the part of the 'masters' or controllers of society, coupled with feelings of shame, envy and guilt on the part of the 'slaves' or those they controlled. Attributions, such as 'Your

Highness, Majesty, Honour or Worship', 'Reverend', 'Very Reverend', 'Right Honourable' and so on, were given to 'masters' and are still used today, while the most derisory attributes to the nameless were and still are heaped on the 'slaves'. Hierarchy became such a powerful way of separating people from each other that it is now believe about 1% of the world's population own more than the remaining 99%. [Oxfam]

In fact, there's much anecdotal evidence that greed, dominance; bullying, victimisation, exploitation, serfdom and slavery were, and still are necessary by-products of hierarchical imbalance.[22] The level of respect people now have for each other depends primarily upon how successful they are in attaining this power of control, so kindness, compassion, care, compatibility and empathy, which at one time were the anly criteria, have little to do with it any more and capitalism reigns supreme.

Under capitalism though, one person's gain implies another person's loss, so "there are two kinds of slaves: the prisoners of addiction and the prisoners of envy" [Ivan Illich]. When an enterprise makes a profit, it's thought to be a 'good thing' by today's standards, but perhaps we should ask ourselves: good for whom? If it's 'good' for its owners, it's bad for its customers because they've paid too much for the products or services it offers them. On the other hand, had we not been thus conditioned over the millennia, it would have been 'good' to charge just enough to break-even and maintain equality and balance between owners and customers all round. Even the economist, John Maynard Keynes, must have been embarrassed by the more cryptic implications of capitalism when he said:

The opportunities for moneymaking ... may find

---

[22] Hoel, H et al: *The experience of bullying in Great* Britain, 2001; Stanghellini, G: *Disembodied Spirits and Deanimated Bodies*, 2004: Sass, L: *Schizophrenia and Modernism*, 2001; Price, J et al: *The Social Competition Hypothesis of depression.* 1994

their outlet in cruelty, the reckless pursuit of personal power and authority, and other forms of self-aggrandisement [but] it is better that a man should tyrannize over his bank balance than over his fellow citizens; and while the former is sometimes denounced as a means to the latter, sometimes at least it is an alternative.[23]

Given this system and the way it's promoted[24] is now so ubiquitous, practically all of us are obliged to participate in some direct, or indirect form of 'profit-making' in order to survive under hierarchical authority. Since the beginning of the Neolithic era, it became so well established that we overlook, deny or just refuse to accept the fact that at one time people survive compatibly without it. Now "shame and its opposite, pride, are rooted in the processes through which we internalise how we imagine others see us",[25] not how we once saw one another intuitively in a non-judgmental way. Sensually recognising our differences is not the same as conceptually ranking them hierarchically.
At one time, it was enough to just feel 'credit where credit was due'; now our egos have to act out their fantasies in a more consciously contrived attempt to gain 'credit, even where credit's not due'. As the 13th century Persian mystic, Rumi must have realised: "The one who is ruled by the mind without sleeping, puts his senses to sleep."[26]
Legitimising reward for being able to influence and control others, as measured by material gain of power, is bound to confuse our natural sense of self-worth because it "entails placing a high value on acquiring money and possessions, looking good in the eyes of others and

---

[23] Keynes, J. M: *General Theory of Employment, Interest and Money*, 1936

[24] Packard, V: *The Hidden Persuaders*, 1957; Pratkanis, A & Aronson, E: *Age of Propaganda. The Everyday use and abuse of Persuasion*, 2004 and many more publications exposing the manipulating power of advertising.

[25] Hyland, T: *Mindfulness and Learning*, 2011, 41.

[26] Helminski, C: *Introduction to Rumi: Daylight*, 2011

wanting to be famous."[27] 'Oh what a tangled web we weave, when first we practice to deceive' [Walter Scott], and deceive not just each other but ourselves too. Since the growth of the ego's claim to authority and hierarchical ranking, it appears to have perverted the way we instinctively feel, with its claims to truth based on reason and objectivity. This alone might have been what initiated the worldwide aspiration for gaining what Montaigne once described as "the most universal of all the follies of the world", namely the "need for reputation and glory".[28]

Putting ourselves first has become our most basic requirement and for psychopaths who are incapable of recognising the needs of others, it's their only need. Amongst the most conspicuous psychopaths throughout history, the twentieth century alone gave us Hitler, who from 1939-45 might have caused as many as 20 million deaths, Stalin, who from 1924-53 ordered the execution of possibly twice as many people, and Mao Zedong, whose 'Great Leap Forward' from 1958-62, could have caused the deaths of as many as 45 million, each in their unstoppable need for 'reputation and glory'. As Stanley Milgrim put it, "these inhumane acts may have originated in the minds of a single person, but they could only have been carried out on such a massive scale if a very large number of persons obeyed [their] orders".[29] And this horrifying show, often in the name of nationalism, politics, economics or religious idealism, continues unabated before our very eyes, often without recognising it. Unless this insatiable need to put one's ego first is recognised and severely restrained before it gains too much power, how many more mass murders will the twenty-first century bring? Perhaps freely elected democratic governments might release us from the manacles of hierarchical control.

---

[27] James, O: *Affluenza*, 2007, vii & 49-112

[28] Montaigne, M de: *Essays*, 1580 Book 1, Ch 41 & Nietzsche's *Beyond Good and Evil*, 1886, para 269.

[29] Milgrim, S: Introduction to his Obedience experiment, 1963

Democracy

Those more extreme forms of hierarchical control, such as autocracy, oligarchy, dictatorship, despotism and totalitarianism have all been tried and tested, but they've all failed. Many monarchies have had equally chequered histories. Democracy however, which has been described as 'a type of political system within which all members have an equal share of power', is generally thought to be a more acceptable form of government but an 'equal share of power' is rarely, if ever, achieved within any form of democracy. It offers a 'share of power' to its citizens to vote but after voting, much of their share immediately becomes transferred to those they voted for.

'Primitive democracy', in which regular consultations with town or city leaders was known to have existed in parts of Babylonia and Mesopotamia as early as 3,000 BC, but the Athenian society around the fifth century BC was where democracy, at least in name, was first thought to have begun. At that time however, out of a city-population of about 250,000, only about 40,000 men were given the vote. This excluded about 30,000 slaves, and the entire female population of Athens. Plato claimed it 'dispensed a sort of equality to equals and unequaled alike' but, by today's standards, this would hardly have been described in the least democratic.

After that, democracy remained fairly dormant for about 2,000 years but is now usually thought to be the fairest form of government, even though it still has its critics. For example, "many empirical studies reveal electoral democracy has no necessary implications for the establishment of legitimacy".[30] Even the most democratically elected governments are never quite as

---

[30] Rothstein, B: *Creating Political Legitimacy* ..., ABS 2009, v 53, No.3. Abstract.

accountable to their citizens as their citizens are to them. They make promises that aren't always fulfilled and are never quite as open, transparent and answerable to their citizens as their citizens are expected to be to them. They also inhibit freedom of speech if it's seen as too threatening, and control is always more top down than bottom up. It has been said, for example, that: "measures are too often decided according to ...the superior force of an interested and overbearing majority",[31] and elections have always "had the obvious disadvantage of merely counting votes rather than weighing them".[32]

In fact, there never was going to be any satisfactory way of representing individual's interests by means of generalised policies.[33] No society could be strait-jacketed thus, without causing frustration, distrust, confusion, and sometimes, in the end even complete breakdown and revolution. After all, a democratic vote is an unwitting acceptance that hierarchical, centralised control is preferable to personal, decentralised control, along with the assumption that, whomsoever the majority elect know better how to manage their voters' behaviour than the voters do themselves. "Government, even in its best state, is but a necessary evil; in its worst, an intolerable one."[34] It is only now being internationally conceded that a top-down government cannot function effectively without at least some form of bottom-up contribution.[35] It has even been said that: "The health of a democracy may be

---

[31] Williams, W: *What's wrong with Democracy*, 2015, quotes Madison, J: Federal Paper No. 10.

[32] Inge, W: *Possible Recovery?* 1941

[33] Arrow, K: *Social Choice and Individual* Value, 1951, showed that there was no consistent way of maintaining social equilibrium in representing individual preferential choices by collective ones.

[34] Paine, T: *Common Sense*, 1776, Ch.1.

[35] 'Open Government Partnership', to which 65 countries now subscribe, is aimed at making governments more open, accountable and responsible to their citizens, along with work of the Equality Trust which aims at less inequality in pay.

measured by the quality of functions performed by private citizens." [Alexis de Tocqueville] In any event, all consciously conceived-of ideas about how a democratic government should act, are bound to favour those who are given the power to do so because their status demands it of them.

When Margaret Thatcher was democratically elected to government in 1979, she quoted St. Francis of Assisi: "Where there is discord may we bring harmony" and "where there is error, may we bring truth". But once in office, her "no, no, no" attitude and "the lady's not for turning" were not going to "bring harmony" and her increasingly autocratic style, typified by statements such as "I don't mind how much my ministers talk, so long as they do what I say", was unlikely to "bring truth" either. Then in 1997, when Tony Blair was also democratically elected, he may have appeared to be less autocratic, with statements such as: "I'm essentially a public service person", yet in 2003 when he ignored the largest protest against war in human history, comprising perhaps 10 million people in 60 countries around the World, he authorised UK military bombing of Iraq. It was claimed to be a legitimate response to Iraq's much publicised: "weapons of mass destruction", even though the advice of the chief UN weapons inspector was that these weapons were fictitious,[36] and who had these 'weapons of mass destruction' anyway?

The argument, that people are happy to comply with the law under a democratic government because they freely accepted a majority vote, is rather like saying they're happy to leave it to the majority to choose a 'big brother' to watch over them because they're incapable of doing so themselves. It boils down to surrendering personal

---

[36] In 2011, a five panel War Crimes Tribunal unanimously decided the former democratically elected US and British leaders' committed crimes against peace and humanity and violated international law when they ordered the invasion of Iraq in 2003.

John Faupel

responsibility to blind obedience. They may be right
because there now appears to be no alternative, but at one
time everyone accepted responsibility for their own
behaviour by monitoring it instinctively, according to how
other's reacted to it, and it worked well enough for
millennia without any form of government. Perhaps the
establishment of an independent judiciary-system, with
courts of law to which everyone is allowed free access,
might help to give democracy the validity it needs?

Justice

Justice has been described as 'the quality of being fair
and reasonable', together with 'the administration of the
law in maintaining this quality'.

The statue of 'Justice' on the dome of the Old Bailey in
London shows a balance scale representing 'equality' in
one hand and a sword for 'retribution' in the other. Yet, by
far the majority of those convicted in such courts of law
are from lower classes, poor and with little education, so,
unless they freely and deliberately chose to be lower
classes, poor and with little education in the first place,
retribution could hardly be described as 'fair and
reasonable'.[37] Not long ago abortion and homosexuality
were subject to retributive justice, and before that, the idea
of 'votes for women' and 'the abolition of the slave trade'
were regarded as almost unthinkable, so isn't our attitude
to 'retributive justice' just a matter of public opinion?
Statute law appears to be valid until such time as case law
considers it invalid.

Perhaps because the concept of 'justice' has been
associated with that of 'retribution' for so long, most
people have become conditioned, or even hard-wired to
believe the latter should necessarily follow automatically

[37] Reiman, J & Leighton, P: *The Rich Get Richer and the Poor Get Prison*,
2015, shows the American retributive justice is aimed at the working
class and does not reduce crime but maintains or even increases it.

from the former. And even though it's claimed no pleasure should follow from administering retribution for unacceptable behaviour, feelings of *schadenfreude*, i.e. 'pleasure or enjoyment in seeing someone suffer', is now commonplace. It only goes to show how frequently revenge now seems to overrule those long forgotten feelings of empathy and understanding of each other's faults and failings.

We like to believe 'justice' is a rational and objective process but everyone, even the legal profession, is biased in one way or another. Although it is commonly felt that 'the punishment should fit the crime', its severity has also been found to relate to differences in social status between offenders and victims. For example, "an upward killing of a social superior attracts more social control than a lateral or downward killing".[38] And even when trial-by-jury is employed to minimise personal bias,[39] either the 'lowest common denominator' or the influence of one or two over-opinionated jurors can determine the outcome. That 1954 play, by Reginald Rose, called the: 'Twelve Angry Men', was all about the deliberations of a jury in a homicide trial. It begins with an 11 to 1 majority verdict of guilty, but feelings of doubt in the mind of the 1 member of the jury, eventually convinces the other 11 of the defendant's innocence. However, another jury with an 11 to 1 majority verdict of innocence, might be reversed by feelings of doubt about the defenders innocence in the mind of the 1 member, might convince the other 11 of his guilt.

Punishment is supposed to act as a deterrent, but levels of recidivism often show how ineffective this can be. It has even been claimed, for example, that: "the most

---

[38] Black, D: *On the Origin of Mortality*, The Evolutionary Origins of Morality, Ed. Katz, L, 2000, 113

[39] Saini, A et al *Rough Justice*, Chance, New Scientist, 2015, 112-129, describes how an ignorance of Bayesian and 'frequentist' statistics can pervert judgment.

effective way of turning a non-violent person into a violent one is to send him to prison",[40] to say nothing of the emotional damage it might cause. In fact, those more punitive systems of justice around the world, such as operate in the USA or UK, correlate with re-offending rates of 60-65%, compared with less punitive systems in Sweden or Japan with re-offending rates of 35-40%.

Long before morality became defined in law, and administered by punitive methods of control, 'restorative justice' was widespread. It was aimed at re-establishing balance and equality within the community, and usually involved trying to help or make good the loss or damage done to injured parties, rather than punish the offenders. Where possible, both victims and offenders were encouraged to come to terms with their differences in order that they might gain more understanding of the experience and compassion for each other from the experience. Retributive justice is primarily concerned with upholding the existing law of the state and maintaining the authority of those who administered it, whereas long before state control,[41] restorative justice was all about sorting out differences between people[42] and was the common practice everywhere.

From the Neolithic era onwards, the emergence of conceived-of aphorisms, such 'I am the way, the truth and the life', helped those who promoted it to establish a so-called justice system that represented how they themselves saw 'the way, the truth and the light' not anyone else. Nevertheless, any such claim could only be validated, if the roles of those who promoted it and those they promoted it

---

[40] Garbarino, J: *Spare the Rod,* 2010, 80

[41] Service, E: *Primitive Social Organisations,* 1962 & Fried, M: *The Evolution of Political Society,* 167

[42] Hinrichs, K: *Follower Propensity* ..., 2007: followers are influenced by a leader to engage in behaviour that they would otherwise consider unethical. Johnstone, G & Van Ness, D: *Handbook of Restorative Justice,* 2007, 55

to, could be freely reversed, in the absence of any change of interpretation.

Obviously, no two people can have the same feelings and thoughts as each other all the time, so an on-going, two-way attempt to adjust and readjust to each other's behavioural practices, based on feelings of empathy, rather than on bigoted beliefs universal truths, is the only long-term solution. Ideas like that however, are beyond the comprehension of narcissists and psychopaths who can only see communication as one-way, in favour of themselves. By insisting on the universal validity of such superficially appealing aphorisms and even punishing those who think otherwise, are simply manifestations of their egos protecting themselves form threat from other egos. In times of war, for example, when both sides believe they are justified in fighting for the 'truth', their motives become self-contradictory and the after-effects of war, rarely if ever, show they had anything to do with being 'fair and reasonable'.

As Tom Paine said: "All national institutions of churches, whether of Jewish, Christian or Turkish, ... appeared to be no other than human inventions, set up to terrify and enslave mankind, and monopolise power and profit."[43] All centralised controllers are there, primarily to protect their own egocentric understanding of the word 'justice' and, if threatened by rival controllers, compel their acolytes to defend it to the death, even though their clarion call is usually 'forward men, I'm behind you'. Alas though, no war determines who is right, only who is left, bathed usually in the blood of their enemy.

The enforcement of any centralised system of justice, isn't justice; it's the absence of any understanding of the different, and ever-changing ways people feel and think and act towards one another. Personal choice is supposed to form "the very cornerstone of our legal system and all

---

[43] Paine, T: *The Age of Reason*, 1794, First Part.

our conceptions of guilt are tightly linked to the notion that the guilty person did it on purpose from free-will".[44] Yet:

> We reward people for doing good deeds and punish them for bad ones. This would seem to be completely misconceived if humans did indeed not have any free will. How can you punish someone for doing something when they are not free to do otherwise? Is our whole moral and judicial system based on an illusion? This just cannot be the case, or at least it is impossible to live with. Can nothing good that I do be attributed to me? Is it all pre-determined by my genes or my history or my parents or social order or the rest of the universe? It seems that we have no choice but to believe in free will[45] ... or at least, not under the present system of retributive justice that is premised upon it.

To attribute behaviour to the 'self', rather than to what makes the 'self' is a fundamental misappropriation of agency. People who commit antisocial acts need help, not punishment because the damage has already been done. 'Retribution' is not 'justice', it's 'injustice'; the whole administration system of justice is what needs help in understanding the human condition.

"By abandoning the free willing self, we're forced to re-examine the factors that are truly behind our thoughts and behaviour and the way they interact, balance, override, and cancel out. Only then will we begin to make progress in understanding how we really operate."[46] And likewise, 'only then will we begin to make progress in understanding' how we have become conditioned, or even

---

[44] Frank, L: *Mindfield: how brain science is changing our world*, 2007, 297

[45] Vedral, V: *Who's in charge here*, Chance, 2015, 140.

[46] Hood, B: *The Self*, This Idea must Die, Ed. J. Brockman, 2015, 147-8.

hard-wired', or simply just deluded into believing we had freely chosen to accept being controlled by a hierarchical system of so-called justice, originally imposed by fear of threat from authority. Nietzsche saw straight through the delusion in claiming 'fear was the mother of morality', upon which justice is supposed to be based.

Morality

The concept of 'morality' is generally understood to mean something like: 'principles concerning the distinction between right and wrong, or between good and bad behaviour'. Unfortunately though, there's no consensus of agreement as to what these 'principles' are. Their distant origins must surely have been premised on trying to establish some kind of equality and balance between people socially and correct any inequalities between them when they occurred. Of course, we all have different attributes, abilities and experiences, and behave in different ways towards each other all the time, so constructing law-like rules of morality by which to judge these differences, is self defeating. "Hunter-gatherers rarely, if ever, handle conflict in a law-like and penal fashion and the society as a whole rarely, if ever, is the agent of social control. Individuals typically handle their own conflicts, and avoidance is more common than punishment."[47]

If 'law is reason, free from passion', as Aristotle thought, he must have assumed this sense of reason upon which he assumed law was supposed to be based, should be independent of our 'passions'. Although we may consciously think we need reason to try and determine the differences between right and wrong, as a guide to controlling our behaviour, it was our feelings or passions that established equality and balance between people

---

[47] Black, D: *On the Origin of Morality*, Evolutionary Origins of Morality, Katz ed., 2000, 105-6.

John Faupel

before determining their differences needed to be determined. In order to understand how the concept of 'morality' and law-like rules of conduct arose, it has been suggested we first need to ask ourselves "whether there were any specific emotions that led to the formation of the concepts of right or wrong, good or bad".[48] But right and wrong meant different things to different people, and to different cultures and societies, which is probably why we have, throughout history, wasted so much time, and spilt so much blood in trying to make them the same for everyone.

If the purpose of morality was to avoid conflict and thereby establish a reasonable level of cohesion and balance between individuals, then the evolution of our passions for each other had already provided us with the answer, long before reason began trying to make sense of them, as:

> Many non-human primates, for example, have similar methods to humans for resolving, managing, and preventing conflicts of interests within their group. Such methods, which include reciprocity and food sharing, reconciliation, consolation, conflict intervention and mediation, are the very building blocks of moral systems in that they are based on and facilitate cohesion among individuals and reflect a concerted effort by community members to find shared solutions to social conflict.[49]

All these methods, which became the principal determinants for resolving differences and maintaining acceptable levels of social behaviour, must have evolved naturally and been maintained by trial-and-error, without

---

[48] Westermarck, E: *Ethical Reality*, 1932, 62
[49] Flack, J & de Waal, F: *Any Animal Whatever*, 2000

any reference to reason. And, just like biological evolution, they gradually established themselves as necessary control-mechanisms for living in harmony and balance with one another. As a social species, we were, and to some extent still are fundamentally gregarious by nature, so evolution had instinctively made us want to share these feelings for each other in order to live comfortably together.

Without conscious thought, this process occurs in a non-judgmental and non-evaluative way and simply evokes feelings of positive or negative reinforcement. Our inter-personal relationships use to be regulated in this way before societies became controlled by the imposition of rules and regulations. All reasoning involved in establishing moral principles to which we complied for fear of retribution, had little to do with being virtuous. Nietzsche realised this when he said: "we had only to follow feelings rather than reason to be virtuous".[50] He called this "pre-moral period of mankind, the imperative",[51] so this self-correcting control mechanism must have been the original way in which our ancestors lived together and maintaind a consistent level of balance and equality within their communities.[52] 'Reciprocity', 'sharing', whether of food or of anything else, 'reconciliation', 'consolation', 'conflict intervention', 'mediation', 'cohesion', and another, not mentioned here by Flack & de Waal, 'avoidance',[53] were instinctive ways of maintaining this need to live and survive in balance together as a gregarious species. It was based on an intuitive sense of trust and understanding of each other's feelings and needs, and an ability to respond to them empathically. Any suggestion that this necessitated law-like rules of conduct is ill-conceived and developed later with language and conscious thought, when trust gave

---

[50] Rousseau, J: *Emile*, 1762, The Fourth Book.

[51] Nietzsche, F: *Beyond Good and Evil*, 1886, para. 32.

[52] Boehm, C: *Egalitarian society and reverse dominance hierarchy*, Current Anthropology, 34, 227.54, 1993

[53] Baumgartner, M: *The Moral Order of Suburb*, 1988, Ch. 3.

way to suspicion and distrust. Even now, "anthropological observations of hunter-gatherers across the world reveal that, typically, they have no explicit conception of law-like rules of conduct."[54]

Perhaps, about 150,000 years ago people began to translate there feelings into thoughts followed much later by written instructions that took the form of 'thou shalt ...' or 'thou shalt not ...'. It was perhaps the earliest conceptually-conscious attempt to highjack the empathic way communities instinctively ran themselves, sparked by the rise of a mutant ego that was incapable of experiencing empathy for anyone but itself, so could only conceive of reason for doing so. Far from clarifying morality, by trying to standardise people's behaviour though, it has only polarised it into what Nietzsche called, a 'master morality' that claimed it was 'good' because it gave the orders, and a 'slave morality' that was only conditionally 'good' if it obeyed them, but always unconditionally 'bad' if it didn't.[55] The 'master morality' exercised a parasitic control over the 'slave morality' by feeding off its subservience. Nietzsche called it "the moral hypocrisy of the commanding class. They know no other way of protecting themselves."[56] By their nature they always discriminated in favour of themselves as representatives of the truth, at the expense of the slave morality that punished itself for its ignorance of the truth. Nietzsche suggested that: "To recognize untruth as a condition of life is certainly to impinge upon the traditional ideas of value in a dangerous manner; and a philosophy which ventures to do so, has thereby alone placed itself beyond good and evil."[57]

After the last few thousand years of what the rational mind conceives of as *a priori* 'building blocks of morality', they still derive [or perhaps 'contrive' would be a better

[54] Black, D: *Sociological Justice*, 1989, 92-3.
[55] Nietzsche, F: *On the Genealogy of Morality*, 1886
[56] Nietzsche, F: *Beyond Good and Evil*, 1886, para. 199
[57] Ibid., para. 1

word] from our sensually-conscious, *a posteriori* experiences of trying to live in balance with one another by means of those self-correcting control mechanisms, identified by Flack & de Waal, i.e. 'reciprocity', 'reconciliation', 'conflict intervention', 'mediation' and 'cohesion'.

Morally 'right' or 'good' people have no need of 'laws concerning the distinction between right and wrong', their sense of empathy for their fellow human beings is all that is required and it's what had been handed down, from mothers to their infants unconditionally through the generations by instinct and example alone. So it is suggested that the increasing need to superimpose inflexible laws upon this natural evolutionary process has not made us more moral but simply overruled empathy at the expense of 'principles concerning the distinction between right and wrong, or between good and bad behaviour' based on reason.

Decision-making

In all so-called decision-making, we tend to assume there is a direct relationship between the person who we think of as 'the cause', and the action that the person performs as 'the effect' of that 'cause' but, by directly linking the two, we overlook the fact that the person's genetic make-up and the sum-total of their life experiences are all that is required to 'cause' the person's actions. There simply isn't anything else that 'causes' this, so-called decision-making process to produce what we call the 'effect', unless, that is, it is a random process but then, by definition, this excludes 'cause' too. We like to think our conceptually-conscious minds can solve problems rationally and determine the future we want, but both the 'infinite regress' that defines our past, and the 'infinite progress' that defines our future, can hardly be handled rationally by a conceptually-conscious mind in the 'now' that produces the action required, or at least it can be given very little credence, because the data involved is far too complex to model by reason and logic alone.

Lateral thinking helps to destroy the myth that "when we think of free will we imagine that 'I' have it, not that this whole conglomeration of body and brain has it ... all human actions, whether conscious or not, come from complex interactions between memes and genes and all their products, in complicated environments."[58] The realization of this would cast a very different light upon, not only our understanding of consciousness but upon how we have changed in our relationship with one another and the nature of ourselves within in the World. In reality, we comprise colonies of molecules and microbes that, from the moment of conception onwards live in us and on us, as they send electro-chemical signals back and forth to each other, in their on-going attempt to function in balance with one another. They do this to keep both them and us alive: breathing air, digesting food, controlling our temperature, blood-flow, heart-rate, fighting off infection, and so on, for as long as possible. We are the amalgam of all these things as they try, not only to coordinate with each other internally, but with our ever changing environmental experiences externally too.

We're a coordinated miracle of molecular and microbial evolutionary processing that tries to keep us healthy and alive but only occasionally do we become consciously aware of a tiny part of all this activity going on throughout our lives. We sometimes reflect on situations before responding to them but isn't it our heredity and environmental experiences that made us reflect on them? D. H. Lawrence would have replied it is: 'not I, not I but the wind that blows through me ... as it takes its course through the chaos of the world'. It is suggested, that our experiences are imprinted into our memories in terms of their positive or negative conditioning of our future

---

[58] Blackmore, S: *The Meme Machine*, 2000, 237

actions, and appear to be inherent in all life-forms, so might be analogous to what has been described as 'morphic resonance'.[59]

Our egos however, are unable to sensually recognise this tangled web of internal and external activity continuously going on all around, and within us; so try emotionally, to treat it rationally in a conceptually-conscious way. "Some scientists might describe the idea of a biochemical basis for the emotions as outrageous ... Neuropeptides and their receptors thus join the brain, glands, and immune system in a network of communication between brain and body, probably representing the biochemical substrate of emotion."[60]

Thinking about all this biochemical activity rationally is premised on judgment and evaluation, so it makes our ego's conception of these experiences emotionally sterile. We may be capable of rationally describing the biochemical processes involved in empathy and love-making for example, but trying to understand these things by reason and logic doesn't recreate the experience of being in love. As Robert Browning expressed it, 'love is more than tongue can speak' and, because what we speak tends to represent what we think, it neutralises the experience. Nietzsche insisted "we really ought to free ourselves from the misleading significance of words", because: "every word is a mask". And, by going even further with the "constant counterfeiting of the world by means of numbers",[61] science constructs an ever more objectively sterile world isolated from the experiences involved in living emotionally and expects us to conform to it own model of them.

The right hemisphere of the human brain experiences an *a posteriori* world directly through its senses and simply

---

[59] Sheldrake, R: *The Presence of the Past: Morphic Resonance ...*, 2011

[60] Pert, C: *Molecules of Emotion*, 1997, Ch. 7-9. Ekman, P: *The Nature of Emotion*, 1994.

[61] Nietzsche, F: *Beyond Good and Evil*, para 4.

goes with the flow in 'the now', in a fundamentally indeterminate way, 'as it takes its course through the chaos of the world'. Its reality however, is entirely non-judgmental, so pre-empts meaning in any conceptually-conscious sense of the word. On the other hand, the left hemisphere can only experience its conception of the world indirectly through reason and logic, on the assumption that by so doing, it can understand and evaluate it by reference to its own consciously constructed *a priori* laws of nature, in order to plan its future. To do this though, "one has to stand back in order to see patterns at all; there is 'necessary distance' for such pattern recognition to work",[62] and this 'standing back' from reality occurs when the left hemisphere becomes introspectively possessive of its own neurological processing. It thinks it understands reality but it only understands the description it has constructed of it from the *a priori* laws it uses to do so. Alas though, the reality it tries to describe is beyond understanding. The right hemisphere does not recognise, nor even need, any of these *a priori* laws of nature, because its processing is premised on the 'null hypothesis' that nature has no meaning, so it simply responds intuitively to its changes. The left hemisphere is premised on the assumption that nature having a meaning, so constructs its own laws to define it and expects the right hemisphere to comply with them.

Although the different ways these two hemispheres of the human brain process data are fundamentally incompatible, they continuously attempt to communicate with one another via the corpus callosum. Whichever hemisphere is triggered first by 'excitatory' chemicals will appear more dominant at the time,[63] so tries to activate the other hemisphere, but is prevented from doing so by the 'inhibitory' chemicals it triggers in response, which testifies

---

[62] McGilchrist, I: *The Master and His Emissary*, 2010 edn. 242

[63] Lisette, J et al: *How does the corpus collosum communicate ...?* Behavioural Brain Research, v223, 211-21, 223

to their incompatibility.[64]

If, for example, we are sitting in a deckchair, intoxicated with the sounds and smells of summer on a lazy Sunday afternoon and are simply going with the flow in a 'default mode' state of sensual-consciousness, we'll automatically inhibit any conceptually-conscious thoughts about manicuring the garden. On the other hand, if we start thinking about how neat and tidy and ordered we could make it, we'll put duty before pleasure, roll up our sleeves, start mowing the lawn and trying to make the flowers behave as we think they should behave.

Reality is either fundamentally indeterminate, in which case it has no meaning, other than the one we ourselves construct of it in our minds. On the other hand, if it is determinate it does have meaning, in which case all our sensually conscious experiences of it are moonshine.[65] More rationally biased people tend to deny their emotions, while more emotionally biased people tend to deny reason, and most of us flit from one form of processing to the other, but never at exactly the same time, so there's no middle ground. No wonder these two mutually exclusive ways of trying to process reality have caused such problems, and schizophrenia, which literally means 'split-mind', might be a major cause.

Irrespective of whether or not we try to conform to conceived-of laws that appear to represent reality, our so-called decisions have a sensual origin and are more like intuitions of an iterative or recursive nature, on the grounds that we could never know, with any degree of certainty, how they were induced, nor even what their outcomes might be. If they are intuitions however, they are

---

[64] Harris-Love, M et al: *Interhemispheric Inhibition* .. J. Physiol. V97, 3, 2007; Putman, C et al: *Structural Organisation of the Corpus Callosum* ... , Journal of Neuorscience, 28 (11) 2912-9, 2008

[65] Feldman Barrett, L et al: *The Experience of Emotion*, 2005 summaries numerous studies in search of an answer, but emotion is a 'first person' experience and no amount of research recreates the experience.

not entirely arbitrary because, at any single point in time, there are infinities within infinites of alternative ways of processing them, ranging from probabilities within narrow parameters of variance, or near complete certainty, to others with widely dispersed parameters of variance, or near complete un-certainty.[66] Even highly probabilistic levels of correlation between just two variables are never entirely reliable, because 'correlation' does not mean 'causation'. And quite apart from unpredictable 'tipping-points' upsetting the whole 'causal chain' model of reality, the way we process data in our own minds at a quantum level doesn't conform to any consciously-constructed law of classical physics at an aggregated level.

If we could see what was really going on at that highly magnified scale during these so-called decision-making moments, we would almost certainly not understand them as the 'uncertainty principle' undermines, not only determinism and the 'cause-and-effect' model of decision-making, but incidentally, also the burdensome attribution of credit or blame to ourselves for our actions to which we have become so deeply committed. But, if we are ignorant of the way our minds process data, there's no reason why we should attribute credit or blame to our ignorance of the way it does so.

It has been suggested that, at the synaptic level, the decision-making process operates more like fractal networking,[67] and because fractals are generated iteratively by chance, our decision-making might be loosely described as guesswork. It dismisses the need for that illusory 'ghost in the machine'[68] that still haunts our long-held conviction that we are in charge of our decision-making. Until such time as it can be proved otherwise, accepting the null hypothesis that reality and all our attempts to process it are

[66] Prigogine, I & Stengers, I: *Order out of Chaos*, 1986, 291.

[67] Dryden, R: *Modelling Process in Fractal Networks: a Possible Substrata for Consciousness*, 1996

[68] Ryle, G: *The Concept of Mind*, 1947.

fundamentally indeterminate and therefore unknowable, might be a safer route to our long-term survival. By dismissing the null hypothesis, the more solipsistic, rational mind's attempt to understand reality is premised on the assumption that it can progress towards the future it wants, even though our more empathic, emotional mind might not like the future it gets when it is has to experiences it.

Progress

Studies of the few remaining indigenous communities, whose lifestyles have been largely unaffected by modernism, shows how intimately they are bound up with their natural environment and each other. Evolution had fine-tuned them to remain in sensual harmony and balance with these experiences and, with the exception of natural disasters their way of life has remained stable and largely unaltered for millennia. The concept of 'progress' would be almost inconceivable to them. With the increasing recognition of 'the self' however, and attempts to translate feelings into words and words into thoughts, that long-held balance between egoism and altruism has changed in favour of the ego's need to progress.

The exchange of goods and services between people, based literally on face-to-face value,[69] was originally for the benefit of the community, but the acquisition of land and chattels that had to be protected against theft was for the benefit of those who claimed its for themselves. This eventually led to the belief that whomsoever owned more than others had a right to control them, and ultimately, to a belief in the 'divine right of kings' to control everyone. It necessitated a change of focus: from 'trust' to 'distrust', from 'intuition' to 'imposition', and from 'cooperation' to 'competition'. It has been said the rational mind has made

---

[69] Graeber, D: *Towards an anthropological Theory of Value* ..., 2001

us the most dangerous of all species, because it has given our egos the power to overcome natural evolution and, thereby become the profit-masters of our own salvation. "Over time the idea of rationality and individualism changed the entire belief system of Western intellectual society, and today it's doing the same to the belief systems of other cultures... Rationality, as economists use the term, means that the individual knows what he or she wants and acts to get it".[70] We call it progress.

After the Dark Ages, the Renaissance movement in Europe began to re-define men's relationship with nature and the fables of a Golden Age, by translating them into what they believed to be a more accurate picture of reality, as expressed in art, architecture and science. The European Enlightenment that followed from it went even further, by claiming reason alone would allow the whole of humanity to 'progress to perfection'. Its doctrine: that 'beliefs should only be accepted if they were based on reason', seemed to have overlooked the fact that reason was based on *a priori* knowledge, which inevitably had its origin in *a posteriori* experience about the elixir of life, thus invalidating the doctrine.

Other, so-called 'enlightenment' ideas, such as: 'everyone should be treated as equal before the law', based on a kind of 'united brotherhood of man', also failed. Even the United Nations has had to match the ever-increasing forces of warring factions in its attempt to achieve this aim. The soliloquy of 'reason' has created what William James referred to as a 'citadel within the sanctuary' of conflicting *a priori* ideologies.

Despite increasing emphasis on using reason to change the world, in order to create a better future for ourselves, seems to have neglected our need to experience its mystery in the 'now'. As George Bernard Shaw realised, 'reason'

---

[70] Pentland, A: *The Rational Individual*, 'This Idea must Die', Ed. Brockman, J, 2015, 317-8

had an altogether different meaning: 'The reasonable man adapts himself to the world; the unreasonable one persists in trying to adapt the world to himself; therefore all progress depends on unreasonable men'. And similar sentiments were expressed in Chekhov's *Uncle Vanya*, when he said: "Man has been endowed with reason, with the power to create, so that he can add to what he's been given but, up to now, he hasn't been a creator, only a destroyer. Forests keep disappearing, rivers dry up, wild life's become extinct, the climate's ruined and the land grows poorer and uglier every day." But "don't worry", said Bertolt Brecht reassuringly in 1922 when the Nazis were to bully their way to power, "they say things will be better for us soon, but I don't ask when".

The rational mind is never satisfied in trying to improve our future, but which it can only measure objectively, usually in terms of material gain but that's a mirage because materialism contains inbuilt obsolescence and changes all the time. After all, what we thinks are tomorrow's luxuries become today's necessities and, what we thinks are today's necessities become yesterday's rejects; the consumers' graveyard where we dump our garbage provides the evidence. Even though 'settling down' and stabilising the present always feels less stressful that 'settle up' on debt forever after, we still seem to think the future is preferable. It has been said that 'we do not inherit the earth from our ancestors; we borrow it from our children [Wendell Berry] and the debts most nations have run up and are forever committed to settling, subscribe to this.

Because we seem incapable of making up our own minds about what we want, the marketers persuade us to climb the never-ending stairway to the earthly paradise they tell us we want. The world's economies are driven only by persuading us what they think we want by ignoring what we feel we need, so we've become hard-wired to believe we can live better alone in a virtual-reality world than together in the natural world of reality.

So what does progress really mean? Oscar Wilde hinted at its real meaning when he said: 'we know the price of everything but the value of nothing'. How has the significance of price, rather than value become so deeply embedded in our psyche? At one time people felt there was a balanced relationship between their worth in terms of the goods and services they exchanged for mutual benefit; then abut 1000 BC it became replaced by coinage, especially if it had the emperor's head on it as proof of its worth, then subsequently by promissory notes and loans borrowed on future expectations.

We used to speak in terms of 'earning money', now we speak in terms of 'making money', so there's no longer any relationship between a person's real worth and their monetary worth, which is all that's left to measure them by. But "an attitude to life which seeks fulfilment in the single-minded pursuit of wealth, in short, material gain, does not fit into this world, because it contains within itself no limiting principle, while the environment in which it is placed is strictly limited."[71] Although this quote appeared long after Andrew Carnegie's claim that: 'the man who dies rich dies disgraced'. So, after making his fortune, he gave most of it away, about a hundred billion dollars by today's standards.

A person might be incapable of evaluating their real legacy, but the evaluation can never be postponed indefinitely. The closer the 'day of reckoning' looms, the more frightening its true implication become. As John Donne expressed it: "I dare not move my dim eyes any way; despair behind, and death before doeth cast such terror". And finally: "when the past no longer illuminates the future, the spirit walks in darkness" [Alexis de Tocqueville]. Indeed, look beneath the cloaks and crowns and jewellery, the honours and titles, the medals and flags and bank balances, along with all the other intoxicating

---

[71] Schumacher, E: *Small is Beautiful*, 1973

possessions our egos have decorated themselves with, and all you will see are a collection of lonely souls, trying to console one another that they must be doing the right thing, out-acting each other's fantasies on the world-stage, blind to the fact that even the "sadly stifled lives many people live ... have missed the chance to be themselves".[72]

These our actors / as I foretold you, were all spirits, and / are melted into air, into thin air: / and like the baseless fabric of this vision, / the cloud-capp'd tow'rs, the gorgeous palaces, / the solemn temples, the great globe itself, / yea, all which it inherit, shall dissolve, / and, like this insubstantial pageant faded, / leave not a rack behind. We are such stuff / as dreams are made on; and our little life / is rounded with a sleep. [*Tempest*]

Could the egoism vs. altruism dichotomy be the principle cause of schizophrenia?

> What evidence there is suggests that schizophrenic illnesses did not appear, at least in any significant quantity, before the end of the eighteenth century or the beginning of the nineteenth. If so, their increasing frequency would have occurred just after the most intense period of change towards industrialization in Europe, a time of profound transition when traditional rural modes of communal life were giving way to the more impersonal and atomised forms of modern social organization.[73]

"It's a remarkable paradox that, at the pinnacle of human material and technical achievement, we find

---

[72] Gray, J: *The Silence of Animals. On Progress and other Modern Myths*, 2013, 109

[73] Sass, L: *Madness and Modernism*, 1992; 364-5; Gehlen, A: *Die Seele im technischen Zeitalter*, 1957

ourselves anxiety-ridden, prone to depression, worried about how others see us, unsure of our friendships, driven to consume and with little or no community life."[74]

"The left hemisphere is fundamentally narcissistic, in the sense that it sees the world 'out there' as no more than a reflection of itself"[75] since it knows no other. And, to illustrate how obsessive its drive to progress itself has become, here are some examples: before the Neolithic era, populations remained sparse and everyone's life-style was essentially cooperative. Now the world's population is nearly seven billion, over half of whom live more self-centred and isolated lives in cities. And to make way for this exponential growth-rate, about 78 million acres of rainforest are being destroyed every year.[76]

In an attempt to understand reality, our egocentric minds are driven to accumulate what we believe are facts about the world, which we can then analyses scientifically, according to what we believes are *a priori* concepts that model it, yet the:

> Corpus of scientific knowledge ... is like an expanding bubble of light in the darkness of ignorance ... but its surface is more important, because that's where knowledge ends and mystery begins. The scientific establishment justifies its existence with the big idea that it offers answers and ultimately solutions. But privately, every scientist knows that what science really does is discover the profundity of our ignorance.[77]

The conceptually-conscious mind has provided itself with, what it believes are fairly reliable mental images of an

[74] Wilkinson, R & Pickett, K: *The Spirit Level*, 2010, 3
[75] McGilchrist, I: *The Master and His Emissary*, 2009, 438
[76] Taylor, L: *The Healing Power of Rainforest Herbs*, 2004
[77] Saffo, P: *The Illusion of Scientific Progress*, 'This Idea must Die', Ed. J. Brockman, 2015, 542-3

outer world,[78] about which our sensually-conscious mind knows nothing. These mental images are like the shadows on the walls in Plato's cave allegory, permanently excluded from experiencing the real world of beauty and wonder beyond the cave, through the intoxicating power of our emotions. Those shadows have produced "a multitude of doctrines, therapies, ideologies, spiritual teachings and belief systems ... to provide the seeker with answers to that which is unknowable."[79]

If the mutation of the ego is some kind of parasite, its 'rise' to power depends on trying to construct and control, not only its environment and even its own evolution, but its 'demise' has been at the expense of empathy for anyone or anything but itself. Yet "pride goes before destruction and the haughty spirit before a fall".[80] As a fundamentally gregarious species alas, the ego's self-centred mind seems incapable of recognising how evolution, long ago, had already provided us with a profound sense of empathy for our World and each other and allowed us to live in harmony with the whole of nature.

---

[78] Kosslyn, S et al: *The Case of Mental Imagery*, 2006.

[79] Parsons, T: *Knowing and Unknowing*, theopensecret.com.

[80] King James Bible, Proverb 16:18

REFERENCE INDEX

Adkins, A: *Merit and Responsibility in Greek Ethics*, 1962: **27**

Alexander, R: *The Biology of Moral* Systems, 1987: **92**

Al-Khalili, J: *Life on the Edge*, 2014: **173**

Alok Jha: *City living affects your brain*, 2011: **194**

Alsop, S (Ed.): *Beyond Cartesian Dualism*, 2005: **153**

Amir-Móez, A: *Discussion of Difficulties in Euclid*, 1959: **164**

Argyle, M, et al: *The Communication of friendly and hostile attitudes*, 1971: **112**

Arrow, K: *Social Choice and Individual* Value, 1951: **212**

Asch, S: *Opinions and Social Pressures*, 1955: **5, 157**

Aunger, R: *The Life History of Cultural Learning in a Face- to- Face Society*, 2000: **59**

Ayer, A J: *Language, Truth and Logic*, 1936: **47**

Babloyantz, A & Lourenço, C: *Computation with Chaos*, 1994: **80**

Baefield, O: *Saving the Appearances*, 1957: **205**

Banaji, M et al: *Blind Spot: Hidden Biases of Good People*, 2013: **166**

Barfield, A: *Saving the Appearances: A Study of Idolatry*, 1957: **193**

Bargh, J et al: *Direct Effects of Trait Constructs*, 1996: **11**

237

Barham, P: *Schizophrenia and Human Values*, 1984: **173**

Baron-Cohen, S: *Zero Degrees of Empathy*, 2011: **180, 198**

Bartlett, F C: *Remembering: A Study in Experimental and Social Psychology*, 1932: **57**

Baumgartner, M: *The Moral Order of Suburb*, 1988: **221**

Baumrind, D: *Are Authoritative families really harmonious?* 1983: **115**

Beaman, R & Wheldall, K: Vol 20, 4, 2000: **18**

Beavers, A: *In the Beginning*, n.d. **202**

Bentley, A & Shennan, S: *Random Copying and Cultural Evolution*, 2005: **59**

Berkeley, G: *A Treatise Concerning the Principles of Human Knowledge*, 1710: **102, 104**

Bettinger, R & Eerkens, J: *Point Typologies, Cultural Transmission*, 1999: **59**

Black, D: *On the Origin of Morality*, 2000: **215, 219**

Black, D: *Sociological Justice*, 1989: **222**

Black, D: *The Social Structure of Right and Wrong*, 1993: **124**

Blackmore, S: *Conversations on Consciousness*, 2006: **54**

Blackmore, S: *The Meme Machine*, 2000: **224**

Blakemore, S & Frith, U: *The Learning Brain …*, 2005: **156**

Blakemore, S: *Left-Brain/Right Brain*, 2015: **157**

Block, N: *Two Neural Correlates of Consciousness*, 2005: **183**

Block, S: *The Bonobo Way: The Evolution of Peace Through Pleasure*, 2014: **191**

Boehm, C: *Conflict and the Evolution of Social Control*, 2000: **15, 33, 124**

Boehm, C: *Egalitarian behaviour & the evolution of political intelligence*, 1997: **205**

Boehm, C: *Egalitarian society and reverse dominance hierarchy*, 1993: **221**

Boltzmann, L: *Populäre Schriften*, 1905: **131**

Boltzmann, L: *Probabilistic Foundations of Heat Theory*, 1877: **72**

Boole, G: *An Investigation into the Laws of Thought …*, 1854: **93**

Boyd, R & Richardson, P: *Punishment allows the Evolution of Cooperation*, 1992: **125**

Brooks, M: *Free Radicals: the Secret Anarchy of Science*, 2011: **82**

Brown, C & Liebovitch, L: *Lévy Flights* , 2007: **55**

Brunner, H et al: *Abnormal Behaviour associated with point mutation*, 1993: **7**

Buchanan, M: *God Plays Dice ...*, 'Chance', 2015: **103**

Buckner, R et al: *The Brain's Default Network*, 2008: **156**

Bugental, D & Love, L: *Nonassertive Expression of Parental Approval and Disapproval*, 1975: **18**

Burton, R: *The Certainty Bias: a potentially dangerous mental Flaw*, 2008: **107**

Carey, N: *The Epigenetics Revolution*, 2011: **52**

Carey, N: *The Epigenetics Revolution*, 2011: **52**

Carling, A: *Equality and Consciousness in Early Human Society*, 2000: **200**

Carnot, N: *Reflections on the Motive Power of Fire*, 1824: **164**

Cashdan, E: *Egalitarianism among Hunters and Gatherer* : **33**

Caspari, R & Lee, S: *Older Age becomes Common Late in Human Evolution*, 2004: **105**

Cavalli-Sforza, L: *Genes, People and Language*, 2000: **54, 55**

Cercignani, C: *Ludwig Boltzmann – The Man Who Trusted Atoms*, 1998: **52, 72**

Chater, N et al: *Restrictions on Biological Adaption in Language Evolution*, 2009: **59**

Coates, K: *A Global History of Indigenous Peoples* 2004: **135**

Curley, E: *A Spinoza reader: The Ethics and other Works*, 1994: **95**

Curry, O. S: *Associationism*, 2015: **79**

Damasio, A: *Self comes to Mind*, 2010: **147**

Darwin C: *The Descent of Man*, 1871: **9, 16, 18, 21, 30, 53, 77, 94 & 123**

Darwin, C: *A biographical Sketch of an Infant*, 1877: **178**

Darwin, C: *On the Origin of Species ....* 1859: **166**

Davis, P: *The Uncertain Future*, 'Chance', 2015: **103**

Dawkins, R: *A Devil's Chaplain ...*, 2004: **47, 108**

Gintis, H: *Group Selection and Human Prosociality*, 2000: **43**

Gödel, K: *Über formal unentscheidbare Sätze der Principia Mathematica*, 1931: **167**

Goel, V: *Anatomy of deductive reasoning*, 2007: **15**

Gold, J & I: *Mental Illness*, 2015: **194**

Gold, J & I: *Suspicious Minds: How Culture Shapes Madness*, 2014: **7, 14**

Goldberg, E et al: *Lateralization of Frontal Lobe ...*, 1994: **159**

Graeber, D: *Towards an anthropological Theory of Value ...*, 2001: **229**

Gray, J: *Straw Dogs*, 2002: **152**

Gray, J: *The Silence of Animals. On Progress and other Modern Myths*, 2013: **233**

Green, J, et al: *An fMRI investigation of emotional engagement in moral Judgment*, 2001: **117**

Greene, J et al: *The neural bases of cognitive conflict and control in moral judgment*, 2004: **92**

Greenfeld, L: *Mind, Modernity, Madness: The Impact of Culture on Human Experience*, 2013: **173**

Greenough, W & Black, J: *Induction of Brain Structures*, 1992: **129**

Guilaine J & Zammit, J: *The Origins of War*, 2005: **190, 192 & 203**

Gullhangen, A & Nøttestad, J: *Looking for the Hannibal behind the Cannibal ...*: 2011: **115**

Hacker, P: *Insight and Illusion*, 1986: **185**

Hamilton, W: *The Genetic Evolution of Social Behaviour*, 1964: **35**

Hamlin, K: *Moral Blank Staleism*, 2015: **116**

Harari, Y: *Sapiens – A Brief History of Mankind*, 2014: **200**

Hare, R: *Psychopathy Checklist – revised technical manual*, 2003: **128**

Harms, W: *The Evolution of Cooperation in Hostile Environments*; 2000: **35**

Harris-Love, M et al: *Interhemispheric Inhibition ..* J. Physiol. V97, 3, 2007: **227**

Hauser, M: *Moral Minds*, 2009: **120**

Haviland, W: *Cultural Anthropology*, 9th edn. 1999: **62**

Heap M: *The Ideomotor Effect*, 2002: **6**

Hegel , G: *Lectures on the Philosophy of World History*, 1770-1831: **147**

Hegel, G: *Phenomenology of Spirit*, 1807: **126**

Hegel, G: *The History of Philosophy*, 1837: **38**

Heinberg, R: *Memories and Visions of Paradise*, 1989: **199**

Helminski, C: *Introduction to Rumi: Daylight*, 2011: **209**

Hill, K & Hurtado, A: *Ache Life History*, 1996: **192**

Hinrichs, K: *Follower Propensity* …, 2007: **216**

Hoel, H et al: *The experience of bullying in Great* Britain, 200: **208**

Hood, B: *The Self*, 2015: **218**

Hull, D: *Science as a Process*, 1988: **59**

Hume, D: A *Enquiry Concerning the Principles of Morals*, 1751: **98**

Hume, D: *A Treatise of Human Nature*, 1739-40: **47, 77**

Hume, D: *An Enquiry Concerning Human Understanding*, 1748: **64, 114**

Hume, D: *Enquiry concerning the Principles of Morals*, 1751: **114**

Hume, D: *Inquiry concerning Human Understanding*, 1748: **170**

Humphries, N & Sims, D: *Optimal foraging Strategies*, 2014: **55**

Hwa Yol Jung: *Transversal Rationality and Intercultural Text*, 2011: **110**

Hyland, T: *Mindfulness and Learning*, 2011: **209**

Inge, W: *Possible Recovery?* 1941: **212**

James, O: *Affluenza*, 2007: **210**

James, W: *Great Men and their Environment*, 1880: **52**

James, W: *The Principles of Psychology*, 1890: **90**

Johnstone, G & Van Ness, D: *Handbook of Restorative Justice*, 2007: **216**

Kahneman, D: *Thinking, Fast and Slow*, 2011: **94, 183**

Kanarek, J: *Critiquing Cultural Relativism*, 2013: **107**

Kane, R (Ed.): *The Oxford Handbook of Free Will*, 2002: **77**

Kant, I: *Critique of Pure Reason*, 1781-7: **162, 167, 168**

Madison, J: Federalist Paper No. 10: 1787: **212**

Malthus, T: A*n Essay on the Principle of Population*, 1798: **56**

Masters, R: *The Nature of Politics*, 1989: **127**

McGilchrist, I: *The Master and His Emissary*, 2009: **156, 159, 226 & 234**

McKenna, T: *Food of the Gods*, 1993: **87**

McKie R: *Chimps with everything: Jane Goodall's 50 years in the jungle*, 2010: **191**

Medows, D et al: *Limits to Growth*, 1976: **56**

Mesoudi, A: *Cultural Evolution*, 2011: **54**

Metzinger, T: *Cognitive Agency*, 2015: **57**

Mikels, J et al: *Should I go with Gut?* 2011: **40**

Milgram, S: *Behavioural Study of Obedience*, 1963: **128**

Milgrim, S: *Introduction to his Obedience Experiment*, 1963: **210**

Milgrim, S: *Obedience to Authority: an Experimental View*, 1974: **5**

Mlodinow, L: *Subliminal*, 2012: **188**

Montaigne, M de: *Essays*, 1580: **210**

Moran, M: *Dopamine serves a positive reinforcer for aggression*, 2013: **126**

Morris, D *Manwatching*, 1977: **5**

Morris, D: *The Human Zoo*, 1967: **5**

Morris, D: *The Naked Ape*, 1967: **5**

Myers, D: *Psychology*, 2011: **7**

Nash, J: *Equilibrium Points in n-person Games*, 1950: **133**

Newman, C et al: *Early understanding of the link between agent and order*, 2010: **67**

Nickerson, R: *Confirmation Bias: a Ubiquitous Phenomenon in many Guises*, 1998: **63**

Nietzsche, F *Beyond Good and Evil*, 1886: **32, 34, 126, 169, 179, 185, 187, 210, 221, 222 & 225**

Nietzsche, F: *On the Genealogy of Morality*, 1886: **222**

Nietzsche, F: *The Birth of Tragedy*, 1872: **88**

Nietzsche, F: *Thus Spake Zarathustra*, 1883-5: **179**

Norris, C: *Psychopathy and Gender ...*, 2011: **205**

Olds, J: *Pleasure centers in the brain*, 1956: **98**

Orwell, G: *Nineteen Eighty-Four*, 1949: **202**

Packard, V: *The Hidden Persuaders*, 1957: **209**

Paine, T: *Agrarian Justice, opposed to Agrarian Law, and to Agrarian Monopoly*, 1795: **205**

Paine, T: *Common Sense*, 1776: **212**

Paine, T: *The Age of Reason*, 1794: **217**

Parsons, T: *Knowing and Unknowing*, theopensecret.com. **235**

Pashoe, S: *A Painter in the Wilderness*, 1999: **49**

Paulhus, D & Williams, K: *The Dark Triad of Personality, narcissism,* …2002: **204**

Pellegrino, G di, et al: *Understanding Motor Events …*, 1992: **89**

Pentland, A: *The Rational Individual*, 2015: **230**

Perrin, J: *Les Atomes*, 1913: **172**

Pert, C: *Molecules of Emotion*, 1997: **148, 151, 225**

Piff, P et al: *Higher Social Class predicts increased unethical Behaviour*, 2012: **32**

Pike, O: *The Psychical Elements of Religion*, 1879: **21**

Pinhas Ben Zvi: *Kant on Space*, Philosophy Now, 110, 2015: **164**

Pinker, S: *The Better Angels of our Nature: The Decline of Violence in History and its Causes*, 2012: **187**

Pinker, S: *The Language Instinct*, 1994: **141**

Popper, K: *Logic of Scientific Discovery* 1977: **60**

Popper, K: *Logik der Forschung*. 1934: **75**

Popper, K: *Objective Knowledge, an evolutionary approach*, 1979: **60, 74, 78, 197**

Popper, K: *The Open Society and its Enemies*, 1945: **129**

Power, M: *The Egalitarians, Humans and Chimpanzees*, 1991: **191**

Pratkanis, A & Aronson, E: Age of Propaganda, 2004: **209**

Price, J et al: *The Social Competition Hypothesis of depression*. 1994: **208**

Prigogine, I & Stengers, I: *Order out of Chaos*, 1986: **228**

Prigogine, I et al: *Order out of Chaos*, 1985: **73**

Putman, C et al: *Structural Organisation of the Corpus Callosum …* , 2008: **227**

Radcliffe-Brown, A: *Structure and Function in Primitive Society*, 1952: **15**

Rae, M & Pojman, L: *Philosophy of Religion, An anthology*, 2015: **145**

Raichle, M: *The Brain's Dark Energy*, 2010: **158**

Ramachandran, V: *The Tell-Tale Brain*, 2011: **11, 40, 89, 140, 149**

Redding, P: *Feeling, thought and orientation: William James and the Idealist ...* 2011: **118**

Reiman, J & Leighton, P: *The Rich Get Richer and the Poor Get Prison*, 2015: **214**

Richman, B: *Some vocal distinctive features used by Gelada monkeys*, 1976: **141**

Robertson, I: *The Winner Effect*, 2012: **127**

Rothstein, B: *Creating Political Legitimacy ...*, 2009: **210**

Rotter, J: *Generalized expectancies of internal versus external control reinforcements*, 1966: **117**

Rouseau, J: *Discourse on Inequality*, 1754: **204**

Rousseau, J. *Discourse on the Sciences and Arts*, 1778: **26**

Rousseau, J: *Confessions*, 1782: **86**

Rousseau, J: *Emile*, 1762: **221**

Rousseau, J: *Social Contract*, 1762: **26**

Rucker, R: *Infinity and* the Mind, 1995: **80**

Ruler, N: *Kant on Causality*, 2011: **168**

Russell, B: *The Principles of Mathematics*, 1903: **166**

Russell, B: *Why I am not a Christian, The Doctrine of Free-Will*, 1967, 1930: **116**

Ryle, G: *The Concept of Mind*, 1947: **228**

Saffo, P: *The Illusion of Scientific Progress*, 2015: **234**

Saini, A et al *Rough Justice*, Chance, 2015: **215**

Sass, L: *Madness and Modernism*, 1992: **233**

Sass, L: *Schizophrenia and Modernism*, 2001: **208**

Schank, R: *Dynamic Memory Revisited*, 1999: **99**

Schultz, W: *The Human Brain Encodes Event Frequencies ...*, 2013: **99**

Schumacher, E: *Small is Beautiful*, 1973: **232**

Semendeferel, K, et al: *Prefrontal Cortex in Humans and Apes*, 2001: **106**

Service, E: *Origin of the State and Civilization*, 1975: **119, 124**

Service, E: *Primitive Social Organisation ..* , 1962: **33, 216**

Sheldrake, R *The Science Delusion*, 2012: **75**

Sheldrake, R: *A New Science of Life*, 2009: **73**

Sheldrake, R: *The Presence of the Past: Morphic Resonance* , 2011: **225**

Shonkoff, J & Phillips, D (Eds.): *From Neurons to Neighbourhooods*, 2002: **7**

Silani, C: *I'm OK, You're Not OK*, 2013: **180**

Silk, J: *Kinship Selection in Primate Groups*, Int. Journal of Prmatology, 2000: **193**

Singer, T. *Are you egocentric? Check your right supramarginal gyrus*, 2014: **180**

Skinner, B: *Beyond Freedom and Dignity*: 1971: **23, 189**

Skyrms, B: *Game Theory, Rational and Evolution of the Social Contract*, 2000: **134**

Slovic, P et al: *Psychic Numbing and Mass Atrocity* 2013: **93**

Smith, A: *The Theory of Moral Sentiment*, 1759: **113, 197**

Smith, A: *The Wealth of Nations*, 1776: **197**

Smith, D: *Why we Lie*, 2004: **112**

Soon, C et al: *Unconscious Determinants of Free Decisions in the Human Brain*, 2008: **95**

Spikins, P et al, A: *From Hominidity to Human Compassion*, 2010: **92**

Spikins, P: *How Compassion Made us Human*, 2015: **92**

Spitzer, M: *On Defining Delusion*, 1990: **187**

Stanghellini, G: *Disembodied Spirits and Deanimated Bodies*, 2004: **208**

Stringer, C: *Human Evolution: out of Ethiopia*, Nature, 2003: **196**

Taleb, N: *The Black Swan*, 2007: **181**

Taylor, K: *Brainwashing*, 2002: **60**

Taylor, L: *The Healing Power of Rainforest Herbs*, 2004: **234**

Taylor, S: *The Fall - The Insanity of the Ego in Human History*, 2005: **55, 199, 205**

SUBJECT INDEX

footnote references in bold

Made in the USA
Columbia, SC
13 April 2017